3/22

LH

DREAMS

AND THE UNCONSCIOUS

IN NINETEENTH-CENTURY

RUSSIAN FICTION

DREAMS AND THE UNCONSCIOUS IN NINETEENTH-CENTURY RUSSIAN FICTION

Michael R. Katz

UNIVERSITY PRESS OF NEW ENGLAND

Hanover and London, 1984

UNIVERSITY PRESS OF NEW ENGLAND

Brandeis University
Brown University
Clark University
Dartmouth College

University of New Hampshire
University of Rhode Island
Tufts University
University of Vermont

The publisher gratefully acknowledges the support of Williams College in the publication of this book.

Copyright 1984 by Trustees of Darmouth College

The following articles have been revised for inclusion in this book:

"Dreams in Pushkin," *California Slavic Studies*, 9 (1980), by permission of the University of California.

"Ivan Fyodorovich Shpon'ka and His Nightmare," copyright 1981 *Dreamworks*, by permission of Kenneth Atchity and Marsha Kinder. An earlier version appeared in *Dreamworks* 1:4 (Summer 1981).

Professor Nicholas Fersen, Williams College, has generously granted permission to quote from his unpublished translation of Pushkin's *Eugene Onegin*.

All rights reserved. Except for brief quotation in critical articles or reviews, this book, or parts thereof, must not be reproduced in any form without permission in writing from the publisher. For further information contact University Press of New England, Hanover, NH 03755.

Printed in the United States of America

LIBRARY OF CONGRESS CATALOGING IN PUBLICATION DATA

Katz, Michael R.
   Dreams and the unconscious in nineteenth-century
Russian fiction.

  Bibliography: p.
  Includes index.
  1. Russian fiction—19th century—History and
criticism. 2. Dreams in literature. 3. Subconsciousness
in literature. I. Title.
PG3096.D73K38   1984   891.73'3'09353   83-40052
ISBN 0-87451-271-9

To Mary Kathryn Dodge

CONTENTS

Acknowledgments	ix
1 DREAMS IN LIFE AND LITERATURE	1
2 ALLEGORY AND POLEMIC PRE-PUSHKIN	16
3 PUSHKIN'S "DREAMS VS. LIFE"	37
4 GOGOL'S "MIXED VEGETABLE SALAD"	66
5 DOSTOEVSKY'S "VARIATIONS AND NUANCES"	84
6 TOLSTOY'S "TRUER FEELINGS"	117
7 CONCLUSION/SUPERSEDURE	147
Appendix of Literary Dreams	153
N. M. Karamzin 153	
V. A. Zhukovsky 153	
A. S. Griboedov 157	
A. S. Pushkin 158	
N. V. Gogol 162	
F. M. Dostoevsky 167	
L. N. Tolstoy 181	
Notes	191
Selected Bibliography	205
Index	213

ACKNOWLEDGMENTS

My thanks to two former students for their enthusiasm and ideas: John Ramsbottom and Douglas Marshall; to my former teachers, colleagues, and former colleagues at Williams College for their various suggestions and objections: Doris de Keyserlingk, Nicholas Fersen, Edwina Cruise, Donald Dragt, Larry Graver, Mark Taylor, Peter Grudin, Dennis Klos, Marianna Torgovnick, and the late Clay Hunt; to colleagues at the University of California, Berkeley and at Dartmouth College for their hospitality and assistance during my sabbatical years: Simon Karlinsky, Robert Hughes, Richard Sheldon, and Barry Scherr; to colleagues at other institutions for their support and suggestions over the years: John Fennell, William Todd, Gregory Freidin, Joseph Frank, Donald Robar, and others; to my typist for her perseverance: Bonnie Blake; and to my spouse for everything: Mary Kathryn Dodge.

Williamstown, Massachusetts
September, 1983

DREAMS AND THE UNCONSCIOUS IN NINETEENTH-CENTURY RUSSIAN FICTION

1. DREAMS IN LIFE AND LITERATURE

> Even dreams contrived by poets partake of the essence of dreams.   Cicero

In virtually every major novel written during the nineteenth century, Russian writers evinced an overwhelming fascination with dreams: their fictional heroes and heroines fall asleep and, almost without exception, witness imaginative night visions. Pushkin's Tatyana Larina, Gogol's Ivan Shponka, and Tolstoy's Anna Karenina are but the most familiar of these literary dreamers. This book analyzes the literary dream in nineteenth-century Russian narrative fiction. It argues that this new technique provided Russian authors with their first access into the human unconscious; with it they explored the "twilight realms of consciousness"[1] in their art as no other European writers did.

Although it is true that the experience of dreaming is universal, the meanings that have been attributed to dreams themselves have long been a subject of dispute. For example, the psychologist Erich Fromm asserts that although

> the views held about the nature of dreams differed vastly throughout the centuries and through various cultures, . . . one idea is not controversial: the view that all dreams are meaningful and significant.[2]

However, scientific investigations seem to be leading researchers toward quite different conclusions. It has recently been argued that "dreams are nothing more than the thinking brain's valiant efforts to weave a coherent plot out of disparate and contradictory signals from

2   Dreams in Life and Literature

lower brain centers during sleep."[3] Thus the universal experience thought to be so "meaningful and significant" may eventually prove to be nothing more than the "psychological concomitant of an essentially biological process."[4]

These views represent two opposite extremes. On the one hand, the scientific approach produces objective knowledge about the process of dreaming through a study of brain waves, rapid eye movements (REM's), and other physiological changes during sleep. On the other hand, the interpretative approach yields subjective knowledge about the significance attributed to dreams in different cultures. Ethnologists and anthropologists continue to collect dream data from nonliterate societies; philosophers and psychologists devise elaborate systems to explain the nature and source of dreams; writers and poets invent imaginative night visions that they ascribe to their fictional characters; and literary critics struggle valiantly to interpret them.

In undertaking a study of dreams in nineteenth-century Russian fiction, it is instructive to survey their prior use in Western literature and to review the ways in which philosophers and psychologists have interpreted them. This chapter begins with a consideration of classical treatises on dreaming and early examples of poetic dreams in Homer, Virgil, and the Bible. From Medieval and Renaissance works, representative dreams in Dante, Chaucer, Milton and Shakespeare will be discussed briefly. Then the chapter attempts to characterize the complex reaction against eighteenth-century rationalism: it examines the psychological theories of Schubert and Carus as well as the poetic practice of the German, English, and French Romantics. Finally it turns to the works of Freud and Jung to compare their methods of dream interpretation, and, in particular, their pronouncements on literary dreams. The chapter concludes with a statement of the scope and the approach adopted in this study of dreams in nineteenth-century Russian fiction.

* * *

Anthropologists attest to the fact that all cultures, almost without exception, have sought to distinguish between two different types of dreams. Lévy-Bruhl in *Primitive Mentality* (1923) states this point succinctly. "Primitives did not accord belief to all dreams indiscriminately. Certain dreams were worthy of credence, others not."[5] This distinction between "credible" and "incredible" dreams also held true for the Greeks. In diverse writings philosophers tried to ascertain the true origin of dreams and to interpret their meaning.[6] Hippocrates' treatise *On Regimen*, Plato's dialogue *The Timaeus*, Aristotle's essays "On Dreams" and "On Divination in Sleep," and Artimedorus's comprehensive *Oneirocritica* are among the most significant attempts to grapple with the problem. As early as Homer, the dilemma that was confronting men in trying to interpret their dreams had also found expression in literary form. The "cautious" Penelope in book 19 of *The Odyssey* explains:

Dreams . . . are awkward and confusing things: not all that people see in them comes true. For there are two gates through which these insubstantial visions reach us; one is of horn and the other of ivory. Those that come through the ivory gate cheat us with empty promises that never see fulfillment, while those that issue from the gate of burnished horn inform the dreamer what will really happen.[7]

This same metaphorical distinction between true and false dreams was restated by Virgil at the end of book 6 in *The Aeneid*:

> There are two portals,
> Twin gates of Sleep,
> One made of horn, where easy
> Release is given true shades, the other gleaming
> White ivory, whereby the false dreams issue
> To the upper air.[8]

After completing his tour of the lower world, Aeneas departs through the ivory portal, the gate of false dreams. Virgil's artistic intention has continued to mystify scholars; nevertheless, this distinction between true and false dreams was maintained throughout classical antiquity and it parallels a similar division between divinely and demonically inspired dreams in the Judeo-Christian tradition.

The Bible contains numerous examples of literary dreams, most of which are followed immediately by attempts at interpretation.[9] Biblical dreams, divine in origin, are always genuinely "prophetic" inasmuch as they eventually come true. However, in sermons and ecclesiastical texts Church Fathers repeatedly warned their faithful flock that only those dreams inspired by God or His angels could be trusted. Dreams could also emanate from the Devil; such deceptive visions were designed to lead virtuous men astray. Both Gregory the Great and Saint Thomas Aquinas, for example, issued grave admonitions about Satan's power to appear to men in their dreams and to cloud their reason.[10] On the other hand, the popular folk tradition continued to produce dream books by amateur interpreters, which attempted to explain in diverse ways the symbolic meaning of confusing dream images.

Literary dreams occur frequently in Medieval and Renaissance texts, where they are used either as allegorical or as narrative devices, or both. Dante's *Divine Comedy* contains three such dreams, all in *The Purgatorio*. In canto 9 (19–42), for example, while still waiting to enter purgatory, the poet dreams that he is being carried aloft by a gold eagle where he is scorched in a sphere of fire, a prophecy of his own imminent purgation.

Chaucer's "Nun's Priest's Tale" not only includes Chanticleer's ironically prophetic dream, but also contains a shrewd discussion of current theories of dreaming.[11] The rooster's loveliest mate, Pertelote, attributes his troubled dream to overeating and advocates a strong laxative. Chanticleer objects, citing a variety of theoretical and practical evidence to validate his own view that "dreams are to be dreaded":

> Dreams have quite often been significations
> As well of triumphs as of tribulations
> That people undergo in this our life.
>   (p. 185)

When Chanticleer fails to heed his own advice and ignores the warning implicit in his dream, he almost falls victim to the sly fox.

In book 4 of Milton's *Paradise Lost*, Satan is discovered in the Garden of Eden late one night:

> Squat like a toad, close at the ear of Eve,
> Assaying by his devilish art to reach
> The organs of her fancy, and with them forge
> Illusions as he list, phantasms and dreams.
>   (800–803)

Indeed, when Eve awakes in book 5 she describes how in her dream she had partaken of the forbidden fruit. Adam replies with what would seem to be a statement of the author's view. He ascribes dreams to "mimic fancy," a lesser faculty of the soul that imitates genuine "fancy." Adam devoutly hopes that Eve will be able to resist the temptation in reality, to which she had already yielded in her demonically inspired prophetic dream.

Shakespeare used literary dreams in various ways, some clearly allegorical, others remarkably poetic. Clarence in *Richard III* relates a magnificent vision to his keeper, which has been described as a "new projection of poetry into the realm of subconscious twilight".[12] In *A Midsummer Night's Dream* the intertwining of dream and reality constitutes the central metaphor of the play. Theseus expounds an ingenious theory of poetic creation when he declares in act 5 that, since all the characters of the play have been aroused from their romantic fantasies, they can finally resume their real lives. Hippolyta counters his argument, assuring her husband that there is more to "fancy" than meets the eye. And, as if to prove *her* point, the fairies return at the end of the play and regain control of the entire stage. Previously, when Bottom had awakened from his dream, he expressed his wonderment comically; nevertheless, his creative impulse is completely consistent with Theseus's theory. Bottom aims to have his dream transformed into a work of art:

> I have had a most rare vision. I have had a dream, past the wit of man to say what dream it was . . . I will get Peter Quince to write a ballad of this dream. It shall be called Bottom's Dream, because it hath no bottom. (IV, i, 211–23)

Shakespeare willingly obliged.

During the Enlightenment, European philosophers and writers showed relatively little interest in dreams or related phenomena. The age has frequently been characterized as one in which "Reason" was the central and unifying factor, "expressing all that it [the Enlightenment] longs and strives for, and all that it achieves."[13] Thus the "proper study of mankind" in the eighteenth century was considered to be man's intellect and the activity of his mind. Novelists wrote primarily about what their protagonists said, what they did, and even about what they thought—all manifestations of the conscious life of their fictional characters.

Toward the end of the eighteenth century there occurred what has been called a "reaction against rationalism."[14] The new movement was founded on the conclusion that, as Dostoevsky's Underground

Man would subsequently observe, "reason is an excellent thing, gentlemen, . . . but it is only reason."[15] It came to be argued that a strictly rational approach to human nature ignored some of its essential components. Both philosophers and poets began to investigate other mental activities: emotions and impulses, intuitive perceptions, imagination, memory, fantasy, and dreams.

Among the most notable intellectual currents of the period was a growth of interest in all manifestations of the supernatural, particularly mysticism and hypnotism. The Swedish theologian Emanuel Swedenborg (1688–1772), after experiencing his own profound spiritual revelation, wrote elaborate descriptions of his personal sojourn in the spirit world. He assumed the role of prophet and explorer of divine secrets and subsequently exerted a powerful influence on the Romantic movement.[16] The Austrian physician Franz Anton Mesmer (1734–1815) devised a theory of rarefied fluids that, he maintained, penetrated all bodies in the universe. He conducted experiments with this new force called "animal magnetism," employing it as a therapeutic agent to cure ailments ranging from blindness to boredom.[17] Hypnotic trances, seances, and hallucinations became the rage in fashionable society.

Related to these manifestations of new curiosity about the supernatural was a revival of interest in dreams, both real and imaginary. Men of diverse backgrounds began to record their own dreams systematically, devise "scientific" theories about their origin, and interpret their dreams as revelations of their unconscious life. The German writer and scholar, G. C. Lichtenberg (1742–99), after ruminating on his own night visions, reached the conclusion that they constituted reminiscences of mental states that had existed prior to the development of individual consciousness. In a prophetic utterance he declared, "I know from experience that dreams lead to self-knowledge."[18] Meanwhile, a kindred spirit in England, a clergyman named D. Simpson, published a *Discourse on Dreams and Night Visions* (1791) in which he asserted the preeminence of such phenomena over all other "most pure and refined concepts."[19] The enigmatic J. G. Hamann (1730–88), one of the first writers to attempt a psychological study of man, described his own "descent into self" on a journey to achieve knowledge. In a letter written in 1759 he alluded perceptively to the ambiguity inherent in his evidence: "For the dreamer everything is true, and, at the same time, everything is illusion."[20] J. G. Herder (1744–1803) argued that dreams constitute man's single most important source for self-knowledge: "The world of dreams gives us the most serious hints about ourselves."[21] In his article on Shakespeare (1771), he noted an intimate connection between the dream and artistic creation and recommended that German poets explore the dream as an expressive example of the sovereignty of the spirit.[22]

Following these preliminary, tentative manifestations of renewed interest and controversy, the dream became an area of investigation by early psychological theorists. The first writer to apply the ideas of Hamann and Herder to the systematic study of dreams was a German physician, G. H. von Schubert (1780–1860). In the introduction to his remarkable treatise, *The Symbolism of Dreams* (1814), he declares, "In a dream . . . the soul seems to speak an altogether different language than it usually does."[23] He characterizes the dream as a form of metaphorical language consisting of images, objects, and persons governed by laws different from those controlling man's conscious life. When he compared the language of dreams to that of poetry, Schubert was struck by many similarities; he concluded, therefore, that poetry must have access to interior regions of the soul, which, in turn, are in touch with cosmic reality. Finally, he suggested what was to become a central tenet of the Romantic theory of dreaming. He speculated that man's conscious life may be nothing more than a dream, and that his unconscious dream may indeed constitute the "true state of waking," when man is in contact with eternal nature.

A more rigorous approach to the study of the unconscious and its manifestations was adopted by another German physician, C. G. Carus (1789–1869).[24] His central work, *Psyche: On the History of the Development of the Soul* (1846), begins with a bold assertion: "The key to knowledge of the essence of the conscious life of the soul lies in the sphere of the unconscious."[25] Carus characterizes dreams as the mental activity of the conscious mind during its nocturnal return to the realm of the unconscious. This leads him to conclude that dreams can often be prophetic. "On this basis we can understand how the conscious, steeped in the unconscious, can perceive in sleep or dreams what would never be accessible to it in the waking state."[26] After studying the relationship between sleep and waking, Carus observes that dream imagery often originates in the individual's internal preoccupations and in the feelings aroused by his external situation. He then compares the soul to the poet, who selects only those images corresponding to the emotions that move him.

Both Schubert and Carus insist on the close connection between the dream and artistic creation. This connection began to attract the attention of European artists and authors at the end of the eighteenth century. Both poets and prose writers began to experiment with dreams as a literary technique to achieve a variety of effects. Perhaps more than any other German author, E. T. A. Hoffman managed to penetrate this mysterious realm. He described a world of dreams that was as real as that of sense perception, but one of a higher, more intense life, where man can transcend both time and space to achieve greater knowledge of the spirit.[27]

The dream became a favorite device of English Romantics. Coleridge claimed that he "dreamed" "Kubla Khan" during a deep sleep but was unable to recollect more than a few fragments upon awakening. Byron's lyric "The Dream" (1816) can serve as a poetic manifesto on the subject:

> . . . Sleep hath its own world,
> And a wide realm of wild reality,
> And dreams in their development have breath,
> And tears, and tortures, and the touch of joy;
> They leave a weight upon our waking thoughts,
> They take a weight from off our waking toils, . . .
>
> (3–8)

Wordsworth, De Quincey, and others viewed the dream as a valuable source for poetic inspiration.[28] While a clear parallel was perceived between them, Charles Lamb expressed the essential distinction: "The . . . poet dreams being awake. He is not possessed by his subject, but he has dominion over it."[29]

In France Charles Nodier regarded the dream not only as an escape from reality, but also as the place where man could discover both the self and the universe: "Dreams are the sweetest and perhaps the truest things in life."[30] Gérard de Nerval's major prose work *Aurélia* (1854) begins with a dramatic statement, whose source is the Homeric metaphor quoted above: "Dreaming is a second life. I have not been able to penetrate without trembling those gates of ivory or of horn that separate us from the invisible world."

By the middle of the nineteenth century, the novel emerged as the narrative form best suited for the investigation of nonrational mental activity. E. M. Forster perceptively described the attractiveness of the genre:

> The specialty of the novel is that the writer can talk about his characters as well as through them, or can arrange for us to listen when they talk to themselves. He has access to their self-communings and from that level he can descend even deeper and peer into the subconscious.[31]

That is precisely what nineteenth-century European novelists began to do. In order to make their fictional characters "more real," they set out to depict not only their external, conscious life, but their internal life as well. This so-called "progession toward greater inwardness"[32] led these novelists to explore more subjective experience. Ultimately they turned to the most subjective of all, the dream of the unconscious mind:

> As though it were not enough to explore the entire world of experience, to capture the precise quality of any event, however subtle and delicate or massive and complex, fiction also lays claim to the vaster and less accessible realm of our fantasies and dreams.[33]

* * *

Numerous critical studies of dreams in fiction have adopted a psychoanalytical approach. L. J. Kent's *Subconscious in Gogol' and Dostoevskij* (1969), G. Devereux's *Dreams in Greek Tragedy* (1976), L. Porter's *Literary Dream in French Romanticism* (1979), and E. Dalton's *Unconscious Structure in "The Idiot"* (1979) all share the same theoretical assumptions. Devereux and Dalton articulate these in similar terms:

> There can, of course, be no question of actually psychoanalyzing a Greek poet long since dead, nor a dramatic personage born from his imagination. What can be shown is that the dreams one encounters in Greek tragedy are authentically dream-like: that the dream Aischylos devised for his Klytaimnestra could have been dreamed by her, had she been a real person. . . . But that demonstration is possible only if one goes through the motions of an "as if" psychoanalysis of the fictitious but plausible Aischylean Klytaimnestra and of her dream.[34]

> Ippolit is not, of course, a patient on the couch who can supply the associations that would lead from this manifest dream to the unconscious dream

thoughts. But if Ippolit's experience is taken to have an internal psychological coherence, and is related as well to the novel of which it is a part, then that context will provide points of correspondence, analogous to relevant associations, that will elucidate the dream. In any case, the dream has essentially the same status as the rest of the text, and may be interpreted by the same methods.[35]

It is essential to return to the works of the founding father of the psychoanalytic movement in order to understand the difficulties inherent in such a psychoanalytic approach to literary dreams. The theory and practice of dream interpretation advanced by psychoanalytic psychology during the late nineteenth century were a direct development both of Schubert's and Carus's ideas on dreams and the unconscious, as well as of the writings of the European Romantics. In defining his own role in the history of the movement, Sigmund Freud (1856–1939) paid fitting tribute to his predecessors: "The poets and philosophers before me discovered the unconscious. What I discovered was the scientific methods by which the unconscious can be studied."[36] Freud established a system by which dreams could be *interpreted* and assigned a meaningful place in man's psychic activity. He would present each image to the patient, who would in turn supply "background thoughts" or "associations." The analyst would then "translate" the manifest content into latent thoughts in order to determine the "meaning" of the dream.

Since Freud insisted that the effectiveness of his method depended on the dreamer's willingness to provide such associations, it would appear that psychoanalysis could have no application to fictional characters. Indeed, in his classic study *The Interpretation of Dreams*, Freud urged that literary dreams should be interpreted *not* psychoanalytically, but "symbolically" (that is, allegorically), by replacing the dream content with one that is "intelligible and analogous." He explains:

> Most of the artificial dreams contrived by poets are intended for such symbolic [allegorical] interpretation, for they reproduce the thought conceived by the poet in a disguise found to be in accordance with the characteristics of our dreaming as we know them from experience.[37]

However, in a footnote to this same passage, Freud acknowledges that there did exist a few "artificial" dreams that lent themselves to his "psychoanalytic" method, namely, those dreams "which were formed with perfect correctness and which could be interpreted as though they had not been invented, but had been dreamt by actual persons."[38] Thus, when a fictional dream appeared to be "genuine" (dreamed by a real person), rather than "artificial" (invented by an author), Freud believed that his method could produce valid results. He went on to summarize his general approach to literature: "I have made use of this correspondence between my investigation and the creative work of the poet as a *proof of the correctness of my method of dream analysis.*"[39] By his own admission then, Freud used literary texts principally to clarify and confirm his own hypotheses about the subconscious.[40]

In only one essay did Freud actually attempt to interpret the "artificial" dreams of a fictional character. "Delusion and Dream" is a psychoanalytic study of *Gradiva* (1903), a novel by a minor German-Danish writer, Wilhelm Jensen. Freud concentrates on the "psychic processes" of the two protagonists, the young archeologist Norbert Hanold and his beloved Zoe (Gradiva). He treats characters, in his own words, as if they were "real individuals and not creations of a writer,"[41] and he analyzes their fictional dreams (dreams "which had never been dreamt"[42]) as if they were genuine. He concludes:

> We can apply . . . the technique which can be designated as the regular procedure of dream interpretation. It consists of disregarding the apparent sequence in the manifest dream, and examining separately every part of the content and in seeking its derivation in the impressions, memories, and free associations of the dreamer. However, since we cannot examine Hanold, we must be satisfied with making reference to his impressions and may, but only quite modestly, *substitute our own ideas* for his.[43]

Regarding fictional characters as real, interpreting their artificial dreams as genuine, but being unable to elicit free associations, Freud was therefore obliged to "substitute" his own ideas for the dreamer's. The novelist is thus transformed into a valuable ally of the psychologist. Thus "Delusion and Dream" is

> the one occasion where [Freud] systematically treated an entire piece of fiction, transforming *Gradiva*, by means of his voracious interpretive method, from an anticipation of psychoanalytic truth into an illustration of it.[44]

Whereas Freud concluded from his research that dreams were essentially wish fulfillments, Carl Gustav Jung (1875–1961) attempted to be more inclusive. He took issue with Freud's "reductive" definition:

> The view that dreams are merely the imaginary fulfillments of repressed wishes is hopelessly out of date. There are, it is true, dreams which manifestly represent wishes or fears, but what about all the other things? Dreams may contain ineluctable truths, philosophical pronouncements, illusions, wild fantasies, memories, plans, anticipations, irrational experiences, even telepathic visions, and heaven knows what besides.[45]

Jung's method of interpretation also diverged somewhat from Freud's; he attempted to establish the entire *context* of the dream image, to understand how each shade of meaning was determined by the conscious associations of the patient. He aimed to establish, in his own words, a "true picture of the [dreamer's] subjective state," a "spontaneous self-portrayal". The dream "shows the inner truth and reality of the patient as it really is: not as I conjecture it to be, and not as he would like it to be, but *as it is*."[46] Just as in Freud's free association, Jung's method also depended on the willingness of the subject to aid in the process of interpretation. He warned that "it is not possible, except under very special conditions, to work out the meaning of a dream without the collaboration of the dreamer."[47] Jung's method would thus seem to be equally ill suited to analyze the literary dreams of fictional characters.

Whereas Freud had designated the dream as the *via regia* or "royal road" to the unconscious and had used art as a means of supporting his theory, for Jung art rivaled the dream as a "road" into the unconscious. He and his followers turned to the products of man's artistic imagination to seek out their corroborating evidence. Jung expressed the point explicitly:

> A great work of art is like a dream; for all its apparant obviousness it does not explain itself and is always ambiguous. A dream never says 'you ought' or 'this is the truth.' It presents an image, . . . and *it is up to us to draw conclusions*.[48]

As Freud had substituted *his own ideas* for the protagonists' in his analysis of literary dreams, so too did Jung *draw his own conclusions* about the meaning of a work of art.

Unlike Freud, Jung evinced little interest in the "intersection" of the two "royal roads" to the unconscious, the place where dreams and art meet, namely, the literary dream. In an essay entitled "Psychology and Literature", Jung elaborated on his dislike for novels written in what he called the "psychological" mode.[49] In such works, where an author took his material from man's "crucial experiences" and "powerful emotions" and raised them to the level of poetic expression, then both the experience and its expression belonged to the realm of clearly understandable psychology; hence there was no role for the Jungian analyst. On the other hand, Jung favored those novels written in the so-called visionary mode, where the artist took his themes from primordial experience. It was from these works created in the "dark recesses of the mind," that Jung and his followers would choose their texts and, like the Freudians, they would use them to support their own psychological theories. One of the best examples is Jung's essay on Joyce's *Ulysses*; he soundly rejects the novel's "dreamlike" quality and declares, "the book seems to me to be written in the full light of consciousness; it is not a dream and not a revelation of the unconscious."[50] It is not surprising, then, that there is no Jungian counterpart to Freud's study of the literary dreams in Jensen's novel *Gradiva*.

Whereas Freud himself was aware of the limitations in applying his psychoanalytic method to the dreams of fictional characters, subsequent writers have shown less reserve. An example of the reductionist conclusions that frequently emerge from their analysis can be found in R. B. Lower's article, "On Raskol'nikov's Dreams in Dostoevsky's *Crime and Punishment*" (1969). The author summarizes his findings thus:

> Analysis of Raskol'nikov's dreams reveals the murder of the old woman to be the defensive acting out of an unconscious sado-masochistic oedipal fantasy. In the murder he identified with the castrating father in order to avoid his anxiety in identifying with the passive, castrated mother, and with the axe he actively attempted to destroy the projected passive-feminine part of himself. The effort failed because, in addition, the woman unconsciously represented his dead father, and the resulting guilt forced him back into a vicious guilt-shame cycle.[51]

Lower contributes little to our understanding either of Dostoevsky or of the human psyche.

A more sophisticated apology for the psychoanalytic method can be found in the introduction to Elizabeth Dalton's study of *The*

Idiot, where the author acknowledges that not all Freudian critics are equal:

> Without denying that there are incompetent psychoanalytic studies, or that psychoanalysts often ignore the specifically literary nature of the text and treat it as if it were the experience or the production of a patient, one must still wonder at the special indignation and derision reserved for psychoanalytic studies and withheld from the reams of boring, trivial, and quite unnecessary criticism of more conventional kinds.[52]

However, her own detailed study of the unconscious structure of Dostoevsky's novel seems schematized in its conclusions:

> In *The Idiot*, all the life of the novel is deeply imprinted with the sadistic conception of the primal scene. There is also evidence of a negative or homosexual resolution of the Oedipus complex, with deflection of the feeling for the father in the direction of passivity and masochism.[53]

Whatever the merits of Freud's and Jung's therapeutic approaches for the treatment of genuine patients, there exist insurmountable obstacles to applying their techniques to literary dreams. The critical method of psychoanalyzing fictional characters and their dreams intentionally mistakes art for life. In novels there are no psyches to be psychoanalyzed, and literary dreams are dreams that have never been dreamed.

* * *

In the introduction to "Delusion and Dream" Freud distinguishes between two approaches to the study of literary dreams:

> One is delving into a special case, the dream creations of one writer in one of his works; the other is bringing together and comparing all the examples of the use of dreams which are found in the works of different storytellers. The second way seems to be by far the more effective, perhaps the only justifiable one.[54]

In spite of his defense of the latter method, his essay is an example of the former, inasmuch as it is limited to the dreams of "one writer in one of his works."

This book embraces the second, more comprehensive approach. It brings together and compares "examples of the use of dreams that are found in the works of different storytellers" in nineteenth-century Russian fiction.[55] The emphasis throughout is on dreams as a literary technique; the analysis is based on the following critical questions. First, how do dreams contribute to an understanding of fictional characterization? Second, what function do dreams fulfill with regard to the narrative structure of these works? Third, how do dreams articulate the author's themes in a given composition?

The critical method employed in this book consists of rendering close readings of primary texts in light of these questions. The theoretical approach is eclectic: it is based on the insights into the origin, nature, and meaning of dreams in life and literature arrived at by poets, philosophers, and psychologists through the ages. It is hoped that this critical method and eclectic approach will yield a wealth of discriminations not only about the use of one technique and the meaning of great works of prose fiction, but also about the characteristics of individual authors and the originality of Russian literature. Finally, this investigation may lead to an understanding of what dreams in Russian fiction can reveal about the concept of the unconscious as it evolves in nineteenth-century European thought.

The scope of this book is deliberately restricted. After a brief survey of Russian Medieval, Classical and Romantic texts, the analysis will focus on the technique of the literary dream in the works of four major Russian authors: Pushkin, Gogol, Dostoevsky, and Tolstoy. This selection is not intended to be exhaustive. Other works of the same period also make use of this technique: Lermontov's fragment "Shtoss" (1841), Odoevsky's collection *Russian Nights* (1844), Goncharov's novel *Oblomov* (1859),[56] Chernyshevsky's *What is to be Done?* (1863), as well as various pieces by Turgenev[57] and Chekhov.[58]

These four authors were chosen for study inasmuch as their collected works include a variety of dreams whose number permits a systematic analysis of each writer's particular use of the device. Furthermore, through the writings of Pushkin, Gogol, Dostoevsky, and Tolstoy, the development of the dream as a technique for psychological characterization, narrative structure, and thematic exposition can be documented from the beginning to the end of the nineteenth century. Finally, the works of these four authors contain the literary dreams—Tatyana's pursuit by the shaggy bear, Shponka's proliferating goose-faced wives, Raskolnikov's nightmare of the beaten mare, Anna Karenina's peasant with a tangled beard—that are the most haunting, powerful, and unforgettable in all of Russian literature.

2. ALLEGORY AND POLEMIC PRE-PUSHKIN

Dreams reveal truth, but not to everyone.

>Russian proverb

During the Medieval and Classical periods of Russian literature, writers used the technique of the literary dream to establish what Northrop Frye describes as "naive allegory," that is, a disguised form of discursive writing.[1] While Medieval dreams tend to convey some moral or didactic message, Classical dreams usually fulfill polemic or satiric functions. These dreams used by early Russian writers differ substantially from those in nineteenth-century narrative fiction.

This chapter will explore some of these differences: first, by surveying examples chosen to demonstrate the variety of allegorical dreams in Medieval and Classical texts; then by selecting three literary dreams in works written during the late eighteenth and early nineteenth centuries, and analyzing them in terms of their narrative, psychological, and thematic significance.

MEDIEVAL AND CLASSICAL TEXTS

Among the earliest works of Russian letters are passages from the Bible, saints' lives, and sermons translated from Greek into Old Church Slavic. These texts served as the basis of the Russian literary tradition and influenced Russian writers when they began to imitate Byzantine models. Both Old and New Testaments contain numerous examples of dreams, often followed immediately by interpretations; these served to establish the motif of the divinely inspired prophetic dream in the Russian Medieval mind.

In Numbers 12, for example, God indicates the use that He will make of this strange form of communication. "If there is a prophet among you, I the Lord will make myself known to him in a vision; I will speak with him in a dream."[2] And indeed God speaks directly to His prophets in dreams, as in Jacob's vision of a ladder with angels ascending and descending (Gen. 28); He also uses allegory, as in Joseph's dream of the sheaves bowed down before his own (Gen. 37). Christ's conception is announced to Joseph directly in a dream (Matt. 1), and Peter sees an allegorical vision, after which he understands his mission to preach to the Gentiles (Acts 10). In all of these biblical examples the dreams are divine in origin and are eventually fulfilled.

In early Church Slavic translations of Byzantine saints' lives (*Chet'i Minei*), dreams and visions were recorded and interpreted. Inasmuch as these dreams could also be attributed to a divine source and were experienced only by holy men, they provided the faithful with additional examples of genuine prophetic dreams.

However, in sermons translated from the Greek, these same Byzantine saints were constantly warning the common folk, lest they attempt to interpret their own dreams as prophetic. Saint Antiochus in his *Prologues* advises his listeners that "it is not fitting to believe in dreams" ("ne podobaet verovati snam").[3] Saint John Scholasticus (or Climacus) in his *Ladder of Divine Ascent* declares that "he who believes [in dreams] is like a person running after his own shadow and trying to catch it."[4] He advises his flock to beware of prophetic dreams since "the demons of vainglory prophesy in dreams. Being unscrupulous, they guess the future and foretell it to us. When these visions come true, we are amazed." According to Saint John, belief in one's own dreams carries yet another risk. "As soon as we begin to believe the devils in dreams, then they make sport of us when we are awake, too." Therefore, he concludes, "He who believes in dreams is completely inexperienced. But he who distrusts all dreams is a wise man."

The reason for the ambiguity is apparent: on the one hand, biblical dreams and those recorded in saints' lives were divine in origin and consequently prophetic; but since ordinary mortals could never be sure about the source of their own dreams, they would do well to disregard all of them, in order not to be led astray by the Devil.

In addition to these sacred texts, secular narratives that entered

Russia by way of Byzantium were also translated into Church Slavic as early as the middle of the eleventh century. Although relatively few examples have survived, several texts contain literary dreams that provide an instructive contrast to those in sacred narratives. The Russian version of Josephus Flavius' *History of the Jewish Wars*, known as *The Narrative of the Destruction of Jerusalem* or *The Narrative of the Capture of Jerusalem*, comprises more of a free paraphrase of the original than a translation. The text contains a number of dreams and omens that contribute to the dramatic quality of the narrative. In one particular instance the Russian "translator" seems to have supplied a dream where there was none in the original text. In book 1, chapter 17, the *History* reads as follows:

> Now when Herod was at Daphne, by Antioch, he had some dreams which clearly foreboded his brother's death, and as he leaped out of bed in a disturbed manner, there came messengers that acquainted him with that calamity.[5]

The Russian version of this same passage contains the following interpolation:

> When Herod was at Antioch, he saw a dream revealing to him his brother's death. And this was the dream: there were four [*sic*] ears of grain—the first was dried up by the frost; the second was standing upright; but the third was fallen upon by wolves, torn apart and dragged along after them. And the interpretation was as follows: the first ear was Phasael, who was dried up by poison; the second ear was he [Herod] himself, safe and sound; the third was Joseph, his brother, who was cut down by the soldiers and dragged along without a burial. And his soul was troubled within him.[6]

Although the allegorical character of this inserted dream suggests a biblical source, its origin remains uncertain. As in sacred narratives, this dream is clearly prophetic and it is subsequently fulfilled.

In one of several dreams in *The Aleksandriya*, a popular biography of Alexander the Great, Philip learns that his wife has conceived a child by Nektanebus, disguised as the Libyan god Ammon. After providing an interpretation, the seer assures Philip that "it is the truth, since you have seen it in a dream" ("istina est', ezhe esi v" sne videl").[7] Other dreams recorded in the text, including those of Alexander himself, substantiate the seer's faith.

The dilemma confronting the Medieval mind can be summarized

thus: sacred narratives provided examples of prophetic dreams, while sermons warned believers not to trust in their own. On the other hand, while secular narratives provided similar examples of prophetic dreams, they tended to foster belief in them.

Original Russian sources reflect the same ambiguity. Various chronicles incorporate literary dreams into their historical narrative. One of the more intriguing is that attributed to Prince Mal of the Derevlians. In the thirteenth-century Pereyaslavl chronicle, his dream forms part of the story of Olga's attempt to take revenge for the death of her husband, Igor. She has just feigned acceptance of Prince Mal's marriage proposal:

And when the Prince was preparing the festivity for the wedding, he often saw a dream: for lo Olga, having arrived, gave him precious scarlet robes, all set with pearls, and black cloths with green ornaments, and tarred boats for them to be carried in.[8]

When the Prince's emissaries arrive to ask Olga's hand, they really are "carried in boats," only to be dropped into a deep trench and buried alive.

The most "troubled" (*muten*) and troubling dream in early Russian literature belongs to Svyatoslav in the famous *Song of Igor's Campaign*:

That night from evening onwards, they were clothing me in a black shroud on a bed of cedar; they poured out for me blue wine mixed with sorrow; from the empty quivers of the pagan tribesmen they scattered large pearls on my breast and caressed me. Now are the beams without a roof-tree in my gold roofed palace. All night from evening onwards dark ravens were croaking; at the approaches to Plesensk there was a wood sledge (?), and it was borne towards the blue sea.[9]

Following the example set by Svyatoslav's own boyars, modern critics have tried to explain and interpret the confusing imagery of his dream.[10] The entire passage is curiously absent from the account of Igor's campaign in the Hypatian chronicle, a fact that has led more than one skeptic to doubt the authenticity of the entire work. However, all the critics, including even the skeptics, concur in seeing Svyatoslav's "troubled dream" as prophetic, foretelling Igor's crushing defeat; it is perfectly consistent with all the other omens and assorted supernatural phenomena described in the *Song*.

Additional examples of prophetic dreams could be adduced to provide further evidence of their didactic function in Medieval literature as well as to explore the question of their reliability. Two seventeenth-century texts will suffice. They contain particularly interesting uses of the literary dream, one of which relates to Medieval theory, while the other anticipates the use of the technique in the Classical period.

In the anonymous secular *Tale of Woe and Misfortune*, the villain, "gray Misery," first appears in a dream.[11] There he urges the young hero to renounce his beloved bride, to spend his money on drink, and to cavort naked through the streets. Fortunately, the hero does not "believe" his dream and manages to resist temptation. But Misery devises yet another plan: again he appears in a dream, this time assuming the disguise of the archangel Gabriel. And the poor lad is deceived; he "believes that dream." He follows Misery's counsel and brings disgrace upon himself.

What better evidence of the ambiguity over the origin and reliability of dreams? The Evil One takes advantage of human uncertainty: rejected in his own demonic form, he can assume a sacred one and achieve his wicked ends. Not even a dream that *appears* to be sent from God is trustworthy, since the Devil has easy access to divine disguise.

Avvakum's imaginative and prolific writings include dreams and visions that anticipate the use of the technique in Classical Russian literature. His autobiography contains an allegorical vision of three ships sailing down the Volga, symbolic of the arduous journey that he is about to undertake. His less well-known fifth petition to Czar Aleksei Mikhailovich, written from his underground cell in Pustozersk in 1669, also includes a vision in the course of its discussion of the great schism. The author claims to have dreamed that the Czar had an enormous ulcer on his belly; as he prays for his recovery, tears drop onto the sore and the Czar's belly becomes healthy. Then the dreamer notices an even larger ulcer on the Czar's back. Again he starts to pray and the sore begins to heal; however, Avvakum awakens from his sleep before being able to complete the cure. That would have to wait until he could meet personally with the Czar in Moscow, after his release from Pustozersk.[12]

Clearly, Avvakum is using the literary dream for a polemic purpose. In his dramatic example of divine retribution for unjust deeds, he presents himself as a possible intermediary between God and the Czar and offers to Aleksei a means of atoning for his previous sins, namely, ending Avvakum's incarceration.

During the Classical period Russian writers used literary dreams for similar polemic purposes. Radishchev includes a lengthy vision in his *Journey from Petersburg to Moscow* (1789), which comprises a scathing attack on Catherine's autocracy as well as on her favorite, Potemkin. Novikov, in a series of articles entitled *The Painter* (1772–73), also uses dreams to satirize the values and morals of Catherine's Russia. In his "News from Helicon," for example, he is wandering about in the "realm of dreams" (*vo snovideniyakh*), fearing that, if he were in fact already dead, he would be unable to complete his ambitious projects. The author had been planning to write "several satirical books by means of which he would rid his country of all vices." But the Muses assure him that he is indeed still alive, and that he has been summoned by them in his dream so that they could express their gratitude to him for his superb use of artistic talent.[13]

Such a selective survey of Medieval and Classical dreams cannot presume to be comprehensive. The examples discussed are intended to demonstrate the diversity of the technique in early Russian literature: moral or didactic in the Medieval period, and polemic or satiric in the Classical era. In both the dreams are undeniably allegorical and constitute a disguised form of discursive writing.

This use of the literary dream differs considerably from that which was emerging in Russian letters at the very end of the eighteenth century and the beginning of the nineteenth. As Classicism was on the wane, Russian writers started to discover, then imitate, and finally create new forms and new styles. The technique of the literary dream underwent an extraordinary transformation. No longer was it used to establish "naive allegory"; instead, it began to assume its own narrative, psychological, and thematic significance.

In order to document the evolution of this literary technique, it is instructive to concentrate on three works selected from the transitional period. These texts are written by three different authors, employing different genres, representing different trends in Russian literature: Karamzin's short story "The Island of Bornholm" (1793), Zhukovsky's literary ballad "Svetlana" (1808–12), and Griboedov's verse comedy *Woe from Wit* (1822–24). In each of these works the literary dream can be said to assume greater complexity and significance.

KARAMZIN, "THE ISLAND OF BORNHOLM"

Dreams are dreadful, but God is merciful.

Russian proverb

Karamzin's short story "The Island of Bornholm" (1793) combines elements of Gothic tales with techniques of Sentimentalist narration. The narrator's literary dream is borrowed from the former genre and influenced by the latter style. The story contains all the characteristic motifs of Gothic fiction: a Medieval setting (castle, armor, dungeon); an atmosphere of mystery and suspense; star-crossed lovers; the theme of incest; and a delight in natural and supernatural terror. In addition, the story contains a dream, a device that in Gothic novels frequently fulfilled a prophetic function, anticipating the resolution of the plot.

But unlike most Gothic fiction, Karamzin's tale is related by a narrator whose sentimental perceptions color the descriptions of setting, characters, and events. It can even be argued that the narrator's subjective consciousness, his own reflections and moods, conveyed with all their emotional nuances, are in fact the compositional and thematic center of the work.[14] The literary dream constitutes one of the principal experiences that serve to characterize Karamzin's narrator.

Before embarking from England, he overhears a young man describe a tragic love affair, which is mysteriously connected with the desolate island of Bornholm. Later, when his ship makes an unexpected stop there, the narrator is free to pursue his curiosity. He stumbles upon an old castle where he requests hospitality. That night he retires to the bedchamber; there, surrounded by moonlit armor, he ruminates on the adventures that he imagines to have occurred within the walls of the old castle: he "mused [*mechtal*], like a man who wanders amidst coffins and graves, gazes at the remains of the dead and brings them back to life again in his imagination."[15]

When the hero finally falls asleep he has two strange dreams. First, the suits of armor are transformed into hostile knights who threaten him with unsheathed swords. "Unfortunate man! How dare you come to our island. . . . How dare you enter the terrible sanctuary of this castle. . . . Die for your pernicious curiosity!" Weapons clang and blows rain down. Suddenly everything vanishes: the narrator has awakened momentarily.

But soon "a new dream [*mechta*] troubled his spirit." Now he hears terrible noises: iron gates crash, windows shake, floors tremble, and a horrid winged monster descends toward the bed. When this second dream vanishes, the frightened narrator is no longer able to sleep. He strolls into the garden, where he comes upon a dungeon within which a beautiful maiden is held captive. It is only the following morning that the narrator can discover the terrible secret of Bornholm from the girl's father.

The dream in Karamzin's story does not convey any didactic or polemic allegorical truths as did those in early Russian literature. Instead, it functions as a component of the Gothic atmosphere, heightening the mystery and suspense, which are never explicitly resolved, even at the conclusion of the tale. The two dream-scenes contain an assortment of Gothic paraphernalia: knights in armor, clanging swords, crashing gates, winged monsters—details that contribute to the mood of foreboding that pervades the work.

Moreover, if the narrator's subjective consciousness is indeed the compositional and thematic center, then the dream represents another, deeper level of his personal experience—his subconscious, where the impact of setting, characters, and events is reflected in a way that differs dramatically from that in the remaining narrative. Only in the dream is the narrator's imagination truly unbridled; the host's resentment at the intrusion, perceived earlier only implicitly, is transformed in the dream into a direct threat to the narrator's well-being. An ominous voice articulates the danger: "You will die for your curiosity!" Armed knights and a winged monster are ready to mete out the punishment.

It would be an exaggeration to assert that this literary dream reveals profound psychological truths about the narrator's subconscious. But by putting his character into a deep sleep and by describing his vivid dreams, Karamzin is pointing toward the potential of such ultimately subjective experience to yield insights about the innermost workings of a fictional character's psyche.

On the other hand, the dream in "The Island of Bornholm" has neither narrative nor thematic significance. It does not anticipate the dénouement in any way, nor does it clarify the thematic intention of the author. To illustrate this point it is useful to refer to the text that may well have served as the immediate source of the narrator's dream in Karamzin's tale.

In 1792 Clara Reeve's Gothic novel *The Old English Baron* (1777) was translated into Russian and published under the title, *The Knight of Virtue*.[16] In it the hero, Edmund Twyford, has a dream in which a bold warrior and his lady appear and acknowledge him as their own son and true heir; then he sees himself walking as a mourner in a funeral procession, and finally, as a husband and father seated at a stately feast. The hero's dream clearly prophesies the remaining events of the fictional plot, and as such it is an important device in the narrative structure of the novel. Furthermore, the dream hints at the author's theme, namely, the reinstatement of virtue both in the family and in society.

The narrator's dream in "The Island of Bornholm" does none of this. Karamzin's tale is actually closer to the genre of the Gothic "fragment" than it is to the novel. It lacks a genuine plot, the narrator's consciousness is its center, and the author has little significant thematic intent whatever. Nevertheless, both in the creation of atmosphere and in the establishment of the potential for insights into a fictional character's subconscious, the dream in "The Island of Bornholm" represents a remarkable stage in the evolution of the literary technique.

Parody can often serve as a reliable indication of artistic innovation. In 1816 the critic O. M. Somov published an amusing review of Gothic literature entitled, "An Outline for a Novel *à la Radcliffe*." It included the following verses:

> While asleep my heroes dream
> Of a fiery dragon, a winged griffin;
> Terror, horror rush along after them . . .
> That's a novel *à la Radcliffe!*[17]

The images in this parodic dream and in the dreamer's implied emotional reaction are uncomfortably close to those of Karamzin's narrator in his castle bedchamber. The dream in "The Island of Bornholm" was clearly an innovative use of that technique.

ZHUKOVSKY, "SVETLANA"

Somov's parody of Gothic novels constitutes a form of indirect literary criticism. The poet V. A. Zhukovsky also uses parody in his ballad "Svetlana" (1808–12), but for a different purpose. There it helps to create his most original work, in which the heroine's frightening dream plays a central role.

"Svetlana" is a variation of Zhukovsky's own earlier ballad "Lyudmila" (1808), which in turn is a sentimentalized "imitation" of Bürger's genuinely Gothic ballad "Lenore" (1773).[18] Zhukovsky's "Lyudmila" begins with the heroine's lament at her lover's long absence in the war. When it appears that he is not among the returning men, the heroine rejects the religious consolation offered by her mother. Later that night when Lyudmila's fiancé finally returns to claim his sweetheart, he carries her off to their bridal bed. But her lover turns out to be a corpse and his home a grave. The ballad ends with the heroine's death as proof of divine retribution.

In contrast to "Lyudmila," Zhukovsky's "Svetlana" was intended to be a much freer reworking of the plot of Bürger's "Lenore." In one of the poet's early plans, the phantom-lover's return occurs within the context of the heroine's nightmare. When she awakens, her dream turns out to be true and the ballad ends tragically, like both "Lenore" and "Lyudmila."[19] But in a later manuscript, a striking transformation has occurred. The heroine sees the same frightening dream, but when she awakens, her fiancé returns home to marry her and she lives happily ever after.[20]

The published version of "Svetlana" begins with a folkloric introduction describing the preparations for the Christmastide ritual of divination, after which the heroine falls asleep and dreams of her fiancé's return. Together they gallop off across a snowy landscape, bypassing a church where a funeral is in progress. Svetlana is then deposited before a little hut: horses, sleigh, and lover vanish. Alone in the midst of a howling snowstorm, she enters to find a coffin inside. The heroine moves toward the icons to offer up a prayer. Immediately a white dove enfolds the heroine in its wings. The corpse gnashes its teeth, directing its threatening glance at the frightened heroine. The dramatic tension reaches its climax:

> Again the pallor on his lips,
> By the white of his eyes

> Death became apparent.
> Behold, Svetlana . . . Oh, Creator!
> Her beloved friend—is a corpse!
> Ah! . . . and she awoke.
>
> (15:9–14)

Instantly Svetlana's terror dissipates; darkness and fear give way to light and sound as her dream yields to life.

But the heroine is deeply troubled by what she has seen; sensing that her dream is prophetic, she is unable to understand its meaning:

> "Ah! a horrible, dreadful dream!
> It does not prophesy any good—
>   But rather a bitter fate;
> Secret gloom of days to come,
> What do you bode for my soul—
> Joy or sorrow?"
>
> (16:6–14)

Fortunately, she does not have to wait long for the answer. In the next stanza her fiancé returns home and the narrator urges her to reject her nightmare:

> What about your dream, Svetlana,
>   That prophet of torment?
>
> (18:1–2)

Svetlana's dream has *not* come true. Her imaginary adventure has been very frightening, but it is only a dream, influenced, perhaps, by her own reading of Romantic novels and Gothic ballads. Zhukovsky concludes with an antifolkloric moral, typical of his own Sentimental poetics and philosophical optimism: both divination and dreams, though quaint customs, are deceptive and do not reveal truth. Instead the poet recommends belief in Providence, the results of which are neatly summarized:

> Here unhappiness is a false dream:
> Happiness is awakening.
>
> (19:13–14)

As Karamzin's short story combined Gothic tales with Sentimental narration, so too does Zhukovsky's literary ballad. The setting, characters, and events depicted in Svetlana's dream, including midnight ride, funeral procession, moaning corpse, and terrifying climax, are motifs common to the world of Gothic fiction and of Zhukovsky's own earlier "Lyudmila." The emotions that precede the dream (loneliness and anticipation), as well as those that it inspires (fear and anxiety), are the ones on which the primary appeal of such literature rests.

As in Karamzin's tale, Sentimentalism pervades Zhukovsky's narration. His "timid" heroine and cavalier hero are sweetly sentimental, the poet's delicate sympathies are made explicit from the outset, the lovers are reunited at the end, and the amorous delights awaiting them in the real world are described in florid Sentimental clichés.

But Zhukovsky goes one step further. The fact that the adventure occurs within a dream, and that the happy ending proves it to be false, constitutes an application of the principles of parody to the genre of the Gothic ballad.[21] Nor is it parody for its own sake alone. Zhukovsky uses it to convey a moral lesson: he advocates belief in Providence instead of in dreams. In one sense, then, the dream in "Svetlana" has a didactic function analogous to that in early Russian literature.

However, in two distinct respects Svetlana's dream differs from its predecessors and anticipates the use of the literary technique in later nineteenth-century fiction. First, the dream plays a central role in the narrative structure of the work. The ballad is divided into three parts: introduction (divination), dream, and conclusion (lovers' reunion). The fantastic adventure of the heroine's dream is the structural center of the work. Later the narrative function of the literary dream will become far more complex, as it will be used both to recapitulate past events of the fictional plot and to foreshadow the future course of action.

Furthermore, Svetlana's dream is "unannounced": she falls asleep in mid-stanza, indicated only by an ellipsis:

> Timidity agitates her breast,
> She is afraid to glance behind,
>   Fear clouds her eyes . . .
>   (5:9–11)

The reader remains unaware that the heroine is dreaming until the terrifying climax and her sudden awakening. Although this device was later to become a standard convention, in Zhukovsky's ballad it was highly innovative and creates considerable uncertainty in the reader's mind as to the existential status of the events being narrated: are they real (as in Gothic tales and ballads), or might they be occurring in a dream?

Second, in "Svetlana" the literary dream is used for the first time to provide direct access to the innermost thoughts and feelings of a fictional character. When the heroine falls asleep, the reader is able to observe the workings of her subconscious and to draw some tentative conclusions about her genuine emotional state and her true psychological motivation. On the one hand, there are Svetlana's secret desires: she longs for the excitement of a mysterious elopement and a midnight wedding, mirroring the plot of a typical Romantic novel. On the other hand, there are her deepest fears: she is terrified by such a prospect and anticipates a tragic outcome, including perhaps, her fiancé's death and her own demise, as in the conclusion of Zhukovsky's earlier ballad "Lyudmila." Thus the dream provides a first view into the subconscious of a fictional character, revealing both her desire for romantic adventure and her fear of the same. It is this profoundly revelatory function of the literary dream that will become central to Russian narrative fiction during the nineteenth century.

There is one further thread that will connect Zhukovsky's heroine to Pushkin's Tatyana Larina in *Eugene Onegin*. Svetlana's dream does *not* come true: in "real life" there is neither Romantic elopement nor Gothic horror awaiting the heroine; instead, there is a Sentimental courtship with her fiancé, followed, presumably, by conventional marriage. Zhukovsky here implies a crucial distinction: life and dreams are different and should never be confused. This was to become one of Pushkin's fundamental themes.

GRIBOEDOV, *WOE FROM WIT*

Like a dream come true
[*Son v ruku*].
    Russian saying

Griboedov's comedy *Woe from Wit* (1822–24) contains the most elaborate use of the dream as a literary technique before Pushkin.[22] Since it belongs to the heroine, its interpretation has contributed to the critical controversy surrounding her characterization. On the one hand both Griboedov and Pushkin point to the paradox in Sofiya's personality. The dramatist admits that "the girl, [although] herself not stupid, prefers a fool to a clever man."[23] Pushkin argues that Griboedov's goal is to create "characters and a sharp picture of manners. In this regard Famusov and Skalozub are superb. Sofiya is not sketched clearly: she is not quite [a whore], and not quite a Moscow cousin."[24] Thus while Griboedov envisions his heroine as intelligent, but guilty of a foolish choice, Pushkin portrays her as a combination of the most insulting term imaginable for a young girl, and a member of the very provincial gentry.

On the other hand it has been argued that the paradox in Sofiya's character is one of the strengths of Griboedov's play. The critic D. S. Mirsky writes, "Sophia is not a type, but she is a person. She is a rare phenomenon in classical comedy: a heroine that is neither idealized nor caricatured."[25] In an elaboration of Mirsky's pronouncement, another critic bases his "defense" of Sofiya on the psychological complexity and subtle ambiguity of her portrayal.[26]

Sofiya's dream is a central component of her characterization and can provide insights into her subconscious that may contribute to a resolution of this apparent paradox. The dream will serve both to distinguish the heroine from her more conventional predecessors in Classical comedy and to connect her to her extraordinary successor in Pushkin's *Eugene Onegin*. In addition, the images in Sofiya's dream reveal the stylistic influences of both Gothic fiction and Sentimentalist narration, similar to those in Karamzin's short story and Zhukovsky's ballad. Finally, the dream plays a leading role in the structure of the work and contributes to a discovery of Griboedov's theme.

Although Sofiya's dream is presented early in the play, its significance extends throughout the entire course of the action. The scenes that precede the dream prepare for its narration; it is subsequently referred to for the remainder of the first act. The climax and dénouement in the last act reveal close parallels to the events that were predicted in the heroine's dream.

Famusov enters; having overheard some music, he knows that it is too early for his daughter to be awake. The maid informs him that Sofiya has just now retired after having spent the entire night reading French novels. Famusov ironically establishes a direct relationship between sleep (and dreams) and "literature":

30　Allegory and Polemic Pre-Pushkin

> She gets no sleep because of French books.
> And I sleep badly because of Russian ones.
>
> (I, ii, 51–52)

After his hasty departure, Sofiya enters followed by her constant companion Molchalin. Noticing that it is already light, she blows out her candle and announces: "Both light and sorrow." The situation itself and Sofiya's words are suffused with Sentimentalism, undoubtedly derived from those French novels she is said to have been reading.

Famusov returns; having surprised his daughter in an awkward situation with a young man, he demands an explanation. When Molchalin offers a lame excuse, Famusov concludes that the suitor's presence must be due to the harmful effects of his daughter's reading:

> All night she reads make-believe,
> And here are the results of these books.
>
> (I, iii, 104–5)

Suspecting that he is being fooled, Famusov demands a fuller explanation.

Sofiya then offers to relate her "troubled dream" (*smutnyi son*), which, she claims, will explain Molchalin's presence. Famusov agrees to listen, thereby allowing himself to be distracted from his accusation and seeming to accept her dream as genuine.

Sofiya has dreamed that she was searching for an herb in the midst of a flowery meadow. Suddenly a "nice man" appears, an acquaintance of hers, "ingratiating, and clever, /But timid," and of limited means. Famusov interrupts her account, objecting to the possibility of acquiring an impoverished son-in-law ("One who is poor is no match for you"). Apparently he has made the assumption that Sofiya's dream will be prophetic and that in it she will learn the identity of her future husband.

Sofiya continues: next she imagines herself in a dark room with the same man; suddenly, from beneath the floor, Famusov appears looking deathly pale with his hair standing on end. Strange monsters enter and separate Sofiya from her companion; while they are tormenting him, Famusov drags his daughter away. Terrible noises follow; her companion screams.

Famusov's reaction to Sofiya's narrative is complicated. Because he recognizes the presence of so many disturbing elements ("devils, love, fears, flowers"), he intuits that she has had a bad dream. But since he is unable to understand it, he abruptly dismisses it as absurd: "Strange dreams occur, but reality is even stranger." As a result he urges his daughter to forget all about her dream: "Put this nonsense out of your mind."

But neither Sofiya nor her father can forget the dream so easily. When Famusov subsequently discovers his daughter together with Chatsky, he exclaims, "Here's the other one," to which she replies, "Oh, father, the dream has come true" (*son v ruku*).[27] When she leaves, Famusov mutters under his breath, "Confounded dream!" Thus Famusov must also now admit that Sofiya's dream cannot be dismissed as nonsense, but he still doesn't like the situation any better.

In the following scene Famusov brings up the subject again, this time with the man who, he now thinks, is his daughter's suitor. Assuming that Sofiya has told Chatsky about everything (including her dream), Famusov asks if perhaps he knows the identity of the "nice man." Chatsky denies having any prophetic powers: "I'm no diviner of dreams." Still not convinced, Famusov warns Chatsky not to believe in Sofiya's dream, since "it's all futile." Thus once again he tries to dismiss it, even though he senses its hidden meaning.

When Chatsky leaves, Famusov stands alone brooding on the mystery: what is the identity of the man who appears in Sofiya's dream? He compares the possible candidates: Molchalin is poor and consequently unacceptable; Chatsky is "a dandy, a spendthrift, a terror,"— that's even worse. For Famusov the problem is insoluble; he disapproves of *both* men as her suitors.

Critics continue to disagree about the identity of the "nice" man and, consequently, about the function of the dream in the play. Belinsky had no opinion on the subject, while Goncharov suggested that the dream was used to indicate to Famusov that Chatsky was Sofiya's real choice.[28] The foremost Soviet Griboedov scholar, N. K. Piksanov, derives his interpretation from a comparison of the final version of the comedy with an earlier redaction. He argues that in the latter Sofiya had fabricated the dream to elicit Famusov's sympathy; she had planned to confess her love for Molchalin and to ask for her father's blessing. Piksanov concludes that during the process of revision the dream lost both its internal coherence and its significance in the plot, and that it should have been eliminated entirely.[29]

The American critic Ralph Matlaw agrees with Piksanov in interpreting the earlier redaction of the dream as a summary of Sofiya's courtship with Molchalin. But he reads the final version as a recapitulation of Sofiya's past containing ambiguous references to both suitors, as a revelation of her present love for Chatsky, and finally, as a foreshadowing of the future course of action. He also maintains that the dream is the single instance in *Woe from Wit* that hints at something deeper in Sofiya's character, and thus provides some indication of what Chatsky finds so attractive in her.[30]

Piksanov's dismissal of the dream in the final version is indefensible; Matlaw's interpretation, while more persuasive, is limited to a brief analysis of its structural function and an even briefer one of its psychological aspects.[31] Much remains to be said about the dream's contribution to the heroine's characterization. Moreover, the dream is fundamental both stylistically and thematically in the context of the entire play, as well as in the evolution of the literary device from Classical comedy to Realistic fiction. Considerably more complex than both the narrator's dream in Karamzin's short story and Svetlana's in Zhukovsky's literary ballad, Sofiya's dream in *Woe from Wit* is the most innovative use of the technique before Pushkin.

On the most superficial level, the heroine's dream seems to be no more than a stratagem to explain Molchalin's presence to her father. In fact, it plays a critical role in the narrative structure of the work. The first dream-scene clearly recapitulates the events of Sofiya's past life: the courtship, either actual or imagined, with her would-be lover. The second dream-scene accurately prophesies the main events of the following acts: Famusov's reaction to Chatsky in act 2, the general consternation in act 3, and the climax and dénouement in act 4, including Famusov's sudden arrival and the forced separation of Sofiya from her suitor(s). Thus the dream connects the events of past, present, and future and serves a unifying function for the entire sequence of actions recounted in the play.

With regard to the heroine's characterization, the dream reveals, in much the same way as Svetlana's nightmare did, Sofiya's deepest desires and worst fears. In the first scene she envisions a conventional courtship and specifies the characteristics of an ideal mate: "nice," "ingratiating," "clever," "timid." But in the second scene she expresses her deep-seated anxiety that her father will prevent such a match from ever taking place.

On a more profound level, Sofiya's dream demonstrates her intuitive perception of her own character as well as those of her suitor(s) and her father. Although the heroine sees herself as "searching" for something, she remains entirely passive throughout her dream as things happen to her: the nice man finds and woos her, her father interferes and carries her off. Sofiya does not act, nor does she even react to the characters and events that she imagines in her dream. In other words, she unwittingly reveals her subconscious awareness of her own indecisive nature.

Precisely because Sofiya is so indecisive, the identity of her dream-suitor must continue to be a mystery, both to her and to the reader. Just as she herself is unable to choose between the two men when awake, so too in her dream his identity remains ambiguous. The first scene seems to refer to Molchalin, the second to Chatsky. This ambiguity is genuine and symptomatic of the heroine's own confusion.

Finally, in her dream Sofiya intuits that her father is opposed to both (any?) suitors, and that ultimately he will prevent her from choosing either Molchalin or Chatsky as a prospective mate.

Sofiya's dream is an expression of truth as perceived in her subconscious. However, neither the heroine herself, nor her suitor(s), nor her father can resolve the mystery. Thus, while the reader is free to interpret the truths revealed to the heroine in her dream, she herself remains unable to use them to solve her personal dilemma.

Griboedov's use of the dream to characterize Sofiya distinguishes her from conventional heroines in eighteenth-century Russian literature. It has long been accepted that *Woe from Wit* is a striking variation on the form of a Classical comedy and that in it the author transcends many of the conventions of that genre.[32] Furthermore, Chatsky has been interpreted as an innovative hero cum *raisonneur*, a genuine character, neither idealized nor caricatured. So too Sofiya must be seen as an innovative heroine, a genuine character, and her dream as a most unconventional method of her characterization.[33]

Sofiya's dream not only transcends the norms of Classical comedy, but it also reveals the influence of two other literary trends discussed earlier. The first scene of Sofiya's dream portrays a Sentimental courtship: bucolic setting (flowery meadow) with a debonair hero of lower social standing (born in poverty). Both the imagery and the language are similar to those that Zhukovsky used to describe Svetlana's reunion with her fiancé after her awakening. Sofiya's reading of French Sentimental novels influences not only her conscious mind and her actual courtship with Molchalin, but also her subconscious mind, and her recalled (or imagined) courtship with her mystery suitor(s).

But the second dream-scene presents a startling contrast. When the idyllic meadows and sky disappear, they are replaced by a dark, gloomy interior with appropriate details: floors open, doors bang, monsters appear ("neither people nor beasts"), and Famusov is "pale as death, with his hair standing on end." There are eerie sound effects: "moaning, roaring, laughing, and whistling of monsters," followed by the suitor's heartrending scream. While the first dream-scene recalls Svetlana's Sentimental courtship, the second suggests her Gothic nightmare, as well as the dream experienced by Karamzin's narrator. If Sofiya's reading of Sentimental novels has influenced the former scene, her familiarity with Gothic tales and ballads has undoubtedly affected the latter.

In sum, Sofiya is an extraordinary and original fictional character whose literary dream distinguishes her from her Classical predecessors, connects her to Karamzin's narrator and Zhukovsky's heroine, and points the way forward to Pushkin's Tatyana.

Although the dream is never mentioned again for the duration of the play, the events of the final scenes closely parallel those in the dream and are essential to arrive at a complete understanding of its function. The climax begins when Sofiya overhears Molchalin's vulgar nocturnal flirtation with the maid. After she finally grasps the essence of his slimy character, Chatsky reveals that he too has been a witness to the entire scene. The general consternation is further compounded when Famusov enters. Deeply distressed at finding his daughter in such immodest circumstances yet again, he decides to send her into exile to the country.

As prophesied earlier in Sofiya's second dream-scene, an enraged Famusov, accompanied by a crowd of servants (monsters), interrupts his daughter's romantic rendezvous and forcibly separates her from her prospective suitors. Famusov also brings "light" onto the stage, and with it, an unintentional revelation of Griboedov's theme. After he has watched the scene between Sofiya and Molchalin, Chatsky's confusion is finally ended: he is "enlightened." At the moment of his illumination he cries out, "Away with daydreams!" ("Mechtaniya s glaz doloi!"). In an early redaction of this scene the hero's exclamation was followed by a further clarification:

> ... I am completely recovered
> From my blindness, from my
>   most troubled dream (*son*).[34]

Just as Sofiya had subconsciously intuited the truth in *her* "troubled dream" (*smutnyi son*), now at last Chatsky consciously perceives the truth and is aroused from *his* "most troubled dream" (*smutneishii son*). He finally realizes that Sofiya is unworthy of his love, as a result of either her own weak character or the influence of her environment, or both. Just as earlier she was unable to choose between her two suitors, so too is she unable to escape from her milieu. Chatsky condemns Moscow and all its inhabitants, bidding it farewell with an angry, frustrated cry, perhaps a realization of the tormented scream foretold at the end of the heroine's dream.

Although Sofiya's "troubled dream" was indeed revelatory, she remains to live out her life in a world of lies. Chatsky, whose "most troubled dream" was so deceptive, finally awakens to the harsh realities of existence. His conscious enlightenment makes Griboedov's thematic intent clear.

Sofiya's dream in the final version of *Woe from Wit*, although edited and abbreviated, lacks neither internal coherence nor significance in the plot. The contribution of the dream to Sofiya's characterization and its structural function are far more complicated than previous critics have allowed. Perhaps the controversy surrounding Sofiya's characterization can be resolved by interpreting her as an unconventionally Realistic heroine in Griboedov's original variation on the genre of a Classical comedy and by seeing her dream as a profound revelation of her conflicting emotions, as well as of her intuitive perceptions. Furthermore, in connecting the events of past, present, and future, the dream unifies the action of the play. Lastly, in the contrast between Sofiya's dream and Chatsky's final awakening, the technique is used to make Griboedov's theme explicit.

Allegory and Polemic Pre-Pushkin

* * *

Thus was the literary dream transformed from its allegorical use in early Russian literature. While in Medieval texts dreams and visions conveyed a moral or didactic message, and in Classical texts, a polemic or satiric one, in Karamzin, Zhukovsky, and Griboedov the dream becomes an increasingly sophisticated device that contributes to an understanding of characterization, narrative structure, thematic statement, and stylistic originality of each author.

Pushkin borrowed the epigraph to Chapter 5 of *Eugene Onegin* from Zhukovsky's ballad "Svetlana": "No longer have these terrible dreams, /Oh, you, my Svetlana!" Subsequently, in Tatyana's narrated dream, the sound effects that accompany the vulgar merrymaking of Onegin's band closely echo those in Sofiya's dream in Griboedov's comedy: "Barking, guffaws, singing, whistling, and clatter."

These are only the most obvious indications that Pushkin's use of the literary dream evolved from that of his predecessors. In fact, the connections are far more complex. Pushkin's nonfictional references to dreams and his historical tragedy *Boris Godunov* reflect both Russian folkloric beliefs and Medieval theories of dreaming; *The Tales of Belkin* develop the disparity between life and dreams, a theme first introduced by Zhukovsky and later developed by Griboedov. Finally, in *Eugene Onegin*, Pushkin combines a variety of Russian and Western sources to create the most original dream in Russian literature.

3. PUSHKIN'S "DREAMS VS. LIFE"

A prophetic dream does not deceive.

Russian proverb

In his commentary on *Eugene Onegin* Dmitry Čiževsky suggests that a possible source for Tatyana's dream may well have been Schubert's treatise *The Symbolism of Dreams*, a Russian translation of which appeared in 1814.[1] While there is little evidence to suggest that Pushkin ever actually read Schubert, there is considerable similarity in their ideas on the nature of dreams. Schubert, it will be recalled, argued first that there exists a special dream language closely related to poetry, and that the dream may actually be the "true state of waking."

Literary dreams in Pushkin's works do indeed constitute a special language, different from that used by the author's fictional characters during their waking states. But Pushkin would never have agreed with the notion that the dream is the "true state of waking," for he never subscribed to the Romantic theory of dreaming first suggested by Schubert, developed by Carus, and embodied in the writings of the European Romantics. For Pushkin, "waking life" or "real life" remained the constant focus of his attention, even when his characters' dreams were in conflict with the realities of that life.

This chapter begins with a survey of dreams in Pushkin's nonfictional writings; then it proceeds to analyze the literary dreams in his narrative works, concentrating on the most significant. The texts are discussed in chronological order, with one major exception: *Eugene Onegin* is reserved for last.

NONFICTION

In a diary entry dated January 7, 1834 Pushkin included a "curious anecdote" related by his old friend F. F. Vigel', who claims to have heard it from the son of Catherine the Great's wet nurse:

> The wet nurse lived in a White Russian village, granted her by the Empress. Once she said to her son, "Make a note of today's date: I saw a strange dream. I dreamed that on my lap I held my little Catherine, dressed in white, just as I remember her sixty years ago." The son carried out her request. Some time later, the news of Catherine's death reached him. He ran for his note: it was dated November 6, 1796. When his aging mother learned of the Empress's death, she did not display any signs of grief; rather she remained silent, and afterwards she said not one word until her own death, which occurred five years later. (XII, 318–19)[2]

The nurse had a dream about Catherine at the same time that her death was occurring. Pushkin was apparently so impressed by this "coincidence" that he recorded it as a genuine example of a prophetic dream.

Later that year, in a letter to his wife dated July 26, Pushkin described one of his own dreams. It concerned the young Princess Polina Vyazemskaya, who was seriously ill and being taken abroad to recuperate. Pushkin wrote: "Today I dreamed that she [Polina] had died, and I awoke in horror." (XI, 182) Not long afterward Pushkin learned that the Princess had succumbed to consumption in Rome. His own dream had prophesied her death.

The last nonfictional example occurs in a review that Pushkin wrote about John Tanner's account of life among a tribe of American Indians. Pushkin characterizes Tanner as a narrator:

> He sometimes poses as a man for whom prejudices are incomprehensible; yet he continually manifests his own "Indian supersition." Tanner believes in the dreams and predictions of old women; both always come true for him. (XII, 121)

Then Pushkin relates a "poetic description" of a dream in which two Indian ghosts, the perpetrator and victim of a violent fratricide, haunt Tanner's sleep.

Death is a common motif in these three examples: the wet nurse dreams of Catherine as her death occurs; Pushkin dreams about the princess's demise shortly before the event; and Tanner is haunted by the Indian brothers. A death in the present, the future, and the past: each is reflected in a dream, recorded, and assumed to be true. Pushkin's belief in the prophetic power of dreams is precisely the attitude against which Byzantine saints warned their flocks in sermons translated into Church Slavic. His autobiographical experience parallels the literary dreams that he ascribes to his fictional characters as well as the belief that they and the reader are asked to place in them.

RUSLAN AND LYUDMILA, "THE GAVRIILIADA," AND "THE BRIDEGROOM"

In three early narrative works written before *Boris Godunov*, Pushkin's use of the literary dream is fairly straightforward. The hero's "prophetic dream" in *Ruslan and Lyudmila*, Mary's "wondrous dream" in "The Gavriiliada," and Natasha's "bad dream" in "The Bridegroom," are central to the narrative structure of each work and contribute to the characterization of the individual dreamer.

In his preface to the second edition of *Ruslan and Lyudmila* (1820), Pushkin lists the questions that contemporary critics posed about the meaning of his narrative poem. The hero's dream was one of the passages that puzzled them most. Ruslan has just defeated the wicked Chernomor and is returning to Kiev with his bride in his arms and the villain strapped over his saddle. During his journey he encounters his former rival Ratmir, who, having abandoned his own search for the heroine Lyudmila, has surrendered to sensual delights. Farlaf, the only remaining challenger, has been rescued from his sulking seclusion by the witch Naina.

That night Ruslan pauses to contemplate his fate; "deep thoughts" and "dreams" (*mechty*) swirl in his head. Finally he dozes off and has a "prophetic dream" (*veshchii son*). In the first scene the hero sees his beloved "motionless and pale," poised on the brink of an abyss. Suddenly she disappears; he hears her voice, a moan, and then follows her.

In the second scene the heroine's father Vladimir sits in his great hall in Kiev surrounded by sons, warriors, and guests. He is furious; silence prevails. The valiant Rogdai, although previously slain by Ruslan, now sits drinking among the guests. Even Ratmir, who had given up the chase, is present. The only sound audible is that of

Boyan's "prophetic" voice and its mournful musical accompaniment. When Farlaf enters leading Lyudmila by the hand, the guests remain silent while Vladimir lowers his head sadly. This scene fades slowly. In his sleep, Ruslan sheds "agonizing tears"; he knows that he is dreaming, but is unable to wake himself up:

> In consternation he thinks:
>   this is a dream [*son*]!
> He pines, but alas, the ominous dream [*greza*]
> He is unable to interrupt.
>
> (IV, 73)

Pushkin's critics asked, "What does Ruslan's dream prophesy?" The critic M. O. Gershenzon interprets it as a reflection of the hero's fear of his own remaining rival Farlaf, as a summary of his past experience (Lyudmila's disappearance and his pursuit), and as a prophecy: while Ruslan sleeps, Farlaf actually steals Lyudmila and subsequently returns with her to a joyless Kiev. Gershenzon concludes that even if one grants Ruslan a deep fear of Farlaf, "such precise foresight of the facts remains an enigma."[3]

In fact, Ruslan's dream recapitulates in reverse order the main events of the narrative as presented in the first canto. There at the wedding feast in Vladimir's hall sit the bride and groom, the three rejected suitors, and the vatic bard. Just as the couple is about to retire, Lyudmila mysteriously vanishes. It is then that Vladimir commissions the desperate Ruslan and hopeful suitors to search for his abducted daughter.

In the hero's dream the disappearance is described first, followed by the pursuit of Ruslan's beloved. The striking image of the "abyss" into which the characters "fall headlong" was to become a leitmotif of Pushkin's literary dreams. Here it reflects the hero's psychological state: his fear of the mystery and his anxiety over the fate of his bride.

The second scene is a direct parallel to the actual wedding, but joy is replaced by gloom. As on that occasion the rejected suitors are present; but when Farlaf enters leading Lyudmila, the dream shifts from recapitulation of past events to prophecy of future ones. In just such a way will Farlaf return to Kiev with the heroine, and his reception will be similarly unenthusiastic. Indeed, at the conclusion of Ruslan's dream Farlaf actually stabs the dreamer and captures his unfortunate bride.

Ruslan's dream, then, plays a unifying role in the narrative structure of the poem inasmuch as it both recapitulates the past and prophesies the future. The parallelism of the three scenes in Vladimir's hall (wedding, dream, and return) establishes a symmetry that brings the action full circle. The hero's emotional state at the time of his dream is represented by the images he sees and by his reaction to them: his despair at the loss of his beloved, his valiant search for her, his fear of the third rival, and his anguish at his own inability to interrupt his vision.

Mary's dream fulfills a similar function in the structure of "The Gavriiliada" (1821), as well as providing irreverent insights into the heroine's state of mind. The Annunciation in the New Testament is presented with no mention of any dream. "An angel was sent [to Mary] . . . he came to her . . . he went away from her." In contrast, Pushkin places the event into a dream framework: Mary dreams that the heavens open; she sees angels, seraphim, cherubim, and archangels; God Himself appears and summons her. Although flattered, Mary cannot keep from noticing the attentions of Gabriel, and she herself is quite taken with his good looks. Upon awakening, the "wondrous dream" (*divnyi son*) lingers in her memory. Later, when Gabriel appears and drives away the Devil, who has himself just taken advantage of Mary's charms, he first delivers the heavenly message, and then proceeds to consummate his own passion for the future Mother of God. At last he is followed by God Himself in the form of a dove: the exhausted heroine's dream is thus finally fulfilled. Thus the dream both unifies the narrative structure of "The Gavriiliada" and contributes to the characterization of the "earthly" heroine, portraying Mary as more infatuated with the handsome archangel than honored by her holy destiny.

Pushkin's literary ballad "The Bridegroom" (1824-25) contains another variation of the dream as narrative device, as well as a means of characterization. The heroine, Natasha, accounts for her poor spirits at the wedding feast by relating her "dream" of the previous night; each of her three installments is followed by an interpretative commentary by the bridegroom. First Natasha describes the setting of her dream, a cottage with booty prominently displayed; the suitor suggests that the scene predicts wealth. Then she narrates the arrival of a rowdy band with a captured girl; he interprets this scene as prophesying merriment. Finally, Natasha depicts the unruly feast, the girl's grief, and the violent severing of her hand. Now the bridegroom objects; he vociferously rejects the validity of her dream-narration. But Natasha heroically challenges him and exposes his crime.

In one sense the dream is no more than a clever stratagem that allows the heroine to complete the telling of her tale. Here Pushkin may be borrowing Sofiya's ruse in Griboedov's *Woe from Wit*; indeed, Natasha echoes a line from her predecessor's second dream-scene: Sofiya talks of "shouting, roaring, laughing and the whistling of monsters accompany us," Natasha of "shouting, laughing, singing, noise and sound. / A wild free-for-all." Like Sofiya's dream, Natasha's tale is organized and narrated as if it too were an actual dream. The bridegroom interprets each scene favorably, until he recognizes the trap. Then he denies the validity of the dream—"But this . . . / Is plain make-believe"—echoing Famusov's dismissal of such phenomena in the early redaction of Griboedov's comedy—"What make-believe that is!"[4]

BORIS GODUNOV

The literary dreams of Ruslan, Mary, and Natasha are central to the narrative structure of their respective works and contribute significantly to the characterization of the dreamers. Grigory's dream in *Boris Godunov* (1825) shares these characteristics; but here the similarity ends. In *Boris* Pushkin introduces the distinction between the conscious dream (*mechta*) and the subconscious dream (*son*); he makes an effort to differentiate the language of Grigory's dream (*son*), and offers a Medieval explanation of its source; and finally, the author does not limit himself to Grigory's dream alone. Dreams and dreamers proliferate: they are woven into the fabric of the work and contribute to the expression of one of its central themes.

Grigory's dream occurs in the scene entitled, "Night. A Cell in the Chudov Monastery":

> The same dream [*son*] yet again!
> It is possible? For the third time!
> Accursed dream!
> (VII, 18)

The young dreamer's first words upon awakening emphasize at once the repetition, his astonishment at such an occurrence, and the superstitious number three, and hint at the possibility of the dream's demonic origin. Grigory himself subsequently refers to his dream as "diabolical" (*besovskoe mechtan'e*) and indicates an awareness of its source: "the Devil was disturbing me" (*"vrag menya mutil"*).⁵

Grigory's dream consists of one short scene: a steep staircase leads him up to a tower from which all of Moscow is visible. On the square below people point up and laugh at him; the dreamer feels ashamed and afraid; he falls headlong from the tower, and suddenly awakens.

The early versions of the play demonstrate clearly the creative process by which Pushkin tried to distinguish the language of Grigory's dream from the surrounding text. The dreamer is gradually transformed into the object of every verb in the passage; first person forms disappear until Grigory is acted upon entirely by external agents (Devil, tower, crowd).⁶ Only the last line of the dream differs dramatically from the pattern: "And falling headlong, I awoke." The personal pronoun returns at the moment of the dreamer's awakening.⁷

Pushkin has introduced Grigory as a character to be contrasted with Pimen. Before recounting his troubled dream, the young monk makes this theme explicit: while he himself sleeps and dreams, Pimen does neither; instead, he labors over his chronicles. Upon hearing Grigory's dream, Pimen attributes it entirely to the monk's youth and urges a regimen of prayers and fasting, from which pleasant dreams would inevitably result. Pimen confesses that even at his advanced age, if he ever neglects his prayers, then bad dreams are sure to follow:

> I dream [*mne chudyatsya*] of boisterous feasts,
> Or military camp, or warlike encounters,
> The senseless amusements of my younger years!
> (VII, 19)

Pimen's dreams, which in an early manuscript are also curiously attributed to a demonic source,⁸ are based on his own personal history and recapitulate the events of his premonastic life.

Grigory's reaction is noteworthy: this is precisely the kind of excitement for which he longs. Only after he had lived life to the fullest would he retreat to a monastery. Grigory thus aspires to imitate Pimen's model. Bored by his tranquil existence, envious of Pimen's glorious past, the young monk adopts as his aspiration or conscious dream (*mechta*) what Pimen now sees only infrequently in his subconscious dream (*son*).

In a subsequent scene that Pushkin had originally intended to follow this one, Grigory was to have complained to a certain "evil monk" about his monotonous existence.[9] Referring once again to his troubled sleep, Grigory also reiterates the diabolical origin of his dream. The "evil monk" exacerbates his young friend's frustration and then proposes that Grigory assume the identity of the murdered Czarevitch. Pushkin later omitted this scene, probably because it depicted Grigory's motivation as too explicit. In the final version the decision to impersonate Dmitry occurs offstage, between scenes; only his escape from the monastery is reported.

Upon learning the awesome news of Dmitry's pretense, the abbot hints at a related theme: "Literacy comes to him not/ From the Lord God." This point of view is echoed by the Patriarch: "I've had enough of these literate ones." When Grigory's outrageous threat is quoted ("I will be Czar in Moscow"), the Patriarch pronounces him to be both a "diabolic vessel" and a "person in league with the Devil," and labels his defection as "heresy." Later, the Czar's edict repeats this judgment: "He fell into heresy and [was], . . . instructed/ By the Devil." Not only Grigory's dream, but also his literacy are presented as suspect.

Belinsky cryptically asserted that the entire future of the Pretender was contained in his troubled dream.[10] Gershenzon characterized the dream as "psychological in content" and "symbolic in form." He first suggested, but did not develop, the distinction between conscious dream (*mechta*) and subconscious dream (*son*).[11]

Pushkin could hardly have believed that the Devil was the real source of Grigory's dream. Rather, in a conscientious attempt to recreate a Medieval world view in his historical tragedy, the dramatist transformed his own conception of irrational forces operating within the human personality and metaphorically attributed his characters' dreams to demonic sources. These same "sources" or "forces" correspond to the modern reader's concept of the subconscious.

Grigory's experiential dream (*son*) actually reveals prophetically *in* the dreamer's subconscious and *to* the reader's conscious the dire consequences of Grigory's pursuing his own conscious dream (*mechta*). In other words, if he will insist on abandoning his monastic existence to experience "battles and feasts," he will undoubtedly be destroyed. Thus, in his subconscious dream (*son*) Grigory sees himself elevated to a position of power over the people, but the crowd's ridicule produces a profound psychological reaction: he feels ashamed and afraid. He falls and awakens.[12] But Grigory ignores this subconscious warning; he chooses instead to pursue his conscious dream (*mechta*). By the end of the play, he has indeed achieved his ambition to become Czar; his "downfall" occurs only afterward and is foreshadowed by Pushkin's final (controversial) stage direction, implying the people's silent acceptance of the "legitimate" heir's death.

Grigory is not the only dreamer in the work. Aside from Pimen, whose dreams were discussed above, Boris Godunov lets escape a startling admission when he learns of the appearance of the Pretender:

> So that is why for thirteen years in a row
> I keep dreaming [*snilosya*]
>   of that dead child!
> Yes, yes indeed! Now I understand.
>   (VII, 49)

Thus, in another repeated dream, with its own superstitious number, Pushkin reveals the powerful subconscious of another fictional character. The villain is haunted by the image of his innocent victim: Boris's dream is a profound acknowledgment of his guilt.

As Grigory's dream was juxtaposed with Pimen's, so Boris's can be contrasted to the shepherd's vision as related by the Patriarch. A poor blind man dreamed that he heard a child's voice directing him to pray for the restoration of his sight. This child identified himself as the Czarevitch Dmitry. The shepherd undertook a pilgrimage to Uglich, and there he miraculously regained his vision. The Patriarch acknowledges that other pilgrims have reported similar cures and consequently advises Boris to transfer the Czarevitch's relics to Moscow to prove not only that Dmitry was in fact dead, but also that he had been accepted among the assembly of saints. Boris is confounded; he knows full well that a child can become a saint only if it has been martyred. Shuisky quickly rejects the Patriarch's proposal, thereby "rescuing" Boris from his embarrassing predicament. Apparently the image of the Czarevitch haunts not only the murderer's dreams; it also returns to plague him through the vision of a simple shepherd, a representative of the people and a spokesman for the truth.

Pushkin articulated his own views on the subject of drama in a review of Pogodin's play *Martha the Mayoress*. "Truth of passions, verisimilitude of feelings in given circumstances—this is what our mind demands from the dramatic writer" (XI, 178). He insists on "psychological realism," that is, the depiction of character in its many-sided complexity.[13] In *Boris Godunov* the device of the literary dream is one means of achieving this goal. The insights provided by Grigory's two dreams (*son* and *mechta*), Pimen's reminiscences, Boris's recurrent nightmare, and the shepherd's vision provide evidence of Pushkin's psychological realism, including profound revelations on the level of the fictional characters' subconscious.

THE TALES OF BELKIN

In *Boris Godunov* Grigory's dreams were metaphorically attributed to the Devil, while the Patriarch suggested that the Pretender's literacy emanates from the same source. From this accurate recreation of the Medieval world view, Pushkin moves next to a debunking of the Romantic one. In *The Tales of Belkin* (1830) he attributes his fictional characters' dreams to literary sources exclusively. These dreams contribute directly to an understanding of one of the author's main themes in the collection: the disparity between art and life.

In "The Snowstorm," the heroine, Marya Gavrilovna, on the night before her elopement with her beloved Vladimir, feigns a headache and retires early. Upon falling asleep, she has two "horrible dreams" (*mechtaniya*). In the first, just as she is about to climb up into Vladimir's sleigh, her father violently drags her from the scene. With a "sinking heart" she "falls headlong" into a "dark, bottomless pit." In the second dream-scene, the heroine sees her pale beloved lying wounded on the grass; he implores her to marry him before he dies. She awakes from these and other "outrageous, senseless visions" "paler than usual," now suffering from a genuine headache.

As in the analysis of *Boris Godunov*, a distinction between the heroine's two dreams (*son* and *mechta*) is essential for understanding the function of the device in the tale.[14] Pushkin describes his heroine as one who was "raised on French novels, and consequently, was in love." Marya's conscious dream (*mechta*) is derived from her reading and reflects the characters and plot of Romantic fiction: a sensitive heroine, dashing hero, and interfering parents; forbidden love, secret elopement, suffering, confession, and finally, parental acceptance. Similarly, Marya's subconscious dream (*son*) is another, more dramatic enactment of this same Romantic paradigm: first by exaggeration, she sees her vengeful father as the insurmountable obstacle to her happiness; second by distortion, she imagines her lover's death on the battlefield. Both scenes in her subconscious dream (*son*) are as literary and as Romantic as the elopment projected in her conscious dream (*mechta*).

But "reality" intervenes. "Life" is unlike "art," the "literary art" reflected in the heroine's two dreams (*mechta* and *son*). The real obstacles to her plan are the forces of nature and of human nature: the snowstorm, an external element, representing the power of fate; and Marya's parents, who respond to her plight with sympathetic understanding, and subsequently become reconciled to her choice of suitor. But the "hero" departs in shame to die in ignominy. Burmin's arrival, his account of the strange "incomprehensible" incident, and his emotional reunion with his long-lost wife are an ironic coincidence, a parody of the conventional dénouement. This twist of fate unexpectedly results in happiness for the heroine in a way unforeseen in either of her two dreams. Thus, both of Marya's dreams (*mechta* and *son*), derived from literary sources, prove to be unrealistic. Life simply does not follow the pattern of Romantic art.

Nor does it follow the pattern of Gothic tales, as Adriyan Prokhorov discovers in "The Coffin Maker." As Pushkin contrasts the conventional portrait of the "cheerful and jocular" gravediggers portrayed by Shakespeare and Sir Walter Scott with the gloomy and cantankerous hero of his own story,[15] so too Adriyan's dream (*son*) reveals that corpses do not conform to the reader's literary expectations.

One night the hero returns from a party, where a toast had been proposed by one of the guests to their respective "clients"; several jokes made at Adriyan's expense had offended him. He decides not to return the hospitality, and instead, plans to invite all his former "clients" to a party. So resolved, he goes to sleep. The narrator observes that it was still dark "when they awoke Adriyan." It is with these words that the hero's unannounced dream (*son*) begins; the reader remains temporarily unaware that the hero is actually dreaming.

The old merchant Tryukhina has died, and the coffin maker is being summoned to make the necessary arrangements.[16] Later, when Adriyan returns home, he discovers that his own house is full of corpses. By moonlight he recognizes his former customers. A brigadier acting as spokesman explains that the corpses are merely responding to the coffin maker's kind invitation. When Kurilkin, the hero's very first client, and one of the many that he had swindled, steps forward to offer an "embrace," Adriyan pushes him away. When this corpse disintegrates, the others threaten the frightened hero, who is almost crushed in the chaos; he "loses consciousness" and suddenly *awakens*.

The hero's dream both serves as the structural center of the tale and also leads to a discovery of Pushkin's theme. Like Svetlana's nightmare and Sofiya's second dream-scene, it is replete with the paraphernalia of Gothic tales (corpses, skeletons, bones). But once again life fails to imitate art. As in "The Snowstorm," forces of human nature intervene. Unlike the literary paradigm that the reader might expect, Adriyan's corpses look and act like ordinary people. Each is dressed according to his position in the social hierarchy. They display a wide range of human emotions (gratitude, friendliness, pride, and shame) and become menacing only after the coffin maker rejects an ambiguous "embrace." It is then Adriyan feels "deafened" and "crushed"; losing his presence of mind, he falls upon the bones and faints dead away. These corpses are not frightening in the conventional macabre manner; instead, their behavior is all too recognizably human.

Just as Marya accepts a "substitute" suitor at the conclusion to "The Snowstorm," Adriyan's life is restored to "normal" with comparable irony. Upon awakening he observes, "Well, if that's the way it is, then bring me some tea at once, and call my daughters." Both Marya's dreams and Adriyan's nightmare illustrate one of Pushkin's main themes in *The Tales of Belkin*: art and life are disparate, and any expectation that reality will conform to literary patterns will inevitably be frustrated.[17]

"THE QUEEN OF SPADES"

In "The Queen of Spades" (1833) Pushkin's thematic focus shifts from the conflict between art and life to that between "imagination" and "calculation."[18] Germann's dreams and the question of their source are fundamental to an understanding of that theme.

Dostoevsky considered Pushkin's tale to be the "acme of the art of the fantastic," precisely because the reader is unable to decide whether the hero's "vision" of the countess (chapter 5) originates from Germann's own mind, or whether he is in contact with another world.[19] While Shklovsky referred to another of the hero's three dreams (chapter 6) as "somewhat unexpected,"[20] the extraordinary dream in chapter 2 seems to have gone largely unnoticed. All three of Germann's subconscious dreams (*sny*) must be juxtaposed with his conscious dream (*mechta*), inasmuch as they reveal the stages in the development of the hero's imagination and accurately depict the conflict between that imagination and his calculation.

Germann's first experiential dream (*son*) results from his overhearing Tomsky's anecdote concerning the three cards. While wandering around St. Petersburg, the hero conceives of a plan to learn the countess's secret and thereby to realize his figurative dream (*mechta*) of acquiring great wealth. But in a sudden reversal, he dramatically rejects both his own plan and Tomsky's anecdote. "No! calculation, moderation, and industry: these are my three faithful cards, that's what will triple, multiply sevenfold my capital and assure me tranquility and independence" (VIII, 235). Germann's "reason" recovers and it repudiates the scheme conceived by his "imagination." He still chooses to realize his dream (*mechta*) by relying on "calculation."

But fate intervenes. Germann mysteriously "finds himself" in front of the countess's house on the evening of a gala ball; the guests are arriving in all their splendor. Under the burden of such a fateful coincidence and with a vision of desired affluence before his eyes, Germann's reason yields and Tomsky's anecdote revives in his imagination. When he returns home to his own "humble abode," he falls asleep and

dreamed [*grezilis'*] of cards, a green table, heaps of banknotes, and piles of gold coins. He played card after card, doubled his stakes decisively, won constantly, and raked in his gold and stuffed his banknotes in his pocket. (VIII, 236)

What has happened is that Germann's conscious dream (*mechta*) has come true in his subconscious dream (*son*), his desire is satisfied, his aspiration realized. When the hero awakens, he sighs at the loss of his imaginary wealth. Clearly his conscious dream (*mechta*) is not so easily fulfilled.[21]

Soon afterward the hero is wandering around the city again, but this time his calculation is no longer able to restrain his imagination. Once more he turns up in front of the countess's house, again drawn there by some "mysterious force." When he notices Liza at the window, the chapter ends with the abrupt announcement, "This minute decided his fate." The power of Tomsky's anecdote, the alluring wish fulfillment of the first dream (*son*), and the set of mysterious coincidences finally cause Germann to forsake his calculation. Instead, his imagination devises a scheme that will lead directly to the realization of his conscious dream (*mechta*).

The nature and source of the "mysterious force" that draws Germann to the countess's house are somewhat problematical. One critic, G. A. Gukovsky, offered a sociological explanation: the hero represents a nineteenth-century bourgeois of modest origins and resources, striving to achieve wealth and status. The power driving him on is the "dark force of money" and his own mania for it.[22] A theory proposed by M. P. Alekseev cites the growing popularity of Mesmerism in vogue in Petersburg society during the 1830s. It was under hypnosis that "mysterious forces" were first revealed in man's waking (nondreaming) existence.[23] Finally, according to Tomsky's pithy characterization, Germann has "the profile of Napoleon and the soul of Mephistopheles." Thus N. W. Ingham argues that Pushkin's supernatural forces are really those of Hell. He maintains that the same "mysterious force" compels the countess to appear to the hero "against her will."[24]

These interpretations are by no means mutually exclusive. In recreating a less complicated Medieval world view in *Boris Godunov*, Pushkin had metaphorically ascribed the "irrational forces" in human nature to a demonic source. In "The Queen of Spades" these "mysterious forces" can be said to originate in a realistic combination of early nineteenth-century trends: historical (the Napoleonic pose), sociological (emergent materialism), ideological (fashionable Mesmerism), and Romantic (the Mephistophelian guise).

Germann's second dream (*son*) in chapter 5 is the central event in the fictional narrative.[25] It follows the funeral, where the hero had imagined that the countess's corpse had winked at him. After drinking a great deal, Germann goes home to bed. But when he "awakens" in the middle of a moonlit night, the countess mysteriously appears and reveals to him the secret of the three cards. When Germann "comes to," his reason temporarily reasserts itself; he concludes that his "vision" was either a manifestation of the supernatural or a subconscious dream. No matter which, Germann records the experience, for he thinks that having either acquired or produced the secret of the cards in his subconscious dream (*son*), he can finally achieve his conscious dream (*mechta*).

Germann's third dream follows almost immediately and reveals the extreme state of his imagination:

Three, seven, ace—pursued him in his sleep [or dream—*vo sne*], assuming all possible forms: the three blossomed before him in the form of a luxurious [cactus] *grandiflorus*, the seven was represented as a Gothic portal, and the ace as an enormous spider. (VIII, 219)

While the first dream depicted the initial impact of Tomsky's anecdote on the hero's fantasy and produced a preliminary vision of wish fulfillment, and his second actually revealed or produced the secret, his third dream shows his imagination run wild, unchecked by his reason, obsessed with the mystery of the three cards. It now transforms real images into fantastic ones and foreshadows the hero's total collapse at the end of the story.[26]

After committing his fatal error at the card table, Germann imagines yet another "wink," this time by the queen of spades; he immediately makes the connection between it and the countess's corpse. It is the hero's last connection. Pushkin's epilogue confirms the diagnosis: "Germann went insane." The form his madness takes is the incessant repetition of his mistake: a punishment to fit his crime. Thus all of Germann's dreams (*sny* and *mechty*) have come to nought. He has ultimately become a prisoner of his own deranged imagination.

THE CAPTAIN'S DAUGHTER

The "mysterious forces" of "The Queen of Spades" are also present in *The Captain's Daughter*,[27] where their power is first revealed in the young hero's experiential dream (*son*). Although somewhat less elaborate than Germann's multiple visions, Grinev's dream plays a central role in the narrative structure of the tale, it contributes to the characterization of both Grinev and Pugachev, and it links Pushkin's personal and historical themes. Curiously, there is no mention of the dream in the author's plans or outlines for the work; the entire passage was inserted into the manuscript on separate sheets, presumably as a later addition.

Grinev has been sent off to the army by his father, whose blessing he receives just before departing. Early on in the journey the innocent hero manages to gamble away a large sum of money. He subsequently asserts his authority over his servant Savelich, commanding him to pay the debt, and over his driver, ordering him to proceed in spite of inclement weather. They soon lose their way in a snowstorm, only to be rescued by a vaguely sinister presence, which first appears "black" against the snowy landscape; then this "something" is described as "either a wolf or a man"; finally it is identified as a bearded peasant.

Once under the peasant's protection, Grinev falls asleep and sees what he himself describes as an "unforgettable" and "prophetic" dream (*son*). Although he may consider it unforgettable, the dream is never mentioned again in the work. It is certainly prophetic, as future events in the narrative demonstrate.[28]

Grinev's dream begins with an extension of his immediate situation ("the storm was still raging and we were still wandering"), thus incorporating external phenomena into his internal vision. When the dreamer recognizes the courtyard of his family's estate, he fears incurring his father's wrath for having "involuntarily" disobeyed him in returning home. He is greeted by his mother, who informs him that his father lies near death. She leads him in to receive a paternal blessing. However, instead of his father, the astonished Grinev sees a peasant with a bushy black beard who looks up at him cheerfully from the bed. When the hero protests, his mother assures him that the peasant is his proxy (*posazhenyi*) father (a stand-in for the father of the bride or groom at the wedding ceremony), and that Grinev should request his blessing anyway. When the lad refuses, the peasant jumps out of bed, takes an axe from behind his back, and starts swinging. The room quickly fills with corpses. Grinev tries to escape, but cannot. The "terrible peasant affectionately" beckons to him: "Don't be afraid, come under my protection." The hero is terrified and confused; he suddenly awakens.

Although the peasant who guides Grinev through the snowstorm also has a black beard, shining eyes, and a "pleasant, but roguish" face, the hero fails to make any connection to his dream-peasant. This same man is recognized by the host of a wayside hut where he engages him in allegorical conversation, urging the host to "hide his axe behind his back," an image analogous to that in the dream. When Grinev repays his guide's kindness by bequeathing him his own fur coat, the peasant invokes God's blessing and swears that he will always remember such a kind gesture. As the chapter ends, Grinev forgets about the snowstorm, the bearded peasant, the fur coat, and even about his "unforgettable" dream.

The reader, however, does not forget. Subsequent events in the narrative closely parallel those in Grinev's dream. When the hero later refuses to swear allegiance to Pugachev, he is dragged off to the gallows by Cossacks who repeat, "Don't be afraid," much as the dream-peasant did. When Savelich intercedes and Grinev's life is spared, he is ordered to kneel and kiss Pugachev's hand. The hero refuses, Pugachev relents, and a general bloodbath ensues. The terrible events foreseen in Grinev's prophetic dream have come to pass.

The hero's first interview with the "villain" provides important evidence of the generous side of Pugachev's nature, only intimated in the dream. In a second interview, the peasant leader agrees to rescue the heroine and even begins to plan a wedding. While Grinev reflects on Pugachev's ferocious cruelty, the "villain" declares that he is "not such a bloodsucker" after all. Following the daring rescue, Pugachev offers his assistance to Grinev, echoing another line in the hero's dream: "I will be the proxy father." But Grinev prefers to return home in order to receive his real father's blessing. He bids farewell to Pugachev, his "proxy father," the "horrible man, monster, villain," with considerable tenderness.[29]

Grinev's dream in *The Captain's Daughter* not only provides essential information about the two main characters but also develops the narrative connection between Pushkin's personal and historical themes. On the personal level, the dream reveals the conflict between father and son: the father, who blesses his son before sending him off to serve, but who then refuses to sanction his marriage; and the son, who fears disobeying his father, but who is unable to be reconciled with him at his deathbed. The dream also reveals the close personal bond between Grinev and Pugachev, the latter who acts as the proxy father for both bride and groom, and as their father figure, replacing both Grinev's father, who has abdicated his role, and Masha's, who has been forcibly removed from his.[30] Thus Pugachev is portrayed as a humane, sympathetic man who sanctions Grinev's marriage, permits him to obtain his real father's blessing, and protects the hero during violent times. But the historical Pugachev remains a merciless villain, a usurper/pretender thirsting for power,[31] and an incarnation of some "mysterious force" that drives him on. The dream provides insights both into Grinev's psychological state and into Pugachev's dual nature, and presents in outline the inextricably intertwined fates of the two heroes, illustrating Pushkin's view of the relationship between personal and historical figures.[32]

EUGENE ONEGIN

Maidens' dreams and old women's tales. . .
Russian saying

Tatyana's dream in *Eugene Onegin* is the best-known and most interpreted dream in all of Pushkin's works and probably in all of Russian literature. Its complexity is borne out by the mass of insights and inanities that have accumulated around it. Amidst this rich and often baffling critical morass, it is possible to discern three major approaches.

First, there are those critics who have investigated the sources of Pushkin's dream imagery. Their conclusions differ widely: Miller traces the bear to Russian fairy tales; Botsyanovsky derives visual images from Russian popular prints (*lyubki*) and Bosch's paintings; Brodsky adds Murillo's picture on the same theme; Čiževsky argues for Schubert's treatise on dreams; Gukovsky and Slonimsky for Russian folklore; Stilman and Mitchell for Tatyana's reading. W. M. Todd argues most convincingly for the presence of folk sources, followed by a literary one, and finally by Pushkin's original conclusion.[33]

The second group of critics has concentrated on the structural function of the dream; they differ as to whether it recapitulates the past or prophesies the future. Samarin cites parallels between Tatyana's dream and her letter to Onegin; Matlaw, between the dream and her flight into the garden; Blagoi considers it a prophecy of the name-day party; Tangl points out parallels with the Moscow ball.

Nabokov describes the dream as a "travesty of the past and a travesty of the future."[34]

The third set has viewed the dream as a means of characterizing the heroine inasmuch as it reveals her inner psychological state. In this category are the interpretations of Gershenzon, who emphasizes Tatyana's newly acquired knowledge; Edmund Wilson, who cites her "subconscious insight into the situation"; Čiževsky, the "revelation of things in her soul"; Müller, the "emotional state of the dreamer"; and finally Gregg, whose Freudian approach leads to the conclusion that the heroine's dream is motivated by her overwhelming fear of eros and her desire for self-punishment.[35]

Among the sources adduced for the imagery in Tatyana's dream, the most relevant texts are those that contain other literary dreams.[36] Brodsky juxtaposes Sofiya's dream in *Woe from Wit* with Tatyana's; Matlaw includes some notes on Griboedov but makes few comparisons between the two heroines' dreams. He also notes parallels between Tatyana and Zhukovsky's Svetlana and suggests that Pushkin may be parodying his mentor.

The connections between Svetlana, Sofiya, and Tatyana are essential for coming to an understanding of Pushkin's use of the literary dream in *Eugene Onegin*. Tatyana's meditative pose is compared to Svetlana's (VI, 53), the epigraph to Pushkin's fifth chapter is borrowed from Zhukovsky, the fortune-telling ritual preceding Tatyana's dream corresponds to Svetlana's divination, and specific images from the novel-in-verse are derived from the literary ballad. The direct links between Tatyana and Sofiya are less obvious, but nonetheless significant, including the bizarre sound effects borrowed from the latter's dream. But more significant than these direct allusions are the parallels in the situations of these three heroines and the reflection of these situations in their dreams.

As regards the role of the dream in the narrative, although Nabokov's suggestion of a synthesis of both past and future is intriguing (though not his idea of "travesty"), much remains to be said about the function of the dream in the work as a whole. As for the characterization of Tatyana, no synthesis has previously been attempted. The principles that underlie this attempt are those developed throughout this chapter: first, a distinction between Tatyana's two dreams (*son* and *mechta*); and second, the proliferation of dreams and dreamers in the work.

Before Pushkin relates Tatyana's subconcious dream (*son*), he describes her conscious dream (*mechta*) in considerable detail. It is derived from two sources: first, the heroine is *by nature* prone to "dreaminess":

> Pensiveness, her companion
> Since her cradle days,
> Decorated with dreams [*mechty*]
> The flow of her rural leisure.[37]
>
> (VI, 42–3)

The other source of Tatyana's conscious dream is her reading, in particular, Richardson's *Sir Charles Grandison* and *Clarissa Harlowe*, Rousseau's *Julie, ou la nouvelle Héloïse* (VI, 44), and Goethe's *Die Leiden des jungen Werthers* (VI, 55). In both stanzas where these titles are catalogued, Pushkin rhymes the word *roman* (novel) with *obman* (deceit), thus intimating the unfeasibility of the heroine's dream (*mechta*).

After her brief initial encounter with Onegin, Tatyana returns to the literary sources of her conscious dream with heightened enthusiasm. Her favorite fictional characters become animated by the power of her imagination and merge with the real-life image of Onegin. He assumes the traits of her Romantic hero while she rereads her beloved novels in search of similar experiences:

> She wanders alone with a dangerous book,
> In it she seeks and finds
> Her secret warmth, her dreams [*mechty*].
>
> (VI, 55)

But the desirable dream (*mechta*) soon becomes her persecutor, as later in her subconscious dream (*son*) the obliging bear will turn against her; "You are pursued by dreams (*mechty*)" (VI, 58). Inspired by such literary models and, even worse, mistaking art for life, Tatyana commits a fatal error: she *believes* in her dream (*mechta*):

> So why is Tatyana guiltier?
> Perhaps because in her sweet simplicity

> She knows nothing about deceit
> And believes in her chosen dream [*mechta*].
>
> (VI, 99)

Thus, the reader can safely assume that she will believe in her own dream (*son*). Indeed, upon awakening, Tatyana is troubled by it and desperately seeks to understand its significance.

What does Tatyana's subconscious dream (*son*) mean? The critics in the third group disagree both about the nature of the heroine's psychological state and about the means of its expression. The dream is said to reveal her "secret knowledge," "subconscious insights," "deep comprehension of hidden realities," and most often, a "relevation of things that lie unperceived in the depths of her [Russian] soul." The "knowledge," "insight," "comprehension," and "revelation" center on the personality of the hero, Tatyana's own character, and the connection between the two. It is alleged that the heroine perceives Onegin's incredible power (possibly even his demonic nature), as well as his deep affection for her. She is said to reveal both her strong attraction for him and her own deep anxiety over the erotic aspect of their relationship.

There is no doubt that the dream does indeed reveal Tatyana's "soul" and with it her perception of Onegin, but only to the reader, not to Tatyana's conscious self. When a further literary source, Martin Zadeka's guide to dreams, fails to explain the "terrible significance" of her "ominous dream" (VI, 108), Tatyana suffers only temporary distress; it soon fades, and she makes no further reference to her dream. Thus it is clearly not that subconscious experience that enables the heroine either to become more self-aware or to understand Onegin's true nature.

That knowledge is achieved only when Tatyana comes to study the sources that formed the hero's character: namely, *his* beloved books. Her visit to his deserted estate, her new awareness of his loneliness and his forced friendship with Lensky, her "recognition" of his heroes—Byron and Napoleon (although she identifies only the former), and ultimately her perusal of his library, including her study of his revealing marginalia, all lead Tatyana to a conscious understanding of Onegin's character. She rejects the Romantic notion of the hero as "demonic," first intimated in her own letter and later reflected in her dream (*son*):

> Creature of hell or of heaven,
> This angel, this proud demon,
> What is he?
>> (VI, 149)

The heroine's conclusion is far more perceptive. Onegin is neither an angel nor a demon: he is rather an imitation, a collage of literary influences, a "parody" of fashionable poses. Tatyana's dream (*son*) had failed to reveal the answer to her; it had to come to her conscious mind through the medium that molded the hero's character.

Miraculously, even after this startling illumination, Tatyana's dream (*mechta*) remains intact. During the ball at which she is spied by the "fat general," her two dreams (*son* and *mechta*) are momentarily juxtaposed. On the one hand, the distinguished company is described in terms that directly recall the bestial orgy in her subconscious dream (*son*). But as Tatyana stands alone in the midst of this chaos,

> . . .in her dream [*mechta*]
> She hastens back to life in the fields,
> Back to the country, to the poor villages,
> To the secluded nook
> Where a pure stream flows,
> Back to her flowers, to her novels,
> And to the dusk of linden avenues
> Back to where *he* appeared to her.
>> (VI, 162)

Her conscious dream (*mechta*) is unchanged: the nostalgic longing for solitude, a rural setting, her favorite novels,[38] and her Romantic hero—the experiences that constitute her past.

In the final chapter of *Eugene Onegin* when the hero rushes into Tatyana's boudoir, expecting to find her transformed into a dazzling princess, he discovers there only a simple country maiden: "With dreams [*mechty*] and heart of days gone by" (VI, 186). In her lecture to Onegin she reveals to him that she conceives of her role in society as merely a role. Outlining a preferable alternative, she reiterates the main elements of her cherished dream (*mechta*): books, garden, country house, and Romantic hero:

> I would be glad to exchange at once
> All the rags of this masquerade,

> All this glitter, and noise, and oppressive atmosphere
> For a shelf of books, a wild garden,
> For our modest house,
> For all those places where,
> Onegin, I first saw you.
>
> (VI, 188)

But the realities of Tatyana's life are different from both of her dreams (*mechta* and *son*). Now she possesses a genuine understanding of Onegin's character and an awareness of her own alternatives. While the awful event prophesied in her experiential dream (*son*) has come true (Lensky's death), Tatyana was previously unable to apply her subconscious insights to her real-life situation. On the other hand, her education in Onegin's study and her experience as a society hostess, while not destroying her figurative dream (*mechta*), leaves it unfulfilled; it is, after all, only a dream.

This is the principal theme by which Pushkin's heroine is connected to her predecessors in Russian literature. Zhukovsky's Svetlana dreams of a Romantic elopement that builds to a Gothic climax, a nightmare influenced by her reading. But when she awakens, real life promises a conventional courtship and a happy marriage. Griboedov's Sofiya reads Sentimental novels and, presumably, Gothic tales. Her dream of sweet courtship followed by forced separation comes true and she is exiled by her father. Pushkin's own impressionable Marya Gavrilovna in "The Snowstorm" is provided with a substitute suitor, instead of the Romantic Vladimir of her dreams; Adriyan Prokhorov in "The Coffin Maker" awakens to resume his "normal" life, after the macabre reunion of his Gothic nightmare. Pushkin insists that dreams and life are different. Tatyana marries the fat general instead of the Romantic hero of her dreams (*son* and *mechta*): she will live more or less happily ever after.

Tatyana is not the only dreamer in *Eugene Onegin*. The hero's subconscious dream (*son*) seems to have been noted by two critics only. Nabokov, remarking on Onegin's special "predormant state," asks rhetorically whether the omens he sees might be related to those that "so beautifully linked up Tatyana's dream with her name-day party."[39] Todd also refers to the mixture of materials in Onegin's dream, with its suggestions of unfulfilled desire, foreboding, obsession, violence, and murder.[40]

Like the heroine, the hero also possesses a conscious dream (*mechta*). In the account of the fictional narrator's own friendship with Onegin, it is stated that one of the qualities that they shared was a propensity for dreaming:

> About that time we became friends.
> I liked his traits,
> An involuntary addiction to dreams [*mechty*]...
>
> (VI, 23)

Time spent together was devoted to reliving the past through their dreams:

> So did we escape in our dreams [*mechty*]
> Back to the beginning of our young lives.
>
> (VI, 24)

The origin of this propensity is identified during Tatyana's visit to Onegin's study. There, just prior to the heroine's entrance, Pushkin describes the main characters of the hero's favorite novels:

> ... And contemporary man
> Is rather accurately portrayed...
>
> Given to excessive dreaming [*mechtan'e*].
>
> (VI, 148)

The source of Onegin's conscious dream (*mechta*) is, of course, a literary one.

Upon receiving Tatyana's letter, the hero is deeply touched: "the language of her girlish dreaming" (VI, 77) stirs his thoughts; he lapses into a "sweet, innocent dream" (*mechta*) (VI, 77), the memory of his "youth." In his extended lecture to the heroine, Onegin uses Romantic clichés to inform her that while his life is over— "There's no return for dreams, for years" (VI, 79)—hers still lies ahead:

> A young maiden will more than once
> Exchange her frivolous dreams [*mechty*] for others.
>
> (VI, 79)

Much later, when Onegin catches a glimpse of the apparently transformed Tatyana, his dream (*mechta*) is suddenly revived, as hers was too by his sudden reappearance:

> His late sleep is troubled by
> Dreams [*mechty*], in turn gloomy and enticing.
> (VI, 174)

What had earlier been a nostalgic yearning for his past has now become a fervent hope for his future.

Onegin's conscious dream is then juxtaposed with his subconscious one (VI, 183–84), just as Tatyana's were (VI, 162). In a valiant attempt to divert his own attention, the hero has turned once again to his reading, but now in vain:

> ... His eyes read,
> But his thoughts were far away;
> Dreams [*mechty*], desires, griefs
> All crowded deep into his soul.
> (VI, 183)

Memories of lost youth and love flood his conscious mind. In addition to these "dreams, desires, and sorrows," Onegin becomes absorbed in a different kind of phenomenon, one completely unfamiliar to him:

> They were the secret traditions
> Of warm, dark antiquity,
> Dreams [*sny*] not connected to anything.[41]
> Threats, rumors, predictions,
> Or the lively nonsense of long folktales,
> Or the letters of a young girl.
> (VI, 183)

These lines clearly echo the introduction to Tatyana's dream (*son*), where it was stated that she believed in "traditions, antiquity, dreams (*sny*), and predictions." The two additions here are significant: folktales (*skazki*), an analogy to Tatyana's penchant for her nanny's stories; and the young girl's letter, a reference to the heroine's moving epistolary confession.

Onegin's actual subconscious dream (*son*; VI, 184) is introduced by a metaphor: his imagination deals images, as a banker deals cards in faro. In an early draft Pushkin had extended this metaphor until the player loses all the "stakes of life." However, in the final version, a brief metaphoric introduction is followed by three distinct dream-scenes each of which has a clear parallel in Tatyana's subconscious dream. Onegin first sees a youth lying on the snow and hears a voice: "Well? He is dead." This refers, of course, to the actual duel with Lensky (including Zaretsky's identical pronouncement) and parallels the climax of Tatyana's dream: "Lensky is smitten in an instant." Then Onegin recalls forgotten enemies, slanderers, cowards, unfaithful women, despised comrades: a catalogue of those insincere inhabitants of his own social milieu, calling to mind the beasts that surround him in Tatyana's dream. Finally, Onegin sees Tatyana in her most characteristic pose: "by the window / She sits . . . forever she!" As Tatyana had identified Onegin sitting at the table in the hut in her dream, now he imagines her at home in the Larins' country estate.

These three images are said to be so powerful that the hero almost "went out of his mind" or "became a poet." Neither occurs; instead, Onegin is driven to action. By throwing himself desperately at Tatyana's feet, he still hopes to achieve some kind of personal happiness through romantic love. But the heroine, who has already reconciled herself to the disparity between dreams and life, realizes that in spite of his heart and his mind, Onegin remains a slave to his dreams, unable to accept the realities of life. Therefore, she must ultimately reject him.

In addition to Tatyana and Onegin, Vladimir Lensky is characterized as a dreamer (*mechtatel'*). His faithful love is described as: "Always, everywhere but one dream [*mechtanie*]" (VI, 40); his romantic verse as: "Mute monuments of dreaming [*mechtanie*]" (VI, 84); and his German ideals as: "Freedom-loving dreams [*mechty*]" (VI, 33). In his oration over Lensky's corpse, the narrator ironically inquires:

> Where are love's stormy desires, . . .
> And where are you, oh secret dreams [*mechtan'ya*]
> (VI, 132–133)

Lensky resides exclusively in the realm of his conscious dreams (*mechty*) and never confronts the reality of life and love, not even in his subconscious dreams (*sny*). For example, just after his wedding date is agreed upon, and he is ecstatically awaiting both the "mystery of the marriage bed" and the "sweet crown of love," the narrator reminds us of what Lensky doesn't know and can't even dream about:

> The worries of Hymen, the sorrows,
> The cold string of yawns,
> Never appeared to him in his dreams [*emu ne snilis'*].
>
> (VI, 94)

Lensky lives and dies in his abstract, Romantic world.

Olga, not surprisingly, has no dreams whatever (neither *mechty* nor *sny*); instead, she sleeps soundly, even while her sister Tatyana lies awake brooding over Onegin's unexpected behavior at the name-day party.[42]

The last dreamer in *Eugene Onegin* is Pushkin-the-narrator. The terminological distinction maintained heretofore breaks down and the two words (*son* and *mechta*) are applied to a wide range of subjects. "Little feet," for example, pursue the narrator not only while awake: "In my dream [*vo sne*] / They trouble my heart" (VI, 18), and "Sometimes in my secret dreams [*mechty*]" (VI, 19).

The source of the narrator's literary inspiration is characterized by various epithets: "creative dreams [*sny*]," "poetic dream [*son*]," "dreams [*mechty*]," and "fruits of my dreaming [*mechtanie*]." When Pushkin writes of love, he confesses:

> It used to happen that dear objects
> Would appear to me in dreams [*snilis'*], and my soul
> Preserved their secret image;
> Later the Muse revived them.
>
> (VI, 29)

Thus, the dream (*son*) is seen as the main source of the images that the poet, together with the aid of his Muse, transforms into literature. In the penultimate stanza, reflecting upon the creation of *Eugene Onegin*, Pushkin confirms this figurative description of his poetic method:

> Many, many days have rushed by
> Since youthful Tatyana
> And with her, Onegin,
> Appeared to me for the first time
>   in a vague dream [*v smutnom sne*].
>
> (VI, 57)

The juxtaposition of traditions, dreams (*sny*), and antiquity recalls the introduction both to Tatyana's and to Onegin's dreams. There these words distinguished both characters' experiential dreams (*sny*); here they are used to characterize Pushkin's own literary aspirations. For Pushkin-the-narrator the distinction between the two kinds of dreams (*son* and *mechta*) has disappeared inasmuch as his dreams are realized in the literature that he creates.

Finally, the narrator refers to all of his earlier youthful desires as dreams, not only those that he had shared with Onegin:

> Oh, dreams, dreams! [*mechty*]
> Where is your sweetness?
> (VI, 136)

> Filled with passions and with indolence
> And with the dreams [*sny*] of a pensive soul.
> (VI, 136)

> Blessed is he . . .
> Who did not indulge in strange dreams [*sny*]
> (VI, 169)

For the narrator, however, these dreams have been tempered by reality:

> Other, cold dreams [*mechty*],
> Other, stern concerns
> Agitate the slumber of my soul
> Both in the midst of social din and in quiet moments.
> (VI, 135)

> And at that time I thought necessary. . .
> Other days, other dreams [*sny*];
> You have become subdued,
> You high-flown dreams [*mechtan'yu*] of my springtime.
> (VI, 200)

Like his beloved heroine Tatyana, but unlike both Onegin and Lensky, Pushkin-the-narrator has also come to understand the profound disparity between dreams and life. And like her, he too chooses life.

* * *

The subconscious dream (*son*) in Pushkin's works can always be said to contain the truth, and it usually reveals the dangers inherent in the characters' pursuing their conscious dream (*mechta*). But since this truth is expressed only on the level of the subconscious, the fictional characters must continue their pursuit until they are either destroyed (Grigory's ultimate demise, Germann's insanity, Onegin's isolation), or until they learn better through real-life experience (Marya Gavrilovna and Adriyan Prokhorov; Grinev; Tatyana and Pushkin-the-narrator). The Pushkinian truth that these characters finally comprehend enables them to keep dreams and life separate; while preserving the former if they choose, they can continue to live the latter.

When Gogol tried to launch his career with the ill-fated *Gants Kyukhelgarten* in 1839, it was based in large measure on Pushkin's *Eugene Onegin*. In the Romantic conclusion of his narrative poem, Gogol's hero and heroine reject their bookish dreams and find true happiness in their mutual love. But the dramatic conflict between dreams and life was subsequently to become a fundamental theme of Gogol's major works, and its resolution would be far from easy.

4. GOGOL'S "MIXED VEGETABLE SALAD"

That which we see when we're awake,
also appears to us in our dreams.

> Russian proverb

The image of a dream has been imaginatively employed as a metaphor for the entirety of Gogol's life as well as for the corpus of his works. At the centenary celebration of the writer's birth, Valery Bryusov recounted Gogol's biography in a poetic manner: "If Gogol's whole life was a dream [*mechta*], if all his *oeuvres* were an exaggeration, then what a fantastic vision [*videniye*], what a majestic hyperbole were his final days!"[1] With an equally original approach to the author's literary career Aleksei Remizov once wrote, "All of Gogol's works from the red caftan [in "The Sorochinsky Fair"] to *Dead Souls* can be conceived of as a series of dreams [*snovideniya*] with awakenings while still in that dream."[2]

On a more literal level, dreams are used as a literary technique in all of Gogol's writings, from his first narrative poem *Gants Kyukhelgarten* (1829), through his Ukrainian tales and Petersburg stories, his comedy *The Government Inspector* (1836), to his novel *Dead Souls* (1842).[3] In Pushkin the conflict between dreams and life first emerged as an important thematic issue in *Eugene Onegin*; in Gogol this disparity becomes the author's principal theme in his major works.

This chapter considers first a personal letter in which Gogol expresses his general attitude toward the meaning of dreams; this attitude will be contrasted to statements in two of the author's short stories. Then the chapter will analyze the literary dreams in Gogol's narrative fiction, ordered according to the resolution achieved between dreams and life; it will concentrate on those works in which the author explores this disparity most profoundly. The chapter will conclude with a comparison of the two versions of "The Portrait" (1835 and 1842), in which the description of the hero's states of consciousness, rather than the actual content of his dreams, is extraordinarily innovative in Russian literature and subsequently exerted considerable influence on novels written during the second half of the nineteenth century.

A PERSONAL LETTER

In November 1835 Gogol wrote to his mother in answer to two letters of hers, one very cheerful, the other somewhat morbid. He chides her gently for paying so much attention to "trifles" including premonitions and superstitions. "Your thoughts are full of conscious dreams [*mechty*]," he says; "You even write to me about your unconscious dreams [*sny*]." "For heaven's sake, mama, all kinds of nonsense appear in our dreams [*snitsya*] . . . You write that you saw a very strange dream. But when are our dreams not strange!" Then he elaborates on this point: "The dream [*son*] is a reflection of our disorganized thoughts. That which we think, that which occupies us—that is what we see in our dreams—only inside out, of course." Finally Gogol sets about interpreting his mother's dreams, demonstrating how each image can be derived from events in her own recent past. The letter concludes with a concise summary, culminating in a splendid Gogolian culinary metaphor: "A dream [*son*] is nothing more than disconnected meaningless fragments of what we have been thinking, which are then combined and made into a mixed vegetable salad [*vinegret*]." (X, 375–77)[4] In spite of its apparent disclaimer, this statement helps to explain the author's use of the dream as a literary technique. Gogol locates the principal source of dream imagery in the thoughts of the conscious mind. These images seem "disconnected," inasmuch as they are not arranged according to the principles of diurnal logic. But they are certainly not "meaningless," either for Gogol's characters or for his readers.

Two short stories contain textual evidence that indicates that this letter belies Gogol's real attitude toward the meaning of dreams. In one of his early Ukrainian tales, "A Terrible Vengeance," the hero,

Danilo, upon hearing his wife's prophetic dream, replies: "You don't know even a tenth of what your soul knows." During sleep the "soul" is apparently privy to deeper sources of knowledge, inaccessible to the conscious mind.[5] This knowledge is expressed in dreams that can both reflect the dreamer's deepest thoughts and feelings and prophesy events that subsequently transpire. Thus this early story provides a statement of Gogol's view of the unconscious and establishes the dream as the principal mode of its expression. Later, in one of his Petersburg stories, Gogol was to include a revealing explanation. When a physician is summoned to treat Chertkov, the hero of "The Portrait," the narrator observes that

> the doctor who attended him and who had heard something of the strange story of his life, tried his utmost to find the secret relationship between the phantoms he saw in his dreams [*grezivshimsya emu provideniyami*] and the events of his life. (III, 116)

With tremendous foresight of later therapeutic methods, Gogol's physician considers using the content of his patient's dreams as one means of medical treatment.[6]

Both Danilo's reaction and the doctor's response reflect the author's genuine attitude. For Gogol dreams are in no way "meaningless fragments"; rather, their images are derived from conscious thoughts, they express knowledge revealed to the soul during sleep, and they can be used as a means of understanding the personality of a fictional character.

GANTS KYUKHELGARTEN

The characters and their dreams in *Gants Kyukhelgarten* (1829), Gogol's first literary endeavor, are clearly modelled on those in the works of his predecessors. The hero is a typical Romantic "dreamer" (*mechtatel'*)—"strange," "restless," "discontent," and "searching." In fact, it is precisely his "diverse dreams" (*mechty*) that cause Gants to forsake both his rural solitude and his sweetheart Luiza in order to undertake some heroic deeds. Totally unaware of his departure, the heroine anxiously awaits her beloved:

> Gants, I suppose, is sleeping
> And dreaming [*snoviden'ya*] of this and that.
> (I, 82)

But the hero is neither sleeping nor dreaming; instead, he has forsaken his sweetheart to pursue his conscious dreams (*mechty*). Subsequently when she comes to look for Gants in his room, Luiza, like Pushkin's Tatyana in Onegin's study, uncovers the origin of her beloved's dreams (*mechty*) through a survey of his library. His Romantic aspirations are derived from his reading of Plato, Schiller, Petrarch, Tieck, Aristophanes, and Winckelmann—an unusual assortment of literary and philosophical texts. But whereas Tatyana carefully studied Onegin's books, including his revealing marginalia, the less intellectual Luiza merely examines the pens with which Gants transcribed his dreams (*mechty*).

At the end of the poem, when the disenchanted hero returns home from the "hateful, stupid world" to his rural retreat and his loving heroine, the narrator vividly describes how Gants bids farewell, not without regret, to those bookish dreams (*mechty*) that led him astray and almost destroyed his chance for happiness:

> And you, perfidious dreams [*mechty*],
> He will no longer worship you.
> (I, 99)

Having renounced all his heroic aspirations, Gants will henceforth content himself with personal fulfillment.

While the hero is preparing to pursue his conscious dreams, the heroine has an unconscious dream of her own also derived from literary sources. She imagines herself standing alone in a thick fog in the midst of a deserted swamp, afraid that she will fall into an enormous abyss. Suddenly Gants appears, all wild and strange, with blood flowing from a wound; he begins to weep, but instead of tears, he sheds torrents of turbid water. Luiza awakens to find herself being rained in upon; a natural occurrence has thus been incorporated into her dream and serves to rouse the sleeper.[7] Deeply distressed, she fears that her vision forebodes some ill for Gants.

Zhukovsky's Svetlana, Griboedov's Sofiya, and Pushkin's Tatyana—all dreamed that they were stranded in some desolate place, searching for their beloveds. The figure of a "wounded hero" appears in a different guise in each of their dreams: Svetlana's fiancé is revealed to be a corpse; Sofiya's mysterious suitor is dragged away and tormented; and Tatyana's Onegin slays his good friend Lensky.

In prophesying her imminent abandonment, Luiza's dream fulfills an important function in the narrative structure; in revealing her fears and anxiety, it contributes significantly to her psychological characterization; in its derivation from literary sources, it leads the reader to a discovery of Gogol's intention: ultimately both characters reject their bookish "dreams" and embrace "life." The hero's conscious dreams (*mechty*) and the heroine's subconscious dream (*son*) can only result in personal suffering.

Gants Kyukhelgarten establishes one of Gogol's fundamental themes, the disparity between life and dreams. The form of the conflict between the two will vary considerably from work to work. In this early poem the resolution takes on a Romantic form. Only by rejecting both kinds of dreams and by choosing real life can Gants and Luiza find true happiness in their love. In subsequent works the "life-choice" is radically transformed and becomes less and less attractive to Gogol's fictional characters.

EVENINGS ON A FARM NEAR DIKANKA

This thematic progression is implicit as early as the dreams in Gogol's first collection of Ukrainian tales, *Evenings on a Farm near Dikanka* (1831–32). In three of the stories the characters' literary dreams are presented as good, but life is somehow shown to be better. However, in both "A Terrible Vengeance" and "Ivan Shponka" the balance between the two is significantly altered.

In "A May Night" the two realms of dreams and life are located in close proximity. The heroine, Ganna, claims to have learned about some awful event connected with a deserted house "as if through a dream." And when the hero, Levko, awakens from his genuine experiential dream, he wonders whether he has really been asleep, since his dream has been so realistic: "It's as if I've been awake." Life is dreamlike and dreams are lifelike. There even are circumstances in which physical objects pass from one realm to the other.[8] Levko awakens grasping a letter given to him during his dream and returns home to share his good fortune with Ganna. He discovers that she is asleep, "whispering his name": she is dreaming about him. He says tenderly, "Sleep, my beauty! Dream of all that is fairest in the world, but even that will not be better than our awakening" (I, 180). Dreams, no matter how good, can never be as wonderful as life.

Two other stories contain variations on this same theme. As

Levko's letter had come out of his dream and into real life, Granddad in "The Lost Letter" pursues a real-life letter into an extraordinary dreamlike adventure. Upon awakening, he discovers that Grandma (like Ganna) has also been asleep. However, unlike Ganna in her peaceful dream of her beloved, Grandma is astride a bench bouncing up and down in a very suggestive manner. But as subsequent events in Gogol's narrative indicate, dreams, no matter how strange, can never be as fantastic as real life.

In "Christmas Eve" the hero, Vakula, is able to win Oksana's love only if he can procure the Czarina's slippers; this feat he accomplishes by tricking the Devil into transporting him to Petersburg. But once again, at the end of the fantastic adventure, nothing can compare with the beauty that real life has to offer. "Never before had Oksana looked so exquisitely lovely. The enraptured blacksmith gently kissed her, and her face flushed crimson and she became even lovelier" (I, 243). Each of these three early tales, "A May Night," "The Lost Letter," and "Christmas Eve," contains an extraordinary adventure: in the first it is clearly a dream; in the second it is "dreamlike"; and in the third it is supernatural. The boundary separating the real world from the world of dreams is palpable, but it is easily penetrated both by characters and by objects. In each tale the hero retrieves some souvenir from his fantastic adventure: Levko's letter, Granddad's cap, and the Czarina's slippers. The resolution of each story is Romantic: the dream/dreamlike/supernatural is good/ strange/lovely, but real life is better/stranger/lovelier. Just like Gants and Luiza, so too Levko and Ganna, Granddad and Grandma, Vakula and Oksana—all live and love happily ever after.

Not so in "A Terrible Vengeance." Although the two realms are once again juxtaposed, the resolution of the conflict between dreams and life is altogether different. Instead of life and love, this story ends in death and destruction. Katerina's prophetic dreams serve as premonitions of the ultimate victory of evil.

When the heroine recounts her first "lifelike" dream (*budto nayavu*), she manages to identify her father as the monster present at the Cossack captain's wedding. There he had vociferously insisted that he would make his own daughter a fine husband. Clearly Katerina recognizes the real source of evil in the tale and perceives her father's incestuous desires.[9]

Danilo interrupts his wife's narrative with a disclaimer: "But I beg you, do not believe in dreams. One dreams all kinds of foolishness." After hearing her perceptive interpretation of the dream, however, he changes his opinion: "Yes, dreams tell many a truth." When Danilo returns from his encounter with the wizard, Katerina recounts her second dream, the one in which she foresees her own death. Then Danilo describes his adventure and shares with her the knowledge that he had acquired from observing a strange conversation between Katerina's "soul" and her father. When she denies having dreamed what her husband reveals (that her father had murdered her mother), Danilo replies: "You don't know even a tenth of what your soul knows."

In her third and last dream Katerina foresees the death of her beloved infant. In it her father threatens that if she refuses to marry him, he will kill her baby. That night she awakens from a deep sleep, runs to the cradle, and discovers that her third dream has already been fulfilled. Within a short time her father comes to take her life as well.

Katerina's dreams express the profound knowledge that her soul perceives during sleep: that her father is evil, that she will soon perish, and that her child will also die. Only when all three of her prophetic dreams have come true, is the terrible vengeance complete.[10]

In the last and least typical of Gogol's Ukrainian tales, "Ivan Fedorovich Shponka and His Auntie," the hero's dream, which is both fantastic and prophetic, envisions a *life worse than death*. Auntie's casual announcement of a plan to marry off her nephew produces a Gogolian equivalent of the prophetic dreams often incorporated into the bridal laments of Russian folklore. There, uncertain fiancées verbalized their vague fears of the unknown in conventional imagery; here, Shponka's fantasy of married life expresses his deep anxiety at the terrifying prospect. His dream provides a summary of his character traits as presented throughout the story and explores his unconscious in great depth. It is essential for coming to understand both the narrative structure of the tale and its theme; in addition, it reveals in concentrated form the style of Gogol's later works.

After Auntie has contrived Shponka's first tête-à-tête at the Storchenkos', she coolly remarks that her nephew "must have a wife." The hero confesses that he is "ashamed" even at the thought of marriage, and pleads both inexperience ("I've never been married before") and ignorance ("I would have no idea what to do with her"). Auntie's provocative response ("You'll find out") does little to soothe Shponka's anxiety. Subsequently he is unable to conjure up more than one image of married life; two people sharing a single room all the time. He responds to his own fantasy with absolute terror (a cold sweat), and retires to bed "earlier than usual." When he finally falls asleep, Shponka's unconscious, far more imaginatively than his conscious, devises four distinct vignettes, Gogolian "scenes from a marriage," each of which alludes to characters and objects from the hero's early life.

In the first scene Shponka feels completely exhausted from "running": suddenly someone grabs him by the ear and identifies herself: "It's me, your wife." The reader recalls the traumatic incident that, according to the narrator, had the greatest influence on the hero's life, when the young Shponka was caught eating a pancake and seized (by the ear) by his stern Latin master. Thus, in the first dream-scene, Shponka's "wife" is identified with the strongest male figure in the hero's youth.

In the second vignette, Shponka's unconscious elaborates on the theme of his presleep fantasy. He and his wife are now sharing one room with a double bed; she is seated on a chair while he sits opposite, not knowing what to do. This situation parallels the contrived "courtship" scene with Mariya Storchenko. Suddenly Shponka is astonished to notice that his wife has the face of a goose, a vicious and delicious fowl, referred to earlier at the Storchenkos' table (where Shponka was also sitting opposite Mariya). There, after the overbearing host had withdrawn, the previously silent hanger-on, Ivan Ivanovich, had emerged as an excessive conversationalist. His final inane topic for discussion was "how plump were the geese running around *his* yard," as opposed to those at the Storchenkos'.

Shponka then finds himself totally surrounded by goose-faced wives. This proliferation produces morbid terror in him (another cold sweat) and an intense feeling of claustrophobia. He flees from the house into the garden, a domain previously associated only with women (Auntie and Mrs. Storchenko). He doesn't escape, but instead his anxiety increases as the proliferation of wives becomes even more threatening. He doffs his hat, and discovers a wife inside; he pulls out a handkerchief, and finds another; he removes a cotton wad from his ear (the same kind that Storchenko uses to keep out cockroaches), and there finds a third. Wives are closing in on Shponka's person. There is no escape.

In the third scene the hero finds himself "hopping"; Auntie informs him that he *must* hop now because he is married. It was she, the central domineering female figure in Shponka's life, who had first devised the plan to marry him off. Now she is forcing him to perform a highly suggestive act against his will. Auntie is then transformed into a belfry, while another wife drags Shponka up the belfry because he has been changed into a bell. When the hero protests his involuntary metamorphosis and tries to reassert his own identity, an innocent "passer-by," the colonel of his former regiment, confirms that he is indeed only a bell, an inanimate object. Earlier, when Shponka had moved from school to the military, the colonel had replaced the Latin master as the strong male authority figure.

In the fourth and final vignette Shponka's wife is changed into a roll of woolen material that a merchant persuades him to buy.[11] The merchant's persuasive order ("You'd better have some wife") echoes Auntie's original suggestion that Shponka marry. But when he takes his "wife" to a Jewish tailor, he is informed that the material is no good at all. Previously, when Shponka had returned from dinner at the Storchenkos', Auntie had evinced particular interest in the sort of dress that Mariya had on: "These days it's hard to find such strong material." The tailor's negative verdict on the same is yet another indication of the doom that the hero's subconscious anticipates.

Shponka awakens from his dream in terror and turns for help to an abridged dream book, part of a volume on divination that was his favorite book, perhaps the only one, in his library. But the narrator informs us that "there was absolutely nothing in it that even remotely resembled his incoherent dream." Just as Tatyana could find no comfort in her beloved Martin Zadeka, Shponka finds neither explanation nor consolation in his dream book.[12]

Ivan Shponka's dream is considerably more innovative than those contained in Gogol's earlier tales. It serves as a coherent summary of the hero's character traits as presented and developed throughout the story. It not only emphasizes his passivity as he submits to others but also reveals his mortal dread of women, marriage, and sexual intimacy. This fear becomes the hero's principal obsession and results in a proliferation of aggressive wives who pursue him and drive him almost to despair. The dream is an incredibly accurate portrait of a fictional character's subconscious.

As the final episode in the narrative, Shponka's dream provides a carefully ordered recapitulation of his past, a biography in telescopic form, with allusions to all the domineering figures in his life: his Latin master, the colonel, the Storchenkos, Ivan Ivanovich, and, of course, Auntie. Each of these has exerted some form of control over Shponka's life: their direct or implied presence in his dream, as they become associated with the hero's images of marriage, further reinforces his fear of emasculation. Just as the main characters of his past appear in his dream, so too do objects and places: ears, beds, geese, gardens, cotton wads, and material. Shponka's dream is a brilliant synthesis of all the paraphernalia in the hero's daily life.

Furthermore, the dream leads to a discovery of one of Gogol's fundamental themes. The author portrays the helplessness of any one individual in the face of inexorable social forces, not the Romantic notions of fate or the supernatural as in his earlier tales, but rather normal societal processes: courtship, marriage, and family.[13] Shponka feels trapped by social conventions; in the dream his subconscious produces a vision of a life far worse than death.

The fact that the hero's dream concludes the story is further evidence of his predicament. Shponka's life had been tolerable, albeit limited, until threatened by the possibility of marriage; then his unconscious fears of women and sex combine with the forces of society to destroy any chance at all for happiness. Since no life is possible for Shponka after his dream, Gogol ends his story abruptly.

The style of Shponka's dream is no less remarkable than its content. All of Gogol's other tales in his first collection are oral narratives, related in a more or less colloquial manner, full of ethnic details and local color. Some are love stories in which handsome Ukrainian lads pursue pretty lasses; others are tragic thrillers in which wizards and witches meddle in human affairs. Throughout, Gogol freely combines farce with fantasy; his Ukrainian tales stand well within the popular Romantic tradition of the period.

But "Ivan Shponka" is the one exception. It is presented as a written work with a literary style more appropriate to the choice of its sophisticated genre. The setting of the tale is fairly realistic: the fictional characters are recognizable as being drawn from the author's own social class and the narrative events occur in the familiar present. In order to differentiate his hero, Gogol emphasizes his verbal incoherence, bizarre obsessions, and limited worldly experience. Such a composite portrait, together with his biting satirical observations about various social institutions (education, bureaucracy, the military), introduces the world in which Gogol would set his major works.

But this seemingly realistic story unexpectedly concludes with a surrealistic nightmare. In it, many of the stylistic devices characteristic of the mature Gogol are previewed: people are transformed into things; images duplicate and proliferate; bizarre hyperboles, hypnotic repetitions, and illogical propositions predominate. Shponka's dream undermines the realism of the preceding narrative and demonstrates that the surface reality of Gogol's world is only apparent. Genuine reality is revealed through the chaos of the hero's nightmare. Albrecht Dürer once gave some advice to his fellow artists: "If a person wants to create the stuff that dreams are made of, let him mix freely all sorts of creatures."[14] This is precisely what Gogol does in Shponka's fantastic dream.

"NEVSKY PROSPECT"

Dürer's advice would also seem to be reflected in a sixteenth-century Italian synonym for "grotesque"—*sogni dei pittori* or "dreams of painters." Gogol's "Nevsky Prospect," one of three short stories published in the collection entitled *Arabesques* (1835), has a painter as its central character and the disparity between dreams and life as its principal theme.

Whereas in "Shponka" the hero's dream concludes the narrative, in "Nevsky Prospect" the young Petersburg artist is initially presented as a "dreamlike" figure (*litso, yavlyayushcheesya nam v snovidenii*), as well as a young "dreamer" (*mechtatel'*), suggesting a coincidence of the two kinds of dreams. In Piskarev's own vocabulary, as well as in the narrator's, the two words are virtually synonymous. Thus when the young artist first catches a glimpse of the beautiful woman, he twice wonders whether or not it's all a dream: "No, it was not a dream [*mechta*]!" "But was it not all a dream [*son*]?"

Later Piskarev has three subconscious dreams (*sny*) that chronicle his desperate attempts to escape from reality into the idealized world of his conscious dreams (*mechty*). In each vision his subconscious artistically devises a different form for his Romantic ideal.

The hero's first dream, one of "aristocratic splendor," is introduced with intentional ambiguity concerning the dreamer's level of consciousness. Piskarev "sits motionless—without sleep, without real wakefulness." A knock at the door causes him to "awaken" into his unannounced dream. The palace to which he is transported dazzles him with its splendor in contrast to the squalor of his own abode: carriages, music, marble, gold, and furs. For the bewildered Piskarev the experience is overwhelming. "It seemed to him that some demon had broken up the whole world into a multitude of different pieces and mixed them all together without sense, without meaning" (III, 27). The hero feels totally disoriented in this fragmented dreamworld until he catches sight of the woman: she stands apart from the rest, "better than all the others, more beautiful." She attempts to reconcile her earlier appearance in a brothel with his innocent expectations. But when the conversation is interrupted, Piskarev's Romantic dream turns into a frustrating nightmare as he runs from room to room in search of her. In desperation, he suddenly "comes to" and finds himself back in his own room. "So he had been asleep! My God, what a dream [*son*]! And why had he awakened? . . . Oh, how disgusting was reality! What was it when compared to dreams [*mechty*]? (III, 27). Gogol's identification of the two kinds of dreams is complete. The hero tries to recover his Romantic vision but instead imagines a variety of figures from his past life: Lieutenant Pirogov, a custodian from the Academy of Arts, a state councilor, and the head of a Finnish woman whose portrait he had once painted. As in Shponka's dream, Piskarev's subconscious brings together an assortment of characters from his early life. Once again he tries to recapture his first dream, but now he can conjure up only a splendid surrealistic image of "some civil servant who was simultaneously a civil servant and a bassoon." Piskarev's dreams have progressed from a Romantic ideal of a beautiful woman, to a realistic recapitulation of his past, to a bizarre surrealistic vision.

In his continued attempts to recover his cherished first dream, the hero reverses the order of his life: "He slept while awake and came to life in his dreams." Finally, when sleep begins to desert him and deny him all dreams, Piskarev resorts to opium, prostituting his art to procure the drug.

The hero's Romantic dream strongly recalls Onegin's vision of the "transformed" Tatyana at the ball, where she too stands apart from all other women. In fact Pushkin's hero also wonders whether he was dreaming ("Is it the same girl—or is it a dream?"). Piskarev's second dream in "Nevsky Prospect" presents a rural idyll, similar to Pushkin's earlier portrait of Tatyana at the Larins' country estate. The artist's simple country lass is now seated at a window (in Tatyana's favorite pose); once again she tries to explain away her presence at the brothel. The hero awakens in tears, bitterly lamenting the disparity between life and dreams: "My God! What is our life? An eternal conflict between dreams [*mechta*] and reality!" (III, 30). Piskarev's third and last dream, his "favorite of all," is one in which the beautiful whore is transformed into the inspiration of his art. Like the image of Pushkin's Muse at the end of *Eugene Onegin*, she too would provide the artist with the motivation to create. Piskarev imagines the touching scene in his workshop: he is busy painting, while his lovely wife looks on admiringly. This is the hero's ultimate fantasy, his paradise on earth, far removed from Shponka's vision of married life. The author observes, "A better dream [*son*] than this he never imagined."

But Piskarev is no longer content to remain in his dream-world. He conceives of a plan to implement this third vision: he will rescue his beloved from her squalid surroundings and marry her. His attempt to realize this scheme, however, results in a devastating confrontation with reality. Piskarev's prospective wife and Muse is drunk and abusive, unsuited and unwilling to fulfill such a Romantic role. The hero's dreams are shattered once and for all, and in despair he decides to take his own life. But even that act is deprived of romance: his unsteady hand results in a painful death.

For Shponka there was no way to escape either during his life or in his dream, nor was there any life possible after his dream. For Piskarev there is no escape in life, in art, in dreams, or in opium, and there is almost no escape in death. While the Romantic heroes of E. T. A. Hoffmann's tales were most often successful in their flight into the realm of dreams, and De Quincey's opium produced and sustained marvelous poetic visions, Gogol offers his heroes no such alternatives. Piskarev's dreams are beautiful, but futile; reality is gruesome, even malevolent; when the hero tries to implement his dream, life intervenes and crushes both the dream and the dreamer. Death is the only escape, and even that is unnecessarily brutal.

"THE OVERCOAT"

There is one other "dreamer" in Gogol's writings for whom death offers the only escape from his wretched life; but this character's dream prophesies neither life, nor death, nor even a life worse than death. Instead it predicts an unusual life after death. When Akaky Akakevich, the hero of "The Overcoat" (1841), returns home from a humiliating reprimand administered to him by the Important Person, the severe emotional shock combined with the Petersburg climate produces a sudden terminal illness; medical attention only serves to hasten his demise. However, before Gogol's hero breathes his last, he has time to imagine a series of visions (*yavleniya*), "each stranger than the last." First he orders the tailor Petrovich to make a new overcoat with special traps to catch all the thieves swarming around his bed. Then he asks his landlady why his old coat is still hanging in front of him, when he already owns a new one. Then he sees himself standing before the general, receiving a stern rebuke, to which he humbly replies, "I am sorry, Your Excellency." In the final scene, Akaky uses such abusive words, each followed immediately by the phrase, "Your Excellency," that the embarrassed landlady hastily departs from the hero's room, never before having heard such language from her meek tenant. One of Gogol's early versions of this same scene actually records some of Akaky's verbal abuse: "'I don't care if you are a general,' he shouted sporadically in a very loud voice. 'I will snatch your overcoat away.'" (III, 456).

The structure of this deathbed delirium (four syntactically parallel scenes) is analogous to the dreams of both Shponka and Piskarev. In addition, Akaky's visions serve a similar narrative function inasmuch as they assemble the main characters of the story during the hero's last moments: tailor, landlady, thieves, and the general. The delirium also recapitulates the major events of Gogol's fictional plot: ordering a new coat, the theft, and the official reprimand.

Furthermore, Akaky's delirium sheds revealing light on his character. In each of these dream-scenes the hero acts more aggressively than during his entire previous life. He "orders" Petrovich to make a more secure overcoat; he "summons" his landlady to render account; he "abuses" the general with vulgar language. Even though Akaky's words were omitted from the final version, the shocking effect is implied by the landlady's embarrassment. Only in this delirium does Gogol finally reveal to the reader the extent of his hero's submerged rage. It is this powerful emotion, which has found no expression during Akaky's life, that becomes the basis of his posthumous revenge in the epilogue. There the hero's ghost returns to lead a strange "life after death" in which he fulfills the threat uttered in the omitted version of the scene: "I will snatch your overcoat away!" The ghost continues his nocturnal search until he successfully locates the appropriate garment. When he does so, it appeases his psychological need for revenge, and the spirit of Akaky Akakevich can finally rest in peace.

Gogol's progress in resolving the disparity between dreams and life is now complete. Both the bookish dreams of Gants and Luiza and the Romantic dreams of the three early Ukraininan tales were soundly rejected in favor of life; in "A Terrible Vengeance" Katerina's prophetic dreams were fulfilled by a series of deaths; Shponka's dream envisioning a life worse than death concluded his story, since no further life was even possible; in "Nevsky Prospect" Piskarev's attempt to flee from his pitiful life into the world of dreams was unsuccessful, and a painful death proved to be his only escape; finally, the submerged rage of Akaky's delirium emerges in his revenge during his strange life after death.

THE GOVERNMENT INSPECTOR, AND "THE PORTRAIT"

In addition to this primary thematic progression, Gogol used literary dreams and dreamlike motifs in several of his other major works. In "Taras Bulba," for example, the image of woman as a destructive force first appears in the Romantic dreams (*mechty* and *sny*) of young Andry Bulba. Khoma Brut's fantastic adventures in "Vii," culminating in a terrifying confrontation with evil, are additional evidence of the author's interest in dreamlike, supernatural phenomena. An early version of "The Nose" leaves little doubt that Gogol had originally intended the story to be interpreted as a dream; even in the final text the hero's repeated "false awakenings" and the numerous dream-references create intentional ambiguity. In the first volume of *Dead*

Souls, both Korobochka and Nozdrev relate troubled dreams in which they imagine themselves persecuted and punished. Chichikov reacts to each dream with appropriate discretion.

Finally, the mayor's dream at the beginning of *The Government Inspector* (1836) and Chertkov's visions in "The Portrait" (1835 and 1842) provide striking examples of how Gogol revised the language of his literary dreams to achieve the intended effect. In his comedy, the evidence comes from a comparison of early manuscripts with the final text; in his short story, from a juxtaposition of the first version with the revised one published several years later.

Immediately after announcing the arrival of the government inspector, the mayor relates his ominous dream to the assembled company:

> I had a sort of premonition: all night long I kept dreaming of two unusual rats. I assure you, I never saw rats like these: black and unnaturally large! They came, sniffed around, and went away. (IV, 11)

In Gogol's earliest draft, instead of rats the mayor's dream contains "unusual black dogs" with "large ears" and "human snouts." In the next version the animals are still dogs, but now their breed is in doubt: "not borzois, but then, on the other hand, not setters either." Only in a variant to this passage, did Gogol decide to transform the dogs into "rats," to limit their number to two, and to add to their "unusual" nature, their "unnatural" size.

The number of rats corresponds to other significant "doubles" in the comedy: two inspectors, two letters, two ladies, two peasant women, two Petr Ivanovich's, and so on.[15] Not only the number, but all the details in the dream are significant: their color (black), nature (unusual), size (unnatural), and activity (they came, sniffed around, and went away) are all vaguely threatening and contribute to the general anxiety; but at the same time the mayor's dream is also extremely humorous and its "connection" with the arrival of the government inspector is illogical, even absurd.[16]

While Gogol's aim in reworking the language of the mayor's dream is primarily comic, in "The Portrait" the author's intention is deadly serious and the result is extremely innovative. In the first published version (1835), when the Petersburg artist Chertkov returns to his apartment, he discovers that a strange portrait has mysteriously appeared on his wall. Unable to fall asleep, he finally enters into a strange state that the narrator describes in considerable detail:

> Not into a dream [*son*], but into some kind of semiunconsciousness, into that painful condition when, with one eye we see approaching visions of dreams [*grezy snovidenii*], and with the other, surrounding objects in an indistinct cloud. (III, 409)

In this "semiunconsciousness" (*poluzabveniye*) or "semidream" (*polusnovideniye*) Chertkov imagines that the lifelike image of the old man emerges from the portrait and approaches his bed. The specter urges the hero to abandon his art in order to achieve commercial success. After a subsequent vision in which the old man is counting his gold, Chertkov decides to accept his advice and to prostitute his talent; he soon becomes both rich and famous. But when he is forced to acknowledge the loss of his own artistic gifts, his career is abruptly terminated. Once again he is plagued by a vision of the evil old man. "The portrait doubled, then quadrupled before his eyes, and finally, it seemed that all the walls were hung with these awful portraits" (III, 425). Like Shponka's wives, Chertkov's portraits proliferate, invading his outer and inner space, producing intense claustrophobia. It is these "visions" that Chertkov's physician unsuccessfully attempts to relate to the events of his patient's life, thereby hoping to treat his madness.

Thus at three pivotal moments in the narrative the hero beholds "visions" of the strange portrait. First, the old man urges him to betray his art and tempts him with a promise of wealth; second, an image of even greater riches seduces him; third, a delirious Chertkov is haunted by the portrait as it becomes the instrument of his demise.

While the early version of Gogol's story contains unusual descriptions of the hero's states of consciousness ("semiconsciousness" or "semidream"), feverish delirium, and actual dreams, the emphasis throughout centers on the role of the supernatural. All the mysterious events are ultimately "explained" by the appearance of the AntiChrist; in an apocalyptic vision the narrator prophesies the total destruction of civilization.

Gogol subsequently reworked "The Portrait" and published a revised version of it in 1842. The focus of the story has now been shifted from the intrusion of the AntiChrist to the conflict between material and spiritual values. In addition, the author completely transformed the dream sequence: the hero's initial dream-encounter with the old man is interrupted by several "awakenings" and accompanied by the dreamer's insightful observations on his own state of mind. The narrator summarizes Chartkov's [sic] dilemma thus:

> The dream as he remembered it became so painfully real in his imagination that he began to wonder whether it really had been a dream [*son*] and a simple delirium, or whether it had not been something else, perhaps a vision [*viden'ye*]. (III, 92)

Gogol now uses the technique of the literary dream to reveal Chartkov's true character, emphasizing his overpowering greed. In his vision the hero steals a packet of gold coins from the old man; subsequently, "gold became his passion, ideal, fear, joy, goal." The dream is also used to prophesy the artist's downfall. As the portrait of the old man threatens to swallow him up, so too will the hero be devoured by his avarice.

Moreover, Chartkov's revised dream represents an innovative depiction of diverse states of consciousness. Unlike the first published version, in which Gogol seemed content merely with "semiconsciousness," here the author explores and charts his hero's journey through the "twilight realms" as no other writer had before.

* * *

Gogol's earliest literary dreams in *Gants Kyukhelgarten* were modelled on those of his predecessors, especially on Pushkin's in *Eugene Onegin*. Beginning with his Ukrainian tales, however, Gogol used the narrative technique as a means of probing the disparity between dreams and life and of exploring the complexity of the human subconscious.

When Dostoevsky's *Poor Folk* was first published in 1846, the young author was heralded by the critic Belinsky and others as a "new Gogol." He deserved this label richly, in part because he was to continue his mentor's exploration of the subconscious in each of his major novels. But the literary dreams that Dostoevsky ascribes to his fictional characters even in his earliest tales were to reveal the powerful influence of Pushkin's narrative works as well.

5. DOSTOEVSKY'S "VARIATIONS AND NUANCES"

What you see in a dream, you rave about when awake.

>Russian proverb

Anna Grigorievna Dostoevsky carefully recorded in her memoirs the events of 8 November 1866, the day on which Fyodor Mikhailovich proposed to her. Their conversation included the following exchange:

> A. G. I am glad to see you . . . especially in such good spirits. Did something special happen to you?
> F. M. Yes, indeed! Last night I had a wonderful dream [*son*]!
> A. G. So that's it! (and she started to laugh).
> F. M. Please don't laugh. I attach great significance to dreams. My dreams are always prophetic.[1]

The critic R. L. Jackson argues that for Dostoevsky the dream represents that area of human experience in which "man's temporal, earthly existence merges with its timeless meaning, where the finite flows into the infinite world of experience and striving."[2] Dostoevsky's belief in the importance of dreams is reflected in the number and originality of those that he ascribed to his fictional characters.

Two classic studies, both written during the 1920s, first called attention to the author's innovative use of this literary technique. Janko Lavrin, in his "psycho-critical" analysis, *Dostoevsky and His Creation* (1920) wrote:

Long before Freud's and Jung's discoveries, Dostoevsky endeavored to arrive at the fundamental nature of dreams and to show their significance in a new light as symbolic projections of our unconscious into our conscious Ego.[3]

And in his formalist work, *Problems of Dostoevsky's Poetics* (1929), Mikhail Bakhtin observed:

Dostoevsky made wise use of the artistic possibilities of the dream in almost all of its variations and nuances. There is surely no other writer in all of European literature in whose works dreams play such a large and essential role.[4]

Dostoevsky himself was also aware of the originality of his use of the literary technique. Both in his first major novel and in his last, he ironically compares the dreams in his writings to the works of other Russian authors. Introducing one of Raskolnikov's dreams, he explains:

A sick man's dreams are often extraordinarily distinct, vivid, and extremely lifelike. A scene may be composed of the most unnatural and incongruous elements, but the setting and presentation are so plausible, the details so subtle, so unexpected, so artistically in harmony with the whole picture, that the dreamer could not invent them for himself in his waking state, even if he were an artist like Pushkin or Turgenev. (VI, 45–46)[5]

In a similar vein the Devil, who appears to Ivan Karamazov, tries hard to convince the dreamer of the reality of his own vision:

In dreams and particularly in nightmares, . . . a man sometimes sees such artistic things, such complex and actual reality, such events, or even a whole world of events, woven into such a plot, full of such astonishing details . . . that, I assure you, not even Leo Tolstoy could have invented it. (XV, 74)

This chapter will consider first the influence of early concepts of the unconscious on Dostoevsky's narrative fiction, including a passage in which the author expounds on his own theory of dreaming. Next it will examine his exploration of the dream as a literary technique in his Romantic tales of the 1840s, emphasizing their connections with dreams in narrative works by Pushkin and Gogol. Finally the chapter will turn to Dostoevsky's innovative use of the technique in his major fiction, concentrating on his first and last novels.

THE INFLUENCE OF EARLY CONCEPTS OF THE UNCONSCIOUS

Through his reading of E. T. A. Hoffmann it is very likely that Dostoevsky became familiar with Schubert's early theory of the unconscious. However, there is no concrete evidence to indicate that he knew Schubert's main treatise, *The Symbolism of Dreams* (1814), nor are there any traces of its direct influence on his work.

Dostoevsky's relation to Carus is more problematical. In 1854 the author's friend Baron Alexander Vrangel, wrote from Semipalatinsk that he and Dostoevsky were planning to translate *Psyche* (1846) into Russian. In a special study devoted to the question of Carus's influence on Dostoevsky, the critic George Gibian concludes that *Psyche* should not necessarily be considered the main source of the author's ideas on psychology. He argues that Dostoevsky arrived independently at conclusions similar to those reached by Carus, and that he found in *Psyche* a theory that coincided with his own view of the subconscious.[6]

The most revealing document for understanding Dostoevsky's attitude toward dreaming and for interpreting the literary dreams that he ascribed to his fictional characters is one of the narrator's extended reflections in *The Idiot*:[7]

Sometimes you dream strange dreams [*sny*], impossible and grotesque dreams; on waking you remember them distinctly and you are amazed at a strange fact. To begin with, you remember that your reason never deserted you all through the dream, you even remember that you acted with great cunning and logic during that long, long time when you were surrounded by murderers who tried to deceive you, hid their intentions, treated you amicably, while they had their weapons in readiness and were only waiting for some signal; you remember how cleverly you cheated them in the end and how you hid from them; then you realize that they are perfectly well aware of your deception and are merely pretending not to know your hiding place; but you have cheated and hoodwinked them again—you remember all that clearly. But why does your reason simultaneously reconcile itself with such obvious absurdities and impossibilities with which, among other things, your dream was crowded? One of your murderers turned into a woman before your very eyes, and from a woman into a cunning and hideous little dwarf, and you accepted it at once as an accomplished fact, almost without the slightest hesitation, and at the very moment when your reason, on the other hand, was strained to the utmost, and showed extraordinary power, cunning, shrewdness, and logic? Why, too, when awake and, having completely recovered your sense of reality, you feel almost every time, and sometimes with extraordinary vividness, that you have left some unsolved mystery behind with your dream? You smile at the absurdity of your dream, and at the same time you feel that in the intermingling of those absurdities some idea lies hidden, but an idea that is real, something belonging to your true life, something that exists and has always existed in your heart; it is as though something new and prophetic, something you have been expecting, has been told you in your dream; your impression is very vivid: it may be joyful or agonizing, but what it is and what was said to you—all this you can neither understand nor remember. (VIII, 377–78)

In this passage Dostoevsky raises two fundamental questions about the nature of dreaming, he describes the material from which dreams are fashioned, and he encloses the entire reflection with references to the all-important theme of memory.

The first question, "But why does . . . reason . . . reconcile itself with . . . absurdities?" expresses the basic distinction between dreams and reality as Dostoevsky defines it. In dreams man's reason accommodates itself to irrational, illogical occurrences that never pass unchallenged during the waking state. There is, as it were, a "willing suspension of disbelief" that takes place on the level of the subconscious, and that distinguishes it from all conscious experience.

The second question, "Why too . . . do you feel . . . that you have left some unsolved mystery behind with your dream?" conveys Dostoevsky's conviction that dreams contain profound truth, some "real" ideal belonging to man's "true" life, which transcends all temporal bounds. Yet this truth is manifested exclusively on the level of the subconscious and remains inaccessible to the conscious mind.

The passage begins and ends with the idea of memory. The dreamer clearly recalls all the narrative events of his dream, both the realistic ones described in the first sequence ("you and the murderers"), and the surrealistic ones related in the second ("murderer-woman-dwarf"). But memory is of no use when it comes to understanding or interpreting the meaning of those same events. When the dreamer recovers his sense of reality, he is left with a vivid emotional impression: "joyful" or "agonizing." Thus while the significance of the dream may be intuited or perceived by the feelings, it can neither be recollected nor comprehended by the intellect.

These reflections reveal with extraordinary clarity the author's attitude toward the experience of dreaming and provide an introduction to his use of the dream as a literary technique. Jackson summarizes the author's view thus: "Dostoevsky regards the phenomenon of dreams as a structure of aesthetic consciousness analogous to art itself, as a phenomenon that gives plastic expression to man's total reality."[8] In each of Dostoevsky's novels fictional characters experience dreams to which they ascribe profound significance; while these characters may not be capable of understanding or interpreting their own dreams, the reader can and will.

THE ROMANTIC TALES OF THE 1840s

Two short weeks after Dostoevsky had been hailed by literary critics as a "new Gogol," *The Double* was published. In a letter written to his brother the author declared that this new work "was ten times better than *Poor Folk*."[9] The critics did not agree; later on Dostoevsky himself admitted that perhaps his tale was an artistic failure. In the first published version of the work which appeared in *Notes of the Fatherland* (1846), the hero's dream is curiously absent and references to "dreamlike" states are few. Only in the revised version, included in Dostoevsky's first *Complete Collected Works* (1886), was Golyadkin's dream, which is so central to the structure and theme of the work, inserted.

While Hoffmann's *Der Doppelgänger* may indeed have been one source for Dostoevsky's double, dreams play no role whatever in that tale. But within the Russian tradition, Gogol's short stories included a rich assortment of literary dreams from which to choose. Shponka's fantastic nightmare of proliferating goose-faced wives, Akaky's delirious rejection of the Important Person's reprimand, and the dreamlike ambiguity surrounding the hero's adventures in "The Nose" all exerted their influence on Dostoevsky's characterization of Golyadkin. Gogol's Major Kovalyov, for example, awakes "quite early," "stretches," examines a pimple in a "small mirror," and then wonders whether or not he is dreaming; he pinches himself to decide. Dostoevsky's Golyadkin also awakens "a little before eight," "stretches," and examines a pimple in a "small round mirror;" he pinches himself in a similar test. While the dreamlike suggestions in "The Nose" remain implicit, Dostoevsky insists on the confusion between dream and reality from the very beginning of *The Double*:

For two minutes or so he lay motionless in bed, like a man as yet uncertain whether he is awake or still asleep, whether all at present going on about him is reality or a continuation of his disordered dreams [*grezy*]. (I, 109)

At the very first glimpse of what subsequently turns out to be his double, Golyadkin wonders whether or not he is dreaming the encounter. Later he continues his anxious speculation. "Is it a dream [*son*], or isn't it? . . . Am I asleep, or am I dreaming [*grezhu*]? . . . No, it wasn't a dream [*son*], and that was that" (I, 109).

It has also been suggested that an even more important source for the underlying idea in Dostoevsky's *Double* was Pushkin's *Boris Godunov*.[10] The historical drama explores in depth the psychological implications of loss of identity and character usurpation. Dostoevsky's Golyadkin refers more than once to Pushkin's Pretender. It is also relevant that Grigory's experiential dream had prophesied his elevation to power, his public humiliation, and his subsequent downfall.

While the events narrated in the first half of Dostoevsky's tale are certainly dreamlike, the hero remains awake throughout and experiences all the fantastic events in reality. But in chapter 10 Golyadkin passes from this dream-like reality into a realistic dream. Shaken to the core by his adventures of the previous day, he spends most of the night in a semisomnolent state; when he finally dozes off, he witnesses "hideous visions" (*videniya*). Golyadkin actually sees three distinct dream-scenes. In the first, he imagines that he is receiving a rebuke from his department head. Whereas Gogol's Akaky had protested (at least in an early version of the scene), Golyadkin's weak attempt at self-justification is interrupted when a "notoriously beastly" person blackens his reputation and occupies both his place at work and his position in society. In the second episode, the hero is recovering from an undeserved blow and reflecting on his own lack of resolution in protesting the affront. Then the "notorious person" reappears and humiliates him once again. In the final dream-scene Golyadkin is occupying a prestigious place in the social hierarchy. But the "notorious person," now identified as "Golyadkin junior," interferes a third time and totally destroys the hero's position by demonstrating that "Golyadkin senior, the real one, was not the real one at all, but a fraud, and that he [junior] was the real one" (I, 185). With this announcement, society turns against Golyadkin senior and accepts the impostor in his place. The distraught hero tries to escape, but each time his feet hit the pavement another Golyadkin appears, as goose-faced wives had proliferated in Shponka's terrifying nightmare. Then the hero's replicating doubles form a line, waddling along behind him "like a gaggle of geese," again recalling Gogol's image. Golyadkin is suddenly horrified to discover that Petersburg is choked with a "fearful multitude" of these creatures, all exactly alike. Finally, a police officer, noting such an appalling breach of decorum, herds them all into his booth.

Golyadkin's dream accurately reveals his subconscious perception of his imminent "displacement" from his position at work and his role in society. In the first scene, his professional security is compromised; in the second, he displays his total lack of conscious understanding, as well as his inability to prevent the displacement; in the third, his role in society is repudiated by everyone; finally he is apprehended, just as he will be in the final scene of the work.

The events of the second half of *The Double* demonstrate the validity of Golyadkin's subconscious insight. Even before the end of chapter 10, the narrator confirms the hero's worst suspicions: "To put it briefly, everything was happening just as it did in Golyadkin senior's dream [*son*]." When the strange figure of Dr. Rutenspitz pronounces sentence in the last lines of the tale, the hero's reaction closely recalls his horror upon awakening from his prophetic dream and it further underscores his own subconscious awareness. "Our hero gave a scream and clutched his head. Alas! He had felt this coming for a long time!" (I, 229).

This idea of displacement, first perceived on the subconscious level in *The Double*, is likewise the subject of an amusing sketch, "How Dangerous to Indulge in Vainglorious Dreams [*sny*]," composed collectively by Dostoevsky, Grigorovich, and Nekrasov, and published in a humorous anthology entitled *The First of April* (1846). It is generally believed that Dostoevsky contributed the section that contains the hero's dream; like Golyadkin's, it is strongly influenced by Gogol.

In one of the three dream-scenes, the anonymous hero imagines a department complete with guards, greatcoats, doormats, and inkwells, not unlike that in Gogol's "Overcoat." The department head instructs Dostoevsky's hero to recopy a document. When he replies that he will pass the job along to Efimov, the hero is reminded that Efimov has already been promoted and now occupies his position, while he, for his general incompetence and "suggestive mode of behavior," has been demoted.

The parallel between this dream and Golyadkin's is striking. Both heroes imagine that they have been displaced from their respective positions; subsequently both awaken to experience these same events in reality. Their dreams are thus used to reveal their subconscious awareness of their predicaments.

Dostoevsky further explored the dream as a technique of psychological characterization in *Mr. Prokharchin* (1846), where the hero's vision comprises the most revealing episode in his unfortunate life. It represents an incursion into the "fantastic," both preceded and followed by a detailed account of his undistinguished existence. It has been argued that Prokharchin's literary dream is the author's single effort to humanize his hero and to demonstrate that he is far more imaginative than all other characters in the work.[11] But the dream also has considerable thematic significance. It introduces two motifs that subsequently receive fuller treatment in Dostoevsky's major novels, and it expounds, for the first time, the theme of the responsibility for suffering.

Prokharchin is carried home in a semiconscious state after witnessing a terrible fire; although he longs to join his fellow lodgers at tea, he suddenly falls asleep. First he dreams that he is actually drinking tea with them, participating in their society. When one lodger proposes a philanthropic project to benefit all "sisters-in-law," Prokharchin, who has supposedly been putting money aside for one of his relatives, objects to the scheme and attempts to justify himself; when his protests are stifled, his first dream-scene ends.

In the second vignette, he is stealthily hiding away half his salary. Apparently he intends to pay the landlady for his lodging, and then to claim that he has no money left to donate to his own poor sister-in-law. Suddenly he catches sight of a colleague with whom he has worked for many years, but with whom he has never spoken. This poor fellow is busy counting his money, lamenting the fact that he hasn't enough to feed his seven children. Suddenly he looks at the hero with indignation, "as if he [Prokharchin] were to blame for this predicament." The hero maintains his innocence, but it turns out that he really is somehow to blame. He starts to run away, but his co-worker pursues him.

In the last dream-scene, Prokharchin is heading toward the conflagration that he had actually witnessed earlier. There he is deeply moved by the sight of a poor old woman who is shouting that her children have driven her away. Suddenly a peasant whom the hero had cheated once, a long time ago, begins to incite the crowd against him. In a terrifying climax that recalls Adriyan Prokhorov's nightmare in Pushkin's tale "The Coffin Maker," the crowd advances on Prokharchin and almost crushes him to death. He makes a tremendous effort and finally awakens.

In the hero's dream, particularly in the second scene, Dostoevsky introduces the psychology of avarice, a motif that later becomes his major preoccupation in *The Adolescent* (Arkady Versilov's dream [*mechta*] of becoming a Rothschild). In addition, the Napoleonic theme, a central component of Raskolnikov's figurative dreams (*mechty*), is first sounded in an impassioned speech addressed to Prokharchin by one of the other lodgers:

Who thinks about you, my good sir? Do you even have the right to be afraid? Who are you? What are you? A nothing, sir, a round pancake, that's what. . . . What are you? . . . Are you Napoleon, huh? Napoleon or not?
(I, 257)

But of even greater consequence is the early emergence of the theme of responsibility, guilt, and conscience. Prokharchin's dream reveals not only his "fantastic" imagination, but also a subconscious awareness of his own guilt for the suffering of others—for all "sisters-in-law," for his colleague's seven children, and for the dispossessed old woman. Prokharchin is first "unfairly" accused by others, but then he begins to realize subconsciously that he is indeed "guilty." The importance of this theme was noted by the critic Konstantin Mochulsky, who saw its connection to the author's later work:

Prokharchin's dream is the most powerful passage in the entire story. This is the first instance in which Dostoevsky touches upon his basic theme: "All men are guilty for everyone," and in which he advances his moral evaluation of solitude as an offense against the human family. Prokharchin's dream reminds us of Mitya [Karamazov's] vision on the road to Mokroye.[12]

But unlike Dmitry Karamazov, Prokharchin does not *accept* responsibility; instead, he equivocates, making excuses to his fellow lodgers, running away from his colleague, fleeing from the victims at the fire. As a result of his unwillingness to heed the inner voice of conscience, Prokharchin is eventually driven mad by the "fire" that rages within. At the conclusion of the work it is intimated that only in death may the hero have gained the insight that Dostoevsky's later characters manage to achieve in life. Prokharchin's final facial expression reveals some "deep thought," as if he had suddenly grown wiser. It appeared that he wanted to say something to his fellow lodgers, perhaps to communicate his insight before it was too late for the rest of them.

While the narrator repeatedly insists that Mr. Prokharchin is asleep and dreaming, in *The Landlady* (1847) the reader is informed that the hero, Ordynov, had been dreaming only at the moment of his awakening. This ambiguity surrounding the events in the fictional narrative was to become a characteristic of Dostoevsky's use of the technique in his major novels. Furthermore, *The Landlady* may be said to represent a synthesis of two earlier Russian stories, "A Terrible Vengeance" and "The Queen of Spades," in that Dostoevsky combines Gogol's folkloric characters with Pushkin's realistic approach to the fantastic.[13] The author himself had attributed the success of the latter story to the ambiguity that surrounds Germann's vision of the countess.[14]

Ordynov's similarly ambiguous dream also introduces two original aspects of Dostoevsky's fiction: the "childhood idyll" and the "incarnation of ideas." These themes emerge only in the hero's last two dream-scenes following a lengthy account of his emotional tribulations.

In one, Ordynov returns to his childhood and experiences all the pleasures associated with his former surroundings. But after he has received his mother's tender blessing, a menacing old man enters the dream. He pursues the child everywhere, becoming embodied in his dolls to make fun of him and turning his schoolmates against him. He frightens Ordynov with a mysterious fairytale, "unintelligible to his childish imagination, yet thrilling, tormenting him with terror and unchildlike passion."

In the following scene, Ordynov sees himself as an adult, alone, surrounded by enemies. To his horror he witnesses his former daydreams (*grezy*), thoughts (*mysli*), and figurative dreams (*mechty*) come to life and assume strange forms: "each of his thoughts, every incorporeal daydream was incarnated almost at the moment of its conception" (I, 279) Ordynov is oppressed by a sense of infinite irony. Feeling that his own dissolution is imminent, he tries to escape; but there is nowhere for him to hide. He cries out and suddenly awakens.

With Ordynov's "childhood idyll," Dostoevsky has initiated a series of dreams in which his characters relive those formative experiences that have so influenced their later lives. But these idylls are almost always "spoiled." In *The Landlady* the scene is shattered by a disruptive figure who has been variously interpreted by critics as Ordynov's father, as Murin, or as the hero's double. In all likelihood the old man does not possess a single identity; rather, he is a collective representation of the male figures in the hero's life who threaten his relationships with women, in particular with his mother and with Katerina.

In the final dream-scene Dostoevsky inaugurates one of his most cherished ideas: that thoughts and figurative dreams have an organic life of their own, that once conceived, they become personified or embodied in forms and images, and that they can then turn against their originator and pursue him to distraction. The destructive power inherent in these thoughts and dreams would subsequently become one of the author's ideological assumptions in his major novels. Furthermore, Ordynov comprehends the power of his own former figurative dreams (*mechty*) only in his experiential dream (*son*); in his later works Dostoevsky will distinguish between the two kinds of dreams in a similar fashion.

This distinction, as well as the ambiguity surrounding the dreamer's state of consciousness, is further explored in *Netochka Nezvanova* (1849), the author's last work written before his exile. Even before completing *The Landlady*, Dostoevsky had begun work on what he hoped would be his first novel on a grandiose scale. Only three parts of it were published before his arrest; afterward he failed to complete the project.

Like Ordynov's dream, Netochka's is announced: it begins with her so-called awakening and ends with her "loss of consciousness." In it, she first hears the sounds of distant music; she makes her way toward its source, a crowded concert hall that she identifies with one imagined in her own earlier figurative dreams. "Then it must be that this was not a dream [*mechta*]! . . . Yes, I have seen all of this before in my dreams [*mechty*]" (II, 195). When the music fades, Netochka bursts into the hall expecting to find her stepfather. Instead, the musician turns out to be his rival and murderer. Terrified, she hears laughter reverberating and suddenly awakens.

As in *The Landlady*, Dostoevsky develops the distinction between two kinds of dreams. The resolution for which Netochka yearns so deeply in her figurative dreams is almost achieved in her experiential dream; but, when the musician proves to be her stepfather's murderer, her figurative dream is shattered. The heroine's experiential dream thus reveals her subconscious perception of truth that is inaccessible to her conscious mind.

From his own reading of Shponka's nightmare, Kovalyov's adventures, Akaky's delirium, Adriyan Prokharov's torment, and Germann's vision, Dostoevsky became aware of the potential of the literary dream. In his Romantic tales of the 1840s he explored and expanded all its possibilities. These early experiments served the author well upon his return from exile. During the 1860s he turned from writing shorter forms to his first full-length novel. It can be asserted that in *Crime and Punishment* Dostoevsky "most sublimely and profoundly exploited the literary and philosophical potential of dreams."[15]

CRIME AND PUNISHMENT

In the epilogue to *Crime and Punishment* Dostoevsky makes a clear distinction between two kinds of dreams, a distinction first suggested in *The Landlady* and then developed in *Netochka Nezvanova*.[16] It occurs in a passage describing Raskolnikov's attitude toward his fellow convicts. He finds himself astonished by their intense love of life in spite of their terrible suffering:

> How could one ray of sunlight mean so much to them, or the virgin forest, or a cool spring in some remote and hidden solitude seen once before, that the tramp dreams about [*mechtaet*], and sees in his dreams [*vo sne*], like a lover's meeting. (VI, 418)

Just as Dostoevsky differentiates between the tramp's "figurative" and "experiential" dreams, so must the reader distinguish among Raskolnikov's different kinds of dreams (*mechty*, *grezy*, and *sny*), as well as those of the other major characters in *Crime and Punishment*.

In the very first chapter of the novel the narrator, using Raskolnikov's own words, refers to the hero's "project" to murder the pawnbroker as an "ugly dream" (*mechta*). Subsequently, after several unsettling encounters, the "project" enters Raskolnikov's mind once again, but this time the narrator explains, "A month earlier, and even yesterday, it had been no more than a dream [*mechta*], but now . . . it was suddenly revealed as no dream, but in a new, terrible and completely unfamiliar form" (VI, 39). Thus the hero's "project," which had originated as a figurative dream (*mechta*), has now acquired a life of its own and has been transformed into a plan of action. Raskolnikov will act upon it and proceed to commit his crime.

In opposition to Raskolnikov's figurative dream there stands a series of five experiential dreams, each of which is narrated in the text.[17] The first and most controversial is that of the beaten mare. Its context provides the background necessary for interpreting it: the hero's three encounters immediately preceding the dream help to explain his traumatic reaction upon awakening from it.

First, Raskolnikov meets Marmeladov in a tavern where he hears the tragic story of his life; next, he returns home to read his mother's letter, which brings to mind both his happy childhood and his deceased father. Finally, he witnesses a "gentleman" molesting an innocent young girl on Nevsky Prospect. In each of these instances, the hero's spontaneous emotional response is one of genuine compassion. But in all three cases this feeling is quickly replaced by intellectual disinterest and growing anger. He returns home and falls asleep. The tavern where he encountered Marmeladov, his childhood as summoned forth by his mother's letter, and the public molestation all merge in Raskolnikov's dream of the beaten mare.

He imagines himself as a child at home in his village, walking along a road with his father past a tavern toward a cemetery. The tavern had always aroused unpleasant impressions, with its raucous singing, laughing, and fighting. Their destination was a little stone church, which had been associated with the boy's love of religious ritual, icons, and priests, as well as with the sacred memory of his late grandmother and brother. The contrast between these two settings (tavern and cemetery) must be interpreted symbolically: they represent the two realms of action, not only of the hero's dream, but of the entire novel. Raskolnikov passes the tavern on his way to the cemetery, through a secular world toward spiritual salvation. As early as the hero's first dream Dostoevsky indicates that in the serenity of the sacred setting and in Raskolnikov's feeling of love are contained the seeds of his rebirth.[18]

When the peasant Mikolka brags that he will give everyone a ride on his old mare, he defends his action by declaring that "she's not worth her salt" ("darom khleb est"), that is, she doesn't earn her keep. This explanation parallels Raskolnikov's own utilitarian estimate of the pawnbroker's worth. Similarly when Mikolka "justifies" his decision to beat the mare even unto death, he declares that she is his "property" (*dobro*), by which he asserts that he has the "right" to dispense with her as he chooses. Raskolnikov argues similarly that his theory has given him the "right" to overstep the boundaries of conventional morality.

The crowd laughs at the spectacle, except for one man who accuses Mikolka of cruelty. But even this man eventually participates; his acquiescence demonstrates that "everyone is guilty," all are responsible for the death of the mare. While Raskolnikov's father does not join in the laughter, he does nothing to prevent the murder. He merely expresses his impotence and indifference ("It's none of our business"), and attempts to lead the child away from the scene.

Nevertheless Raskolnikov experiences at close range the victimizer's determination and the victim's resilience. He breaks through the crowd and gives vent to his deepest emotions: on the one hand, his profound compassion for the innocent victim, and on the other, his intense hostility toward the oppressor. His subsequent inquiry resounds with a total lack of comprehension and initiates Dostoevsky's insistent "dream-questions": "Why on earth did they kill the poor horse?"

While the child's emotional reaction to the mare's death recalls the adult Raskolnikov's earlier display of spontaneous pity for Marmeladov, his own mother and sister, and the innocent girl on Nevsky, in the dream his compassion is not superseded by any intellectual withdrawal or revulsion. Instead, it is the boy's father who drags him away, providing his son with a most unsatisfactory explanation.

The dreamer wants to cry out; suddenly he awakens and mutters with relief: "Thank God, it's only a dream [*son*]." Yet in spite of this disclaimer, the dream has had a powerful effect not only on the hero's "troubled" and "confused" soul, but also on his body. He feels as if he himself had suffered a beating, indicating an identification with the victim of his dream, not with the victimizer.

It is at this moment that the hero makes explicit the connection between his experiential dream (*son*) and his figurative dream (*mechta*). First, he consciously switches his empathetic identification from the victim to the beater-victimizer. "God—is it possible, is it really possible that I will take an axe and beat her on the head, smash open her skull?" (VI, 50). This is actually the first accurate description of the hero's plan to murder the old woman.[19] It is articulated or made conscious as a result of his dream. Once he has formulated the thought, Raskolnikov becomes aware of the full horror of his scheme and rejects it resoundingly. "Lord!—show me the way, and I renounce this accursed . . . dream [*mechta*] of mine" (VI, 50). With this declaration, a "terrible burden" is lifted from the hero's soul and he feels both tranquility and freedom. Thus Raskolnikov's first experiential dream (*son*) is the crucial experience that enables, even compels him to renounce his figurative dream (*mechta*). His subconscious reveals both to the dreamer and to the reader the "real" Raskolnikov—the child who feels compassion for the victim as well as hostility for the victimizer, and who asks the penetrating question. Raskolnikov's "conscious" appears to heed this message from his "subconscious." The hero seems to understand the meaning of his experiential dream (*son*) and renounce his figurative dream (*mechta*).

But this renunciation is short-lived. "Circumstances" intervene: Raskolnikov "overhears" that the pawnbroker's sister, Lizaveta, would not be at home that evening. The hero turns back to his figurative dream (*mechta*) and carries it out, totally ignoring the meaning of his experiential dream (*son*). But the reader does not forget it: he knows better than the hero that Raskolnikov's figurative dream will ultimately lead to his demise.

The hero's second experiential dream occurs immediately after overhearing a conversation between two students about the pawnbroker's "uselessness"; their views "happen" to coincide with his own. Raskolnikov returns home and spends most of the day in bed; toward evening he begins to doze. The narrator relates one of his "very strange" dreams (*grezy*):

> In the one that recurred most often he was in Africa, in Egypt, at some oasis. A caravan was resting, the camels lying peacefully, and the men eating their evening meal; all around, palm trees stood in a great circle. He was drinking water from a stream that flowed babbling beside him, clear and cool, running marvelously bright and blue over the colored stones and the clean sand with its glitter of gold. (VI, 56)

Unlike the hero's first experiential dream, this one occurs when the dreamer is in a semisomnolent state; furthermore, it describes a condition rather than narrates a succession of events. The scene is an idyllic and exotic paradise where all physical needs are satisfied (rest, food, drink). The dreamer's sensations are expressed in a series of miraculous transformations: desert yields to oasis, stones appear multicolored, sand seems like gold, and water becomes an instrument of life.[20] In Raskolnikov's first dream, the cemetery and church were said to represent the "sacred" as opposed to the "secular" of the tavern. The same opposition exists here in the hero's recurrent dream; another "sacred" paradise stands in contrast both to the sordid conditions of his life and to the horrible reality of his impending crime. The dream serves as a spiritual "oasis" in the "desert" of Raskolnikov's chaotic thoughts. Furthermore, as the tranquility and compassion of the first dream were said to contain the seeds of the hero's rebirth, so too the serenity of the second dream foreshadows his ultimate salvation in the epilogue. There, after his fifth and final dream, Raskolnikov will glimpse a similar paradise.

The hero is abruptly roused from this soothing dream by the sound of a clock striking; he has "overdreamt" and is late in making the necessary preparations for carrying out the murder.[21] As the result of his first experiential dream (*son*), Raskolnikov had renounced his figurative dream (*mechta*); after his second, he does not hesitate even for a moment. He pursues his plan to its ultimate and horrifying conclusion.

Both of the hero's first two dreams are "announced" by the narrator. His third dream, however, is not: the reader is left uncertain about the reality of the episode until the moment of awakening. The dreamer himself remains confused until the imagined events are dismissed by a servant who plays the role of "objective" observer.

Once again the context provides the clues needed to interpret the dream. Raskolnikov has just left the police station where he has "confessed" not his crime, but his earlier failure to marry the landlady's daughter. While crossing the Nikolaevsky Bridge, he almost bumps into a carriage; as a result he is whipped across the back by a coachman. Bystanders laugh, but a merchant's wife, mistaking him for a beggar, hands him some money.

Her charitable act occasions an intense experience for the hero. He stands overlooking the Neva: the golden dome of a cathedral dominates the cloudless sky. Suddenly Raskolnikov feels tremendous distance from his former self, his past ideas and thoughts; his spirit soars upward and he flings the woman's gift into the water. Once again the hero experiences a moment of sacred serenity, a spiritual oasis, an alternative to the chaos of his ideas.

He returns home and immediately falls asleep, only to be "roused" by unnatural noises. He manages to recognize his landlady's voice imploring the assistant superintendent of police not to beat her, while he hears a crowd assembling on the landing. Raskolnikov seeks an explanation for the events, just as he did at the end of his first dream. "But what is it for? What is it for? . . . And how is it possible!" (VI, 91). But instead of interfering, he cowers in fear of becoming the next victim. At last the noise abates, the superintendent leaves, the landlady slinks away, and the crowd disperses. In the ensuing silence the hero's questions reemerge: "But, God, can all this really be possible? And why on earth, why did he come here?" The dream ends abruptly; Raskolnikov awakens in a state of "anguish" and "unlimited terror."

In Raskolnikov's first dream Mikolka clubs his mare to death, the crowd jeers, and the boy expresses compassion. Upon awakening, the dreamer feels as if he had suffered a beating. On the Nikolaevsky Bridge the hero is inadvertently whipped by a coachman, bystanders laugh, and an old woman takes pity. In his third dream it is the landlady who is beaten by the assistant superintendent, the crowd watches, and the hero fears that he will be next. Raskolnikov either identifies with, is cast in the role of, or fears becoming the victim.

In the hero's fourth dream the roles are dramatically reassigned: Raskolnikov himself is now cast as victimizer with the pawnbroker as his victim in a reenactment of the actual murder. The dream follows Raskolnikov's return to the scene of the crime. There he encounters the mysterious "bourgeois" who accuses him of being a murderer. The hero returns home in a state of frenzy. Just before falling asleep, he drifts into a strange state of consciousness that the author characterizes as "daydreams" (*grezy*):

> He could not think. His mind held ideas, or fragments of ideas, disconnected and incoherent images—the faces of people he had known as a child or seen once and never remembered again, the belfry of the Church of the Ascension, the billiard table in some inn, with an officer playing at it, the

smell of cigars in a basement tobacco shop, a tavern, a back staircase, sloppy with dishwater and strewn with eggshells, the Sunday sound of bells drifting in from outside . . . all changing and whirling in dizzy spirals. (VI, 210)

As in Raskolnikov's first experiential dream, these fragments juxtapose images of sacred and secular; the church belfry and the sound of bells enclose the other sordid details. And similar to the episode overlooking the Neva preceding his third dream, the hero experiences a momentary release from his thoughts and takes refuge in his feelings.

But he soon returns to the realm of theory. Reflecting on his crime, Raskolnikov concludes that he did not in fact murder a person, rather, he killed a principle; that he failed to "overstep" any boundary, rather, he remained "on this side." He decides that if it were possible he would kill the old woman again.

The hero's fourth dream provides just such an opportunity. In it the mysterious "bourgeois" reappears and leads him back to the pawnbroker's apartment. Upon entering he observes that the old woman is sitting in the corner of her room, hunched over and acting as if she were "afraid." He moves swiftly, hitting her over the head with an axe, but the victim remains stationary. Observing her more closely, he discovers that she is laughing; he becomes enraged and beats her even harder. But no matter how ferociously he brings down his axe, he cannot kill the old woman. Her laughter grows louder and the landing fills with people standing in silence. Raskolnikov is unable to escape: he wants to scream, and suddenly he "awakens."[22]

Having concluded that he failed to kill the pawnbroker the first time, Raskolnikov returns in his dream to try once again, but in vain. Whereas Mikolka had succeeded in killing the mare, and the assistant superintendent had given the landlady a sound thrashing, Raskolnikov has failed to murder the old woman. Each of the hero's three dreams is a symbolic reenactment of a "murder"; in the first two the victimizer achieves his goal. It is only in the third, when the dream replicates reality, that the victim not only survives, but emerges victorious to humiliate the victimizer. The message from Raskolnikov's subconscious is clear: he cannot "kill" the pawnbroker, he cannot "overstep" any boundaries, he is not an extraordinary man.

Raskolnikov's fifth and final dream differs dramatically from all his others. It neither recalls events and people from his past life, nor reflects his thoughts and emotions. Instead, it is an allegorical "dream-vision" which results in the spiritual transformation and religious conversion of the hero. Through a series of experiential dreams reenacting his crime, Raskolnikov's subconscious has reiterated with increasing urgency that he is ultimately incapable of fulfilling the role that was assigned to him by his theory. Now, in his last dream, the hero becomes witness to a graphic demonstration of the logical consequences of this theory.

The vision occurs while Raskolnikov lies ill in the prison hospital. He dreams of a world that has fallen victim to a terrible plague caused by a new strain of infectious trichina, "spirits" with minds and wills of their own. Its victims become insane, yet consider themselves infallible in their knowledge of scientific and moral truth. Wars, fires, famine, and cannibalism ensue; everyone is doomed except for a chosen few destined to found a new race.

Raskolnikov's first experiential dream of the beaten mare had compelled him to renounce temporarily his figurative dream of killing the pawnbroker. But now, only after his last experiential dream, can he finally move toward the renunciation of that figurative dream and toward the acceptance of his own salvation.

Not long after his dream Raskolnikov undergoes another moment of sacred spirituality, the culmination of all previous similar moments:

A broad landscape was revealed from the high bank. From the opposite side, far away, the sound of singing was carried faintly. There, in the immensity of the steppe, flooded with sunlight, the black tents of nomads were barely visible dots. There was freedom, there dwelled other people so utterly unlike those on this side of the river that it seemed as though time had stood still with them, and the age of Abraham and his flocks was still the present. (VI, 421)

The church and cemetery of the hero's first dream, the cathedral dome described before his third, the belfry and the church bells preceding his fourth—these are the experiences that comprise the foundation of Raskolnikov's religious conversion. But the hero's last allegorical vision most resembles his second dream, the caravan at the oasis, which had occurred immediately before the murder.[23] There the details of the sacred paradise were conveyed through a series of miraculous transformations. Here Raskolnikov moves beyond the images to their inherent spiritual qualities: happiness, freedom, eternity. Just as the hero is completely absorbed by his vision of the nomads, Sonya appears unexpectedly at his side. Only now, having recognized the appalling consequences of his figurative dream, and having experienced a glimpse of paradise, is Raskolnikov finally ready to make the sudden leap of love and to follow the slower path toward faith.

At the same time as Raskolnikov was awakening from his fourth experiential dream, the one in which he failed to kill the pawnbroker, Svidrigaylov had stood perched on his threshold, ready to enter the hero's life. At first he is mistaken for a hallucination, a continuation of Raskolnikov's vivid dream. Later Svidrigaylov himself testifies to the power of dreams and provides a vivid description of their consequences: "Common folk get drunk, while educated young men with nothing to do consume themselves with unrealizable dreams [*sny*] and daydreams [*grezy*], and stultify themselves with theories" (VI, 370). Svidrigaylov's explanation can be read as an ironic characterization of Raskolnikov, whose crime has resulted precisely from his own most "consuming," "unrealizable" dream, from his "stultifying" theory.

Following Dunya's final rejection and before taking his own life, Svidrigaylov has an elaborate experiential dream of his own, which closely parallels Raskolnikov's fourth dream. It synthesizes the major elements of his character and defines the spiritual abyss that separates him from the hero.

In his first dream-scene Svidrigaylov experiences great discomfort upon discovering that a mouse is in his bed and is running up and down his body. In the second, he enters a lovely cottage where he comes upon the coffin of a little girl. She lies like a marble statue, with a smile "full of infinite, unchildlike grief." To his distress he recognizes the victim of his previous crime of passion; she had taken her own life. In the next scene, he walks out into the corridor of his hotel where he discovers a young girl hiding in a dark corner whom he takes back to his room, undresses, and puts to bed. Suddenly, regretting his involvement, he wants to escape. But then he notices that the girl is flirting with him. Appalled by her unchildlike behavior, the sleeper screams and suddenly awakens.

Svidrigaylov's dream expresses in symbolic form the dichotomy between his ideas and his emotions. His reason had led him to suppose that he could overstep moral boundaries and commit crimes with impunity. But his feelings had continued to manifest themselves in his magnanimous gestures toward Sonya and in his final desperate appeal to Dunya. As in Raskolnikov's fourth dream, Svidrigaylov "returns" to the scene of his most heinous crime. Just as the hero was unable to kill the mocking old woman in his dream, so Svidrigaylov fails to ravish the flirtatious young girl in his. Svidrigaylov's dream concludes with another significant parallel: as Raskolnikov had "overdreamt" his murder of the pawnbroker, Svidrigaylov "overdreams" his own suicide. Whereas Raskolnikov ends by choosing Siberia, Svidrigaylov goes out to put a bullet through his head.

Raskolnikov's choice is inspired principally by the example of Sonya's selfless love and her steadfast faith. She too has an experiential dream that foreshadows the hero's transformation in the epilogue; she also has a figurative dream dominated by a strong religious theme. The night before Raskolnikov confesses his crime to Sonya, she spends a feverish night dreaming about Polechka, Katerina, Lizaveta, *and* Raskolnikov, "with his pale face and burning eyes. . . . He would kiss her foot and weep." In the epilogue after the hero's last dream and his glimpse of paradise, when Sonya appears at his side, he does indeed throw himself at her feet and weep, a gesture that marks the first stage of his repentance.

Only one day earlier, during Sonya's inspired recitation from the Gospel, just as she was about to reach the climactic moment of Lazarus's resurrection (John 11:1–45), the narrator describes her intense involvement in the experience as a "figurative dream" (*mechta*). Sonya is not merely a passive witness to the miraculous event; rather, she is an emotional participant in it, much as Alyosha will partake of Christ's miracle at Cana of Galilee in *The Brothers Karamazov*.

* * *

The elaborate use of both figurative and experiential dreams in *Crime and Punishment* represents an enormous expansion of the possibilities of the literary technique. Dostoevsky has built on the foundation of his own earlier explorations in his tales of the 1840s. Thus, as Golyadkin's dream formed the structural center of *The Double*, Raskolnikov's dreams provide a narrative thread that extends from the first chapter through the epilogue; in addition, the dreams of Svidrigaylov and Sonya are used to clarify the two alternatives available to the hero. Mr. Prokharchin's dream was employed primarily as a means of characterizing the hero; Raskolnikov's dreams plumb the depths of his psyche and chart his progression toward love and faith. His dream of the beaten mare and his theory of the extraordinary man are in one sense elaborations of Ordynov's final dream-scenes in *The Landlady*. In *Netochka Nezvanova* Dostoevsky uses the unannounced dream to create intentional ambiguity and he juxtaposes the two kinds of dreams. In *Crime and Punishment* announced dreams alternate with unannounced ones, and the disparity between the hero's experiential dreams and his figurative dream is the motivating force that finally leads to the renunciation of his theory and the transformation of his spirit.

THE IDIOT, THE POSSESSED, AND THE ADOLESCENT

In his three middle novels Dostoevsky uses literary dreams primarily for thematic purposes. Raskolnikov's figurative and experiential dreams give birth to the conflicting dreams of Prince Myshkin and Ippolit in *The Idiot*. These dreamers, in turn, are followed by Stavrogin, the hero of *The Possessed*, who first beholds a vision of the "golden age," the greatest of Dostoevsky's figurative dreams. This vision subsequently undergoes a radical transformation in *The Adolescent*, where it is conveyed by the hero's father, Versilov. The dreams in Dostoevsky's last and greatest novel synthesize the complex explorations in all previous works; in *The Brothers Karamazov* the full potential of the literary technique is realized.

Aside from references to Ganya's nightmare and Nastasya's recurring dreams about Rogozhin, the two principal dreamers in *The Idiot* are Prince Myshkin and Ippolit.[24] Myshkin first recounts his figurative dream (*mechta*) during a long conversation with Mrs. Epanchin and her daughters. Diverging from a straightforward account of his experiences in Switzerland, the prince describes his extraordinary vision by the waterfall:

> It was there that I seemed to hear some mysterious call to go somewhere, and I could not help feeling that if I went straight on and on, . . . I should reach the line where the sky and the earth meet and there find the key to the whole mystery and discover at once a new life. (VIII, 50–51)

This dream recurs at two critical moments in the narrative: during the hero's discussion of nihilism with Ippolit and during his wait in the park for Aglaya. It represents an idyllic setting in which Myshkin longs to find refuge and escape from the exasperating experiences of real life. As such it serves a function analogous to Raskolnikov's vision of the oasis in *Crime and Punishment*.

Myshkin's experiential dream (*son*) of Nastasya, the "woman-sinner," is first recounted as he awaits Aglaya. When he falls asleep in the park, he dreams about a woman whom he knows, but whose identity he chooses not to acknowledge. Although her face reflects remorse as if she had committed some crime, he refuses to admit that she is in fact a "sinner." She beckons to him and he follows; then he suddenly awakens to find Aglaya's hand resting on his.

This dream subsequently reappears to the prince. When he falls asleep before reading Nastasya's letters to Aglaya, the figure of the "woman-sinner" returns and beckons to him tearfully. Myshkin awakens and, with a painful recollection of the woman's face, finally begins to read the letters before him. Whereas the prince's recurrent figurative dream seems to offer him refuge from reality, his repeated experiential dream intimately links the two dissimilar women with whose lives he becomes so entangled.[25]

Although Ippolit, the other dreamer in *The Idiot*, lacks a figurative dream, he has two related experiential dreams that juxtapose the principal moral opponents in the novel. The first forms part of his "Necessary Explanation," a lengthy discourse on nihilism. Ippolit dreams of being enclosed in a room with a scorpionlike animal. When his mother fails to catch the beast, she summons their dog, who, sensing a "mystery," enters into combat nevertheless. The dog crushes the skull of the animal but gets stung in the struggle. When white juice appears on her tongue, the dreamer awakens suddenly and Prince Myshkin enters his room.

Ippolit's dream is an allegorical representation of the struggle between the forces of good and evil and it results in tragedy: although good destroys evil, it is itself destroyed. Similarly, Prince Myshkin enters the distraught world of the novel to do combat with the forces of evil; by the end he too will be destroyed.[26]

Ippolit's second dream follows his visit to Rogozhin's house, where he becomes fascinated by Holbein's morbid portrait of Christ. In his dream he confronts a disgusting tarantula. When he awakens, his door opens and Rogozhin enters his room.

In the first of Ippolit's two dreams, good combats evil and is destroyed in the process: enter Myshkin. In the second, only evil is present: enter Rogozhin. Whereas the prince possesses both a consoling figurative dream and a sustaining religious faith, Ippolit lacks the two. His experiential dreams reflect the process of his own moral degeneraton. Not even Myshkin can provide him with an escape from disease, despair, and death.

Raskolnikov's vision of the oasis and Myshkin's dream of the waterfall are further developed in Dostoevsky's third novel, *The Possessed*. In his desperate farewell note to Dasha, the hero, Stavrogin, writes, "I am not well, but I hope the mountain air will help me get rid of my hallucinations. That takes care of the physical side; as for the mental side, you know everything" (X, 513). The nature of his hallucinations was clearly revealed in the suppressed chapter entitled "At Tikhon's," where Stavrogin not only confesses his willful crime against Matresha but also recounts for the first time the vision of the "golden age."

Just as Ippolit's dream of the tarantula was provoked by a painting (Holbein's Christ), Stavrogin's vision is inspired by Claude Lorrain's "Acis and Galatea." In it Stavrogin is transported from his wretched hotel to that corner of the Greek archipelago depicted on the artist's canvas. There he finds himself a witness to the sunset in Lorrain's idyllic landscape on the "first day" of European civilization. In this pre-Christian paradise, Stavrogin confronts the innocence and happiness of its childlike inhabitants.

He awakens with tears of joy to gaze at the flowers on his windowsill, similarly illuminated by the rays of the setting sun. When he tries to recapture his dream, Stavrogin notices a tiny red spider, which calls to mind a similar insect glimpsed during his final meeting with Matresha. Suddenly he visualizes the young girl exactly as she was then: standing on her threshold, shaking her head, and raising her fist. Stavrogin's dream of earthly paradise vanishes, but the image of Matresha reappears to haunt him daily. In *Crime and Punishment* Svidrigaylov's dream was plagued by the victim of his most heinous crime; in *The Possessed* Stavrogin's vision of the golden age is obliterated by the image of his prey, dragged up from his memory by the tiny red spider.

In Dostoevsky's next novel, *The Adolescent*, the elder Versilov also witnesses the dream of the golden age, but here the context is altered and its meaning transformed. The sun, which Stavrogin saw setting on the first day of European civilization, becomes in Versilov's vision the "last day" of our era, the end of Western civilization. Thus the former's utopian vision is transformed into the latter's apocalyptic nightmare out of which a new messianic conception of Russia would emerge. After the old European order had vanished, Russia's mission, her supreme intellectual contribution, would be to reconcile all existing ideas. This dream represents the ultimate statement of Versilov's so-called Geneva ideas of humanitarian atheism or "virtue without Christ." The dreamer acknowledges the loss of God in his secular ideal and even wonders whether men will be able to survive without Him.

Then Versilov describes a second vision, one in which "all the battles have been fought and the struggle is over." Men have rejected their former beliefs in God and immortality; now, human love is directed toward nature, the world itself, and other men. Unfortunately the inhabitants of this brave new world, having been left to their own devices, feel like abandoned children. This vision concludes with an unexpected reference to Heine's dreamlike image of "Christ on the Baltic Sea" from the lyric poem "Frieden." Versilov is finally forced to admit that men were unable to manage without God altogether. Christ appears and holds out His hands; the scales fall from men's eyes and everyone joins together in a hymn of resurrection.

Stavrogin's vision of a pre-Christian paradise in *The Possessed* was destoyed by the recollection of his own crime; Versilov's dream of a post-Christian utopia is inherently evil. Any attempt to restore earthly paradise, to dispense with God, or to organize society along atheistic-humanitarian ideals is doomed to failure. The reemergence of Christ at the end of Versilov's vision demonstrates conclusively that both the "Geneva ideas" and the dream of the golden age represent the ultimate deception of mankind and can only result in spiritual death.[27]

The younger Versilov, Arkady, the main character of the novel, pursues a different figurative dream ("becoming a Rothschild"), but one that similarly leads him astray. His several experiential dreams, however, reveal a genuine attachment to his father, a deep love for his mother, his perception of Lambert's true character, his sexual attraction toward Katerina, and his awareness that his precious "letter" can be used for selfish as well as altruistic motives.

It is, however, neither Versilov nor Arkady who represents the spiritual and artistic culmination of *The Adolescent*; rather, it is Makar, Arkady's "other" father figure, whose pilgrimages to Russian monasteries, whose parables and letters, and whose own life represent the values of genuine Russian faith: the communality of believers, the beauty of the world, and the mystery of God. His profound faith in a Russian Christ is Dostoevsky's answer to the dream of a golden age; the resolution of the conflict between these two forces is most graphically depicted in the author's last and greatest novel.

THE BROTHERS KARAMAZOV

In *The Brothers Karamazov* each of the three brothers has an experiential dream that expresses his emotional state at a critical juncture in the narrative and that helps to define his ultimate spiritual achievement.

Alyosha's dream is related in what Dostoevsky once described as perhaps the "most essential" chapter in the whole novel.[28] Driven to despair by Zosima's "odor of corruption," Alyosha had deserted the monastery. He decides to yield to temptation at Grushenka's, but she takes pity on him and insists on respecting his grief. Upon his return to the elder's cell, his soul is "overflowing with mingled feelings" of sweetness rather than sadness. Fragments of ideas rush into his head; he finds himself unable to concentrate but feels something "whole, steadfast, comforting." Thus, standing on the threshold of his dream, Alyosha is torn between disturbing thoughts and reassuring emotions.

During her dramatic reading of Lazarus in *Crime and Punishment*, Sonya had participated emotionally in the miracle of resurrection; here, during Father Paissy's recitation of Cana of Galilee (John 2:1–10), Alyosha will partake in the miracle of transformation at the marriage feast. Initially the words of the Gospel are intertwined with Alyosha's personal recollections as he moves from full consciousness into a state of semidream. The first phrase describing the guests at the wedding brings to mind his recent encounters with Rakitin and Grushenka. The Virgin Mary's declaration that "the people wanted wine, but have none," enables Alyosha to identify the passage and to recall both the elder's teachings and Dmitry's words about joy and forgiveness. Jesus' assertion that His "hour has not yet come," and Mary's counsel ("Whatsoever He says unto you, do it") are followed by Alyosha's commentary on the parable. He reflects on the poverty of the people and is struck by the fact that Christ has come to share in their joy.[29]

When Jesus commands the servants to "fill the pots" and then the water is miraculously transformed into wine, Alyosha moves from semidream into dream and is transported from the monastery to the actual scene of the marriage feast. This signals the end of the complex interweaving of biblical phrases, personal recollections, and interpretative commentary. Father Zosima, who is seated among the guests, invites Alyosha to participate in the miracle of transformation. When the elder directs the young monk's attention toward Jesus, the dreamer extends his arms joyfully and suddenly awakens.

Alyosha, who had previously abandoned the monastery in despair at the "odor of corruption," now, after his joyous dream, leaves the elder's cell in ecstasy and throws himself onto the earth. "He longed to forgive everyone for everything, and to beg forgiveness. Oh, not for himself, but for all men, for all men and for everything." (XIV, 328). When Alyosha rises from the earth, he has been spiritually transformed from a "weak youth" into a "resolute champion."

What has occurred as a result of this dream is nothing less than a genuine "miracle." Having expected a "false" miracle after Zosima's death, Alyosha almost despaired when the corpse began to stink. But then he falls asleep and in his dream not merely witnesses but participates in Christ's first miracle. At Cana of Galilee Jesus transforms water into wine not to compel faith, but to celebrate it. Thus only on the subconscious level, when his reason is suspended, can Alyosha discover the true power of belief.

Upon awakening from his dream, he undergoes a genuine religious conversion. The characterization of his emotions, his desire "to forgive everyone for everything," constitutes a total acceptance of the teachings of Father Zosima.[30] Earlier the elder had urged Alyosha to leave the monastery, to go out into the world, and to begin his work there. Only now, as a result of his miraculous transformation, can Alyosha accept Zosima's advice. He will attempt to practice what the elder preached, the doctrine of "active love," during his sojourn in the world.

While Alyosha's experiential dream is obviously related to Sonya's reading of Lazarus, his conversion is a further development of Raskolnikov's climactic epiphany following his own fifth dream. Whereas in *Crime and Punishment* the event occurs only at the end of the epilogue, in *The Brothers Karamazov* it happens early enough in the narrative for Alyosha to spend the rest of the novel attempting to apply the insights that he has acquired as a result of his profound experience.

Alyosha is the first of the three brothers to undergo conversion as the result of a dream. The ideas of Ivan and Dmitry both influence his transformation and lead to a clearer understanding of their own divergent spiritual paths. On the way to Grushenka's house, Alyosha echoes Ivan's blasphemous words in declaring that he too seeks "justice" and no longer "accepts the world." The genuine miracles at Cana of Galilee and of Alyosha's conversion, as well as the genuine mystery of his ecstatic communion with nature, stand in stark opposition to the ideas of Ivan's Grand Inquisitor, who advocates *false* "miracle, mystery, and authority."

During his state of semidream, when Alyosha identifies the Gospel passage, he readily connects Zosima's teachings to the words of his older brother. Dmitry, who is next to begin his spiritual transformation, is thus closely linked to the elder in Alyosha's mind. The parallel between Alyosha's conversion and Dmitry's regeneration is also made explicit in one of Dostoevsky's notebooks. In a description of Dmitry's arrest and "torments" during the interrogation, the author notes: "He [Dmitry] remembered Grushenka and her cries; the spiritual purificaton began (emotionally as in the chapter on Cana of Galilee)."[31]

Even before the investigation, Dmitry refers to his vivid experiential dreams: he frequently sees himself "falling down a precipice," "being chased," or undergoing various "humiliations." He always appears as the victim whose suffering is gratuitous. Toward the end of the preliminary inquiry, Dmitry has a genuine experiential dream, which, like Alyosha's vision, initiates the process of his religious conversion.

The narrative context is essential for understanding the dream. As the witnesses are busy presenting their evidence, Dmitry gazes out the window at the rain, the muddy road, and the unattractive rows of peasant huts. When Grushenka eloquently testifies to his innocence, Dmitry feels somewhat relieved. Overcome by physical weakness, he lies down on a large wooden chest.

In his dream Dmitry imagines that he is being driven through the steppe by a peasant on a snowy November day. As the cart approaches a small village, he notices that all the houses are burned and blackened. Pale old women stand along the roadside; one with a long, bony face is holding a baby.[32] Dmitry inquires of his driver, "Why are they crying? What are they crying for?" When no explanation is offered, the dreamer persists:

Why are those poor mothers standing there, why are the people poor, why is the babe poor, why is the steppe barren, why don't they hug each other, kiss each other, why don't they sing songs of joy, why are they so dark from black misery, why don't they feed the babe? (XIV, 456)

From the immediate and specific (baby), Dmitry progresses to the general and abstract (mothers, poor people, barren steppe). Then he expresses his profound incomprehension of all human suffering. Finally he returns to the specific and insists: "Why don't they feed the babe?" He feels compelled to ask these questions, yet he receives no answers. Suddenly the dreamer is overcome by tender emotion. He wants to do something immediately so that the baby will stop crying and so that no one will ever cry again. In the dream Grushenka appears unexpectedly at Dmitry's side, assuring him that she will stand by him throughout his life. He yearns to live, to move toward the light, and suddenly he awakens.

Discovering that while he slept (and dreamed) someone had placed a pillow beneath his head, Dmitry asks ecstatically, "Who was that kind man?" When this question also goes unanswered, he joyfully announces to all present: "I have had a good dream [*son*], gentlemen." He agrees to sign the deposition without any hesitation.

At the end of his first dream in *Crime and Punishment* the young hero asks: "Why on earth did they kill the poor horse?" At the conclusion of his third dream, Raskolnikov insists on finding out why his landlady was beaten: "What is it for? . . . And how is it possible?" His questions go unanswered. Raskolnikov's conversion occurs much later, in the epilogue, after his fifth dream (a vision of the utopia), and after the fortuitous appearance of Sonya.

Like Alyosha's vision of Cana of Galilee, Dmitry's dream of the babe represents the beginning of his "spiritual purification." Whereas Alyosha will seek to implement Zosima's "active love" in the world, Dmitry is led both to confess to his actual crime and to accept the burden of suffering. Just as Alyosha's miracle occurs on the level of his subconscious, so too Dmitry's dream leads to his feeling compassion and to his eventual rebirth.

It has been argued that Dmitry's dream symbolizes his desire to become the poor baby's "father."[33] Having attacked other "fathers" in the novel (Fyodor Karamazov, Grigory, Snegirev, and Zosima), Dmitry perceives in his dream that the baby is "fatherless" and he now wants to assume that role. But by the end of his dream, Dmitry has progressed beyond the concept of "fatherhood" to that of "brotherhood," from the suffering of one child to that of all humanity. He openly declares his willingness to accept this ultimate burden of responsibility.

Dmitry's subsequent references to his dream during the remainder of the novel shed further light on the importance of the babe in the process of his spiritual purification. During his actual trial, Dmitry declares to the court, "We're all cruel, all monsters, we all make men weep, and mothers and babes at the breast." (XIV, 458). Later, when he keeps repeating, "It's for that babe that I'm going to Siberia," Grushenka begs Alyosha to explain: "Tell me, Alyosha—what babe?" But even he is unable to provide a satisfactory answer. Finally Dmitry himself attempts to interpret the mystery to his younger brother:

Why was it I dreamed of that babe at such a time? "Why is the babe so poor?" That was a sign to me at that moment. It's for the babe that I'm going. Because we are all responsible for all. For all the babes . . . all the babes. I go for everyone, because someone must go for everyone. (XV, 31)

Here, in his characteristic style, Dmitry reiterates the central theme of the novel.

While Alyosha's conversion immediately follows his miraculous vision, he achieves his greatest success by implementing Zosima's doctrine in his interactions with the children. Dmitry's spiritual purification begins as a direct result of his dream of the babe; subsequently he accepts responsibility for the suffering of humanity. Ivan, whose intellectual contemplation of the torments of little children leads him to spiritual revolt, also has a dream; however, his experience serves only to reveal the failure of his rational approach to reality.[34]

On the way to his third meeting with Smerdyakov, Ivan encounters a drunken peasant, whom he leaves face down in the snow. During the interview Ivan acknowledges his own responsibility for the death of his father and resolves to confess his guilt openly at Dmitry's trial. With a great feeling of relief, he comes across the same peasant on his way home; lifting him out of the snow, he sees to it that the man is provided for. Ivan's spontaneous emotion ("something like joy") and his compassionate action (rescuing the peasant) parallel the experiences of his two brothers: Alyosha's ecstasy after his vision followed by his decision to "sojourn in the world," and Dmitry's tender emotion after his dream followed by his acceptance of the burden of suffering.

However, as soon as Ivan arrives home, his joy vanishes. Memories begin to haunt him and he feels ill. When he lies down for a little rest, his "nightmare" (*koshmar*) begins. In it, the Devil appears and engages in an intellectual debate with Ivan, some of which concerns the reality of the nightmare itself.[35] Trying to reject the theological implications of his vision, Ivan protests:

> You are a lie, you are my illness, you are a phantom. . . . You are my hallucination. You are the incarnation of myself, but only of one side of me . . . of my thoughts and feelings, but only the nastiest and stupidest of them. (XV, 72)

The Devil rises to his own defense; he eloquently explains how it is possible in a dream for a character to expound some new idea, about which the dreamer was previously unaware:

> In dreams and particularly in nightmares, . . . a man sometimes sees such artistic things, such complex and actual reality, such events, or even a whole world of events, woven into such a plot, full of such astonishing details . . . that, I assure you, not even Leo Tolstoy could have invented it. (XV, 74)

Dostoevsky was eager to establish the verisimilitude of Ivan's nightmare; at the same time he strove to exploit the ambiguity concerning the Devil's appearance. In a letter to N. A. Lyubimov dated August 10, 1880, he wrote:

> I consider it my duty to inform you that I have gotten opinions from doctors (more than one) long ago. . . . This is not only a physical (diseased) trait, when a man begins at times to lose the distinction between the real and the imagined . . . but it is also a spiritual trait, corresponding to the hero's character. Denying the reality of the phantom, he insists on its reality when the

phantom disappears. *Tormented by disbelief, at the same time he (unconsciously) wishes that the phantom were something real and not a fantasy.*[36]

The climax of Ivan's nightmare occurs when the Devil confesses his sincere admiration for the figurative dreams (*mechty*) of young men. As an example, he cites Ivan's early article, "The Geological Cataclysm," in which the author had attempted to destroy both the idea of God and the outmoded conception of morality. There Ivan had argued that men must begin anew, uniting in the joyful present, conquering nature by means of science, and ultimately accepting death. As a result, ordinary man would be transformed into a man-god, and paradise would be realized on earth.

The theme of Ivan's article is a restatement of the dream of the golden age, which had originated in Stavrogin's confession in *The Possessed* and was transformed into Versilov's vision in *The Adolescent*. Here the godless utopia is ascribed to an earlier stage of Ivan's own intellectual development. As in Dostoevsky's previous novels, the figurative dream (*mechta*) of the golden age is conveyed within the context of an experiential dream (*son*). But Ivan's "dream" is mercilessly mocked by the Devil, who makes light of its consequences:

Since there is no God and no immortality anyway, the new man may as well become the man-god . . . and promoted to his new position, he may lightheartedly overstep all the barriers of the old morality of the old slave-man, if necessary. . . . That's all very charming. (XV, 84)

Here the Devil reiterates a theme that has occupied Dostoevsky from *Crime and Punishment* to *The Brothers Karamazov*. Raskolnikov's figurative dream (*mechta*), outlined in his early article on crime and illness, was later discredited and finally rejected after his last terrifying experiential dream (*son*). Ivan's figurative dream of the golden age, expounded in his early treatise, is finally exposed in his nightmare as the ultimate error of human thought.

Upon awakening, Ivan meditates on his own state of consciousness, somehow still hoping to deny that what he had seen was a dream:

I was asleep last time, but this dream (*son*) was not a dream (*son*). And it has happened before. . . . I have dreams now . . . they're not dreams, but reality: I walk about, speak, see, . . . but I'm asleep. (XV, 86)

Alyosha's arrival and announcement of Smerdyakov's suicide abruptly thwarts Ivan's plan to save his brother Dmitry by confessing to the crime himself. During the trial, Ivan's delirious speech reflects in a confused way the principal themes of his nightmare. His "attack of brain fever" and his vociferous removal from the courtroom symbolize his unfortunate spiritual predicament at the end of the narrative.

Thus it is by means of an experiential dream that Dostoevsky defines the spiritual culmination or epiphany of each of the three brothers. Alyosha's religious vision of Cana of Galilee marks his transformation into a "champion" resolved to implement Zosima's teachings. Dmitry's emotional dream of the babe, which concludes in a crescendo of questions, leads him to genuine compassion and to the beginning of his spiritual purification. Ivan's intellectual nightmare, in which the Devil himself refutes the figurative dream of the golden age, reveals the ultimate failure of his rational approach to reality. It is always the experiential dream emerging from the subconscious that contains the truth that must eventually be recognized and implemented in the characters' lives.

* * *

Ivan's Devil wonders whether "even Leo Tolstoy" could have invented such artistic things as people imagine in their dreams and nightmares. Not long after Dostoevsky's death, Tolstoy was asked if he had ever read *The Brothers Karamazov.* "I couldn't stick it out to the end," he confessed.[37] In a letter to Mrs. Chertkov written a few days before his own death, Tolstoy expressed his opinion of Dostoevsky's masterpiece: "I cannot overcome my dislike for all that is antiartistic, superficial, affected, and irrelevant to the great problems."[38] In spite of this criticism, Tolstoy's use of literary dreams as a technique in his own fiction would rival Dostoevsky's in terms of its psychological, narrative, and thematic significance.

6. TOLSTOY'S "TRUER FEELINGS"

People are not afraid of what they do while awake, but they are afraid of what they see in their dreams.

    Russian proverb

In a diary entry for December 1851 Tolstoy recorded a "horrible" dream in the course of which he was confronted by the corpse of his brother Dmitry:

> It was one of those dreams that are not easily forgotten. Can it really mean something? I wept a great deal afterward. Feelings are truer in a dream than in the waking state. False reasoning awakes poetic feeling.[1]

The young author accepts the validity of his dream entirely and asserts that "feelings" are more authentic in a dream because in the waking state, the powers of reason distort and falsify emotions. This insistence on the authenticity of feeling is reiterated in the epilogue to *War and Peace*, where Tolstoy observes, "In a dream everything is uncertain, senseless, and contradictory, except for the feeling that guides the dream" (XII, 291). Such a conviction is reflected throughout his major works in the literary dreams that he ascribes to his fictional characters.

This chapter first surveys representative dreams and analogous experiences selected from Tolstoy's works of the 1850s in order to document his early experiments with the literary technique. Then it analyzes the dreams in the author's two major novels, *War and Peace* and *Anna Karenina*. Finally, the chapter will attempt to characterize the allegorical dreams in Tolstoy's late works.

EARLY WORKS

Maksim Gorky, in his *Reminiscences of Tolstoy*, reports an illuminating conversation with the author; after hearing Gorky recount "the most terrible dream he ever had," Tolstoy replied, "That is terrible. . . . Did you really mean that? You didn't invent it? . . . Empty boots marching—that really is terrible. Even if you did invent it, it's good. Terrible!"[2] Tolstoy acknowledges the power of Gorky's recollected dream, whether or not it was real. Observing that the dreamer is offended by his suspicion, Tolstoy continued:

> Don't be annoyed; sometimes, I know, one invents something without being aware of it, something that one cannot believe, that cannot possibly be believed, and then one imagines that one dreamed it and did not invent it at all.[3]

By emphasizing the emotional impact of the experience, Tolstoy seems to be obliterating the distinction between genuine and invented dreams.

The first chapter of *Childhood* (1851–52), part of the author's autobiographical trilogy entitled *Childhood, Boyhood, and Youth*, also contains an invented dream. When the tutor, Karl Ivanovich awakens young Nikolai by tickling his feet, the hero suddenly bursts into tears. He explains the reason for his distress:

> I told him that I was crying because of a bad dream [*son*]: I had dreamed that mama was dead and they were taking her away to bury her. I invented [*vydumal*] all of this, for I really could not remember what I had been dreaming that night; but when Karl Ivanych, affected by my story, tried to comfort and soothe me, it seemed to me that I actually had dreamed that awful dream and now I shed tears for a different reason. (I, 4)[4]

As in the recorded conversation with Gorky, Tolstoy underlines the emotional impact of the experience. The power of the invented dream is such that the creator comes to believe in its reality. Later on in the same chapter Nikolai admits that "the melancholy thoughts occasioned by the dream that I had invented [*vydumannyi son*] still haunted me" (I, 4). When the boy greets his mother, he describes to her how he cried in his sleep, "remembering my invented dream [*vydumannyi son*] in all its detail and involuntarily shuddering at the recollection" (I, 9). Subsequently, when he learns that he is to be sent off to boarding school in Moscow, Nikolai reflects, "So that is what my dream [*son*] foreboded . . . God grant that there may be nothing worse to follow" (I, 13). Here the epithet *invented* (*vydumannyi*) has been omitted: Nikolai's dream was indeed invented, its impact persists, and then it seems to be fulfilled.

In fact, the dream turns out to be more prophetic than even he suspects. The awful event that it foretold actually occurs; toward the end of *Childhood* the young hero's mother dies in dreadful agony. Thus Nikolai's invented dream, which never really occurred, finally comes to pass. In Tolstoy's major works literary dreams will be "invented"; they will be ascribed to fictional characters, communicated with extraordinary conviction, and almost always fulfilled in the course of the narrative.

In other works of this same period Tolstoy experimented with various ways of representing dreams and related phenomena in literature. In "A History of Yesterday" (1851) he catalogues his sensations upon falling asleep: all the associations of his mind and the transformations of phrase into image. After recording individual dream images, he specifies the external stimulus that produced each one. He argues that people fall asleep in three stages: first, they lose consciousness of intellect, then, of feeling, and finally, of body. The moment before a sleeper is aroused, he gathers impressions into a dream (under the influence of some external stimulus), and awakens gradually, in three stages, reversing the order of the process described above.[5] Thus in "A History of Yesterday" Tolstoy insists on the connection between external stimuli and dream imagery, and also maintains that dreams are formed at the moment of awakening. These two principles will be clearly reflected in his major novels.

Tolstoy's autobiographical story "The Snowstorm" (1856), the setting of which strongly recalls the situation of Grinev's dream in Pushkin's *Captain's Daughter*, demonstrates the connection between external stimuli and dream images and also provides examples of other dreamlike states. The narrator's logical sequence of "memories and visions" drawn from his childhood (chapter 6) is followed by an illogical collection of "daydreams" (chapter 8), which culminates in an "experiential dream" of extraordinary transformations (chapter 9), reminiscent of Gogol's innovative technique:

I slept soundly; but the ringing of bells was constantly audible and appeared to me in a dream [*son*] in the form of a dog who was barking and hurling itself at me, then as an organ, in which I was one of the pipes, then in the form of French verses, which I was composing. Then it seemed to me that this sound was some kind of instrument of torture. (III, 140)

The dreamer awakens with the sensation that his foot is being crushed by that same instrument; it is actually the onset of frostbite, an external stimulus incorporated into the dream, which awakens the sleeper. The narrator's increasing physical distress is reflected in his psychological deterioration, which in turn is expressed as an intensifying series of dream images.

In the final chapter of "A Landowner's Morning" (1856), a fragment of Tolstoy's unfinished "Novel of a Russian Landowner," the hero Nekhlyudov follows a similar psychological progression. He is disillusioned with life, and

his main pleasure was provided by the intensified activity of his imagination, which at this time presented to him in a disconnected and abrupt manner, but with striking clarity, the most diverse, intermingled and incongruous images and pictures from his past and his future. (IV, 169)

Then Nekhlyudov drifts into a dreamlike reverie, which concludes with a "dream-within-a-dream": he imagines that he has fallen asleep and is dreaming of exotic places.

In "Albert" (1858) a mad musician's aborted romance unleashes the forces of his bizarre imagination. Tolstoy follows the hero's decline until a "multitude of unconnected but related visions" carries him off into the "free and wonderful realm of dreams [*mechtaniya*]."

The nature of these dreams may perhaps be deduced from the author's curious prose poem simply called "Dream" (*Son*) (1857–58), the first version of which is thought to have served as the original conclusion to "Albert."[6] In it a character similar to the mad musician is pronouncing an inspired speech before a responsive crowd. He is interrupted by a simple woman who seems to be in possession of some indeterminate force and who destroys the speaker's hold on his audience. Although she listens to him with love and compassion, she is unable to comprehend his message. Suddenly he understands everything and bursts into tears.[7]

Tolstoy establishes a dramatic contrast between the narrator's intellectual "inspired speech" and the woman's spontaneous "love and compassion," thus implying that enlightenment can be achieved not through thoughts and words, but through feelings and emotions. This theme becomes a fundamental truth of the author's later work and is frequently revealed through the dreams of his fictional characters. In fact Tolstoy tried to incorporate a revised version of this same prose poem into his unfinished work "1805," into an early draft of *War and Peace*, and finally into the novel itself.

During the 1850s Tolstoy explored the creative possibilities of the literary dream. He insisted on the primacy of feelings, eliminated the distinction between "invented" and genuine dreams, documented the connection between external stimuli and dream imagery, and investigated other dreamlike phenomena. In his two major novels *War and Peace* and *Anna Karenina*, he would invent extraordinary literary dreams and ascribe them to his most original fictional characters.

WAR AND PEACE

The two principal dreamers in *War and Peace* (1865–69) are Andrei Bolkonsky and Pierre Bezukhov, both major figures—both male, and both nonhistorical characters. Minor players either have no dreams, or, if they do, theirs parallel those of the major figures. Women do not have dreams, nor do they seem to play significant roles in any.[8] Nor do historical characters dream, although both Napoleon and the Czar enter into the dreams of others.

Andrei and Pierre have two dreams each, separated by years of experience. Andrei's first dream occurs during the battle of Austerlitz; his second as he lies on his deathbed, following the battle of Borodino. Pierre's first dream occurs at Mozhaysk, shortly after the battle of Borodino; his second, at Shamshevo, before he is rescued from captivity. All of these dreams result from the two characters' experience of war and serve to reveal their opposite spiritual progressions, the one toward death, the other toward life.

On the evening of the battle of Austerlitz, Prince Andrei leaves the council of war preoccupied with morbid thoughts. His vivid imagination recalls a series of intimate family scenes, after which it conjures up a battle in which he alone excels. Meditating on the idea of glory, he comes to acknowledge that his own desire to become famous is more important than either death or the loss of his family.

All of these conscious thoughts lay the groundwork for Andrei's first experience of war and his subconscious dream on the battlefield.

There, he advances heroically against the enemy, just as he imagined that he would; but instead of distinguishing himself in battle, he is seriously wounded. He falls, flagstaff in hand, and suddenly looks up to behold the sky with gray clouds gliding slowly across it. That immeasurably lofty, peaceful scene inspires what Tolstoy refers to in an early manuscript as Andrei's "dream and delirium [*son i bred*] on the battlefield" (XIII, 28–29). Lying there in a semiconscious state, he experiences the infinite in a sudden spiritual manifestation. He declares ecstatically, "Yes! Everything is vanity, everything is falsehood, except for this infinite sky. There is nothing, nothing but that. But even that does not exist, there is nothing, except quiet and peace" (IX, 344). For the first time in his life Andrei hears the "voice of death and suffering" and he begins to understand its message.

When Napoleon, the supreme embodiment of Andrei's own desire for personal fame and military glory, approaches the wounded prince, he is immediately incorporated into this "dream and delirium." Andrei juxtaposes his hero with this sudden glimpse of the infinite and concludes that Napoleon is insignificant by comparison. Tolstoy's hero has begun to grasp that fame and glory, victory and defeat, are trivial matters; nothing can compare to the infinite, lofty sky.

Following his profound spiritual revelation, Andrei is transferred to Napoleon's bivouac where he slides deeper into unconsciousness. There his "feverish fancies" and "dreams" (*mechtaniya*) recapitulate his shattering experience of battle, including the family memories of the preceding evening and the vision of Napoleon juxtaposed against the lofty sky. Then, in a final flourish, Andrei's subconscious combines these images into an extraordinary vignette: the French emperor is transported back to the Bolkonsky estate at Bald Hills. When Napoleon displays his disapproval of the peaceful family scene, Andrei realizes that the emperor's success must be founded on the unhappiness of other people. The contradictions seem irreconcilable: only the lofty sky offers serenity. Tormented by doubt, Andrei descends into the chaos of oblivion.

Fame and glory, military heroism, triumphant bravery—these are the values that Andrei carried with him into the battle of Austerlitz. But as a result of his dream and delirium, he is carried off the field having concluded that these things are worthless; on the other hand, family scenes, concern for his child, memories of home life—these values have become profoundly meaningful. But Andrei does not yet achieve inner peace; he loses consciousness before reaching a final resolution.

After seven long years filled with diverse experience, on the eve of the battle at Borodino, Andrei's imagination is hard at work again. Before Austerlitz he had dismissed family memories in order to dwell on the idea of fame; now he confronts the possibility of his own death with equanimity, acknowledging his own insignificance. He tries to fall asleep, but his mind is haunted by recollections of Natasha and Anatole.

During the battle of Borodino Andrei is mortally wounded. But instead of experiencing a "dream and delirium" as he had at Austerlitz, he regains consciousness in the military hospital to discover that Anatole was also wounded during the battle and has had a leg amputated. Andrei responds to his former enemy with genuine love and compassion. His second dream occurs much later, when he lies at home dying, there attended by the devoted Natasha, the woman whom he still loved dearly. His conscious mind was still preoccupied with "thoughts, only thoughts" leading nowhere. Andrei tries unsuccessfully to reconcile the disparity between his own imminent death and the life and love demonstrated by Natasha. Finally the wounded prince falls asleep.

In a vivid dream (*son*) he sees himself lying in his own room, but now completely recovered from his wound. The people around him talk about trivial matters and then depart. He becomes obsessed with the door leading into his room; he rises from his bed and goes to lock it. But suddenly he realizes that death is standing behind the door, pushing it open, entering the room, and about to overtake him. At the very moment that Andrei dies in his dream, he awakens and remembers that he was asleep. He thinks to himself; "Yes, it was death! I died—and I woke up. Yes, death is an awakening!" (XII, 64).

The profound understanding that he could not achieve through conscious thought, through rational, intellectual processes, finally comes to Andrei in a subconscious dream. Twice he was wounded in battle and twice he almost died; but the author does not allow him to die until he has come to understand the meaning of death. Andrei's spiritual transformation is accomplished in two stages: first, his vision of the lofty sky at Austerlitz, and second, his dream of an encounter with death. Tolstoy's hero has finally achieved enlightenment:

> From that day there began for Prince Andrei, together with an awakening from sleep, an awakening from life. And compared to the duration of life, it [this awakening from life] did not seem slower to him than an awakening from sleep compared to the duration of a dream [*snovidenie*]. (XII, 64)[9]

Having understood the simple and solemn mystery of death, Andrei can finally enter into its kingdom.

The other principal dreamer in the novel, Pierre Bezukhov, also progresses toward enlightenment as a result of his two experiential dreams.[10] But whereas Andrei learns the meaning of death so that he is able to die, Pierre comes to understand the meaning of life so that he can live.

Pierre's first dream occurs shortly after the battle of Borodino. Plagued by memories and surrounded by wounded men, he sets out on foot for Mozhaysk, halting at night along the roadside. Three soldiers who settle down near him subsequently conduct him safely to his destination. In one of Tolstoy's early manuscripts this scene continues as follows:

> They brought Pierre to Mozhaysk. There were no quarters. He lay down in a carriage, putting his legs on the coach box, and he slept until late morning. They roused him with the news that the troops were departing. Pierre awoke and witnessed the continuation of yesterday's events. (XIV, 267)

Whereas the original version of this episode contains no dream, in the novel Tolstoy first records Pierre's thoughts before sleep and then recounts his extraordinary experiential dream.

Pierre begins by contrasting his own fears during battle with the soldiers' tranquility and he comes to feel envy for their "communal life." Then he sinks into reminiscences of his own recent past, including a dinner at the English Club where he had challenged Dolokhov, and a meeting with his benefactor at Torzhok. As Prince Andrei's first dream had imaginatively transported Napoleon to Bald Hills, Pierre's now summons his benefactor to the club.

He dreams that a solemn meeting of the Masonic lodge was taking place at the English Club in the presence of his benefactor as well as Anatole, Dolokhov, Denisov, and some "others." Above the raucous shouting and singing, the benefactor's voice can be heard distinctly; his speech is profound and comforting. Pierre reacts to his words in the following way: "He did not understand what the benefactor said, but he knew that he was talking about goodness and about the possibility of becoming what they [the "others"] were" (XI, 293). He tries to understand intellectually, but his mind is cluttered with "thoughts, clearly expressed in words, only thoughts that someone was uttering or that Pierre himself formulated." Finally, the light begins to dawn:

"War is the most difficult subordination of man's freedom to the law of God. . . . Simplicity is submission to God; you cannot escape from Him. And *they* [the "others"] are simple. *They* do not talk, but act. A spoken word is silver, but an unspoken one is gold. Man can be master of nothing while he fears death. And he who does not fear it possesses all. If there were no suffering, man would not know his limitations, he would not know himself. The most difficult thing . . . is to be able to unite [*soedinyat'*] in one's soul the meaning of everything. To unite everything? . . . No, not to unite. It's impossible to unite thoughts, but to *harness* [*sopryagat'*] all these thoughts—that's what is needed! Yes, *one must harness, one must harness!*" he repeated to himself with internal rapture, feeling that only with these words could he express what he wanted to express, and could he solve the problems that tormented him. (XI, 294)

The phrase *one must harness* represents the intrusion of an external stimulus into his dream; Pierre's groom employs the phrase to awaken the sleeper. But Pierre resists, still longing "to see," "to understand" (*ponimat'*), and "to grasp" (*ponyat'*) the meaning of what was being revealed to him. The groom persists; upon awakening, Pierre laments, "One more second and I would have grasped it all [*vse ponyal by*]." But the spell is broken: "Pierre felt with horror that all the meaning of what he had seen and thought in his dream was destroyed" (XI, 294). The groom hastens to convey the urgent news that the French are nearing Mozhaysk, and that the Russians need to depart immediately. Pierre sets out for Moscow.

Although intuiting that his benefactor is talking about "goodness" and about the "possibility of becoming what they [the "others"] were" (that is, good), Pierre can comprehend neither the benefactor's words nor the "others'" actions. Recognizing this failure, he nevertheless makes substantial progress toward a solution. First he enumerates his philosophical concerns: freedom, divine law, simplicity, death, suffering, self-knowledge. All the important themes are present, but in no coherent order. Pierre strives to *unify* ("harness") them, to discover an organizing principle, to break through the complexity and arrive at a simple solution. But try as he does to "understand" and "grasp" (*ponimat'/ponyat'*) the meaning of his dream, he fails to achieve that final resolution.

In one of Tolstoy's manuscript versions of this scene Pierre actually comes to understand too much. Over and above the drunken shouts of Dolokhov and Anatole, the speech of his benefactor, and the words of the proverb, Pierre discerns the advice of a biblical injunction: "Give away all that thou hast and follow me." Upon awakening, Pierre hears someone say, "Give away all, God be with him. Well then, give it away" (XIV, 347). He watches as a soldier donates his supply of water to an old woman and concludes that this spontaneous act is an example of the "unspoken word"; it can be found neither in the shouts of Dolokhov and Anatole nor in the eloquent "silver words" of the benefactor. Instead, the solution lies in unspoken "golden words," in exemplary actions, in good deeds performed by the "others." Pierre awakens from this manuscript dream to proclaim, "Yes, now I understand." But the author decided that it was too early for Pierre to understand so much. The final version includes no such example of the "unspoken word." The hero does not discover Tolstoy's solution yet; instead, he must continue his search.

Although Pierre's second dream occurs several months later at Shamshevo on the eve of his rescue from French captivity, Tolstoy's manuscript contains yet another dream that was supposed to have preceded these events. Although it too was rejected in the final version, it resembles the early variant of Pierre's first dream at Mozhaysk and also relates it thematically to his second dream at Shamshevo.

In the final text Tolstoy describes Pierre's return to Moscow and the evening spent at the Rostopchins' discussing the subject of Freemasonry. Upon returning home Pierre discovers a letter from his wife and subsequently reflects:

They, the soldiers at the battery, Prince Andrei killed . . . that old man. . . . Simplicity is submission to God. Suffering is necessary . . . the meaning of everything . . . one must harness . . . my wife is getting married . . one must forget and understand. (XI, 300)

This presleep meditation reiterates the principal motifs of Pierre's first dream at Mozhaysk and also alludes to subsequent narrative events (Andrei's supposed "death" and Hélène's intended marriage). Pierre then lapses into a dreamless sleep. But in one early version Tolstoy actually recorded the details of Pierre's "long series" of dreams that night:

> He lay alone, weak and powerless, and a tall old man in a white robe stood over him and said, "Let those who have ears, hear. It is easier for a camel to pass through the eye of a needle, than for a rich man to enter the kingdom of heaven. Give away all that thou hast and follow me." (XIV, 350)[11]

"But to whom?" Pierre wonders, and "How?" Suddenly he awakens; and, "as if in answer" to his dream, he learns that Moscow is to be abandoned.

As in Pierre's first dream, there is an implicit contrast between "spoken" words and "active" goodness. The biblical injunction to "give away all" that appeared in the early version of the Mozhaysk dream here forms the conclusion of the old man's speech. Similarly, in the Mozhaysk manuscript, when Pierre awakens, he is witness to an example of the soldier's practical charity; here Pierre discovers that now he too will be obliged to follow the same biblical injunction: Moscow is to be left to the enemy and everyone will have to give away everything. But it is still too soon for Pierre to discover Tolstoy's truth: this dream is rejected outright. The hero is now to be arrested by the French and taken prisoner.

As a result of the trials and tribulations that he endures as a captive, Pierre loses his faith in the cosmic order, in his own soul, and in his God. But before long his encounter with Platon Karataev, a simple God-fearing peasant-soldier, initiates the dramatic process of the hero's spiritual rebirth. In contrast to the contemplative Pierre, Karataev is a man of action: "He did not understand [*ponimat'*] and never could grasp (*ponyat'*)" the meanings of words. Pierre had awakened from his dream at Mozhaysk feeling a desperate desire to "understand" and to "grasp" its meaning; Karataev simply lives the good life, practicing virtue. He is one of "them," the "others," sent, as it were, to teach Pierre how to live.

At Shamshevo, on the eve of his rescue from captivity, Pierre falls asleep "as he had at Mozhaysk after the battle of Borodino." Tolstoy makes explicit the connection between the hero's two dreams: "Once again events of reality merged with dreams and again, someone, he himself or someone else, spoke thoughts to him, and even those same thoughts that had been spoken to him at Mozhaysk" (XII, 158). In his second dream, Pierre finally learns the answers to the questions which had been tormenting him for so long: "Life is everything. Life is God. Everything changes and moves, and this movement is God. And while there is life, there is joy in consciousness of the divinity. To love life, to love God" (XII, 158). Karataev suddenly appears, an embodiment of this newly discovered attitude toward life and God. Then Pierre's former tutor shows him a globe that seems to be alive and pulsating. Its surface is composed of droplets constantly moving, merging, dividing. The tutor explains, "This is life." Pierre is stunned: "How simple and clear it all is. In the middle of the globe is God, and each droplet tries to expand so as to reflect Him to the greatest extent." The tutor commends his pupil: "Vous avez compris, mon enfant." This phrase represents another intrusion of an external stimulus that serves to rouse the dreamer. A Frenchman shouting "Vous avez compris, sacré nom" awakens him. He attempts to dwell on the memory of Karataev, and seems ready to grasp (*ponyat'*) the fact that the peasant-soldier had in fact been executed by the French, when suddenly Pierre remembers an evening with a beautiful Polish woman:

And not linking up the memories of the day or drawing a conclusion from them, Pierre closed his eyes; the picture of nature in summer was mingled with memories of swimming, of the liquid pulsating globe, and somewhere he sank into the water, so that it closed over his head. (XII, 159)

With this strange, soothing feeling of envelopment the hero falls into a dreamless sleep.

Pierre's dream at Shamshevo furthers the progression toward enlightenment initiated by his first dream at Mozhaysk. Now his Swiss tutor has superseded the Masonic benefactor as the source of one kind of wisdom (words), while the peasant Karataev replaces the simple soldiers as an example of virtuous action. At Mozhaysk Pierre was striving to "unite" and to "harness" his thoughts in order to "understand" and to "grasp"; at Shamshevo he realizes how "simple and clear" everything is; the tutor explains what goodness means and Karataev exemplifies the virtuous life. The solution that Pierre was seeking so desperately at Mozhaysk is almost achieved at Shamshevo; the tutor commends his former pupil, and even the author concurs that his hero was very close to full understanding. But Pierre is still unable to make the necessary connections, he fails to reach the final conclusions; instead, he sinks into sweet oblivion. At Mozhaysk Pierre had resisted being aroused so that he might "understand"; he awoke in horror, feeling that he had lost the meaning of his dream. Here at Shamshevo he almost achieves that understanding, but mysteriously retreats into a pleasant memory. While the solution is imminent, it still cannot be expressed within the hero's experiential dream.

The solution emerges only in the first epilogue to the novel. There Tolstoy describes Pierre's trip to Petersburg, during which he becomes completely disenchanted with the emperor and the Russian bureaucracy. Upon his return home, he outlines his own ideas on the urgent need for social and political reform to the unsympathetic Nikolai Rostov. Both Natasha and young Nikolai Bolkonsky listen rapturously. Rostov later comments unfavorably on the child's fascination with Pierre's "dangerous" plans and ends by declaring that "Pierre always was and always will be a dreamer [*mechtatel'*]." In one sense Pierre has only just become a "dreamer" inasmuch as he now has a new figurative dream (*mechta*), a vision of the way things ought to be, and he has decided to work toward realizing it.

In his subsequent conversation with Natasha, Pierre tries to define the central role that he played during his meetings in Petersburg. He admits, somewhat immodestly, that the whole business was going to pieces before he arrived. "But I succeeded in uniting them all [*vsekh soedinit'*] and then my thought was so simple and clear" (XII, 292). Here Pierre provides conclusive proof that he now possesses the solution he had been seeking for so long. He has finally managed to synthesize the meaning of his two experiential dreams: from Mozhaysk, he has extracted a unifying principle; from Shamshevo, he knows that this principle is "simple and clear." These two insights have become the foundation of his new figurative dream. He proudly declares the conscious conviction that he has been chosen to provide "a new direction to all Russian society and to the whole world." Natasha does not and cannot respond to his figurative dream; transformed by marriage and motherhood, she remarks on some insignificant domestic detail and takes her leave. While the heroine is fated to be completely fulfilled by family, the true Tolstoyan hero will always retain his intellectual and spiritual pursuits.

Thus it is that both Andrei and Pierre, the two principal male nonhistorical characters in the novel, progress toward their respective enlightenments through their experiential dreams. Andrei's juxtaposition of Napoleon and the lofty sky during his "dream and delirium" on the field at Austerlitz, followed by his dream encounter with death after the battle of Borodino lead him to an understanding and tranquil acceptance of death. Pierre's dream of his benefactor at Mozhaysk and the combination of his Swiss tutor and Karataev at Shamshevo, lead him to an understanding of life and a courageous mission in society.

Nikolai and Petya Rostov, two secondary nonhistorical characters, have dreams that reflect the central themes of Andrei's and Pierre's dreams in a minor key. Nikolai's first dream occurs shortly after the battle of Schön Grabern. Crossing the Ems, he too gazes up at Prince Andrei's lofty sky and reflects on the disparity between life and death. "Fear of death and of the stretchers, and love of the sun and life, all merged into a feeling of sickening agitation" (IX, 180–81). At Schön Grabern Nikolai gallops bravely into battle and is wounded immediately. Carried back to the Russian camp, he subsequently dozes by the fire. In his dream he recalls the characters of his "distant" family past (his mother, his beloved Sonya, and his sister Natasha), as well as those of his "recent" military past (Denisov, Telyanin, and Bogdanich).

In one of Tolstoy's early versions of this scene, Nikolai awakens to notice a white object hanging in front of the fire. "Here it is," he thinks to himself, "my death" (XIII, 471). Nikolai's reflection prompted by the lofty sky, the figures recollected in his dream, and the omitted image of his death are all analogous to Andrei's experiences: his meditation on the eve of Austerlitz, his delirium on the battlefield, and his dream-encounter with death. But Nikolai Rostov is a minor, "ordinary" character whose development is but a vague reflection of Andrei's profound spiritual travail.

Nikolai's second dream occurs on the eve of the battle of Austerlitz. As he rides up and down the line, his eyes close involuntarily; in his imagination "the emperor [appears], then Denisov, then Moscow memories" (IX, 325). Just as in his first dream at Schön Grabern, Nikolai combines figures from home and from the front; but here the Russian emperor assumes a central role. The dreamer imagines himself receiving an order and then pictures the enemy whom he must kill in order to win the Czar's admiration. Next Nikolai pursues a chain of associations connecting battle images to Moscow memories: white spot, snow, *une tache*, Natasha, *tashka* (saber). Finally all these elements merge into one: the emperor, sabers, hussars, mustaches, Gurev, Denisov, and Natasha. Nikolai is awakened abruptly from his dream by the sound of gunfire.

At the battle of Austerlitz the wounded Prince Andrei had incorporated the historical figure of Napoleon into his dream; the French emperor was perceived as insignificant compared to the lofty sky. Nikolai Rostov's dream of serving the Russian Czar further reveals the limited nature of his character. At the conclusion to the novel he will stubbornly defend the regime against the social and political reforms advocated by Pierre.[12]

While Nikolai's dreams mirror the themes in Andrei's, Petya Rostov's dream parallels Pierre's. The night before a guerrilla raid Petya dozes while a Cossack sharpens his saber, grinding the blade against a whetstone. In his dream the military encampment is transformed into a magical kingdom in which nothing resembles reality. Night sounds become those of musical instruments in a fantastic orchestra playing a fugue, "first solemnly ecclesiastical, then dazzlingly brilliant and triumphant" (XII, 147). Although Petya admits to himself, "This is just a dream," he begins to conduct the imaginary instruments in a splendid victory march. His dream is interrupted by a summons from the kindly Cossack.

In Pierre's dreams at Mozhaysk and Shamshevo, he had progressed toward a solution, which he conclusively demonstrates in the epilogue. Petya Rostov, another "ordinary" character, cannot attain anything like Pierre's resolution; nevertheless, in his dream he too gains a fleeting glimpse of eternal harmony and experiences a brief moment of transcendental ecstasy.[13] During the next day's skirmish, Petya rides recklessly into enemy fire and is shot through the skull. The guerrilla raid succeeds in rescuing a group of Russian prisoners among whom is Pierre.

Both Nikolai's second dream and Petya's ecstatic vision glorify the experience of war; Nikolai remains a staunch supporter of the Russian Czar, and Petya dies a hero's death in his name. On the other hand, Prince Andrei in his dreams had become disabused of his naive heroism and his previous views on fame and death, while Pierre had moved toward his unifying principle and a simple solution to the mystery of life. After Andrei dies peacefully and Natasha appears to be fulfilled by family, Pierre seems to be left alone in a state of total spiritual isolation.

But *War and Peace* concludes not with a feeling of isolation, but with an experience of communion embodied in a final experiential dream. Young Nikolai Bolkonsky, after overhearing the political debate between his Uncle Pierre and Nikolai Rostov, asks whether or not his father, Prince Andrei, would have agreed with Pierre. His uncle's affirmative response exerts a major influence on the boy's "terrible dream" (*son*) recounted on the final pages of the first epilogue.

Nikolai imagines that he and Pierre are in the vanguard of a large army consisting of white lines resembling the threads of a cobweb. As they advance on their goal, the threads become entangled; the army can move no further. Before them stands the threatening figure of Nikolai Rostov, who claims to have orders from Arakcheev to kill anyone who advances. Nikolai Bolkonsky looks up at Pierre, but his uncle has been somehow transformed into his own father, who now tenderly caresses his son. Rostov continues to advance; the young dreamer is seized with terror and suddenly awakens.

When Nikolai reflects on the meaning of his dream, he comes to the conclusion that Andrei's spirit had actually visited him that night. He interprets his dream as a sign that his father would indeed have approved both of him and of Pierre. As a result Nikolai decides to join forces with his uncle and resolves on an admirable course of action: "I will learn—but then I will do something—everyone will know me, love me, and be delighted with me." (XII, 295).

Young Nikolai's dream reveals the Romantic heroism in his character, which can be seen as a parallel to the martial enthusiasm manifested earlier in the dreams of both young Rostovs, Nikolai and Petya. On the level of political allegory, this dream has also been said to provide evidence of the author's prediction that Nikolai would ally himself with Pierre against Rostov in the coming uprising of December, 1825. One critic cites this dream as further evidence of Tolstoy's general pattern of "strong resolution followed by a hint of irresolution," "thus giving suggestions of future turmoil and change a privileged place in the novel."[14] Finally, by declaring himself on the same ideological side as the two protagonists, Pierre and Andrei, Nikolai Bolkonsky becomes the spiritual heir of both his father and his uncle; as such, he represents Tolstoy's hope for the future of Russia.

Tolstoy's description of Prince Andrei's enlightenment following his second dream is thought to be based on Schopenhauer's idea of death as expressed in his major treatise, *The World as Will and Idea*: "One day a sleep becomes the last one, and its dreams . . . —we dream them now. . . . In general the moment of dying must be very similar to that of awakening from a heavy oppressive dream."[15] During the summer of 1869, the year in which he finished work on *War and Peace*, Tolstoy noted his "unending ecstasy over Schopenhauer . . . the most brilliant of men."[16] He was especially fond of a collection of short philosophical essays entitled *Parerga and Paralipomena*, which he maintained was "much stronger than Schopenhauer's systematic exposition." Tolstoy read and reread one essay in particular, "On Spirit Seeing and Everything Connected Therewith." In it Schopenhauer argues that the graphic abilities of the dream far surpass those of the normal human imagination. On the one hand, he notes the dream's objective clarity and vivid reality, on the other, its "undeniable resemblance to madness." The author concludes that the dream is a source of "second sight," intuitive perception unlike that acquired through the senses.[17]

Tolstoy's theoretical interest in dreams, as well as his use of the literary technique in his fiction, has been traced back to the early works of the 1850s, which predate his infatuation with Schopenhauer. The dreams in *War and Peace* not only express the divergent spiritual progressions of the two protagonists but also reflect parallel developments in the secondary characters and point toward a thematic synthesis as a result of a child's dream in the epilogue.

As Dostoevsky had uncovered some coincidence between his own ideas on dreams and those presented by Carus, so it can be argued that Tolstoy found in Schopenhauer a congenial approach to dreams and related phenomena. In his next major novel, *Anna Karenina* (1875–77) Tolstoy exploits the literary technique to its fullest extent; as in *War and Peace* the two protagonists have dreams that reveal their opposing spiritual progressions; the minor characters' dreams reflect parallel movements; and the author suggests a thematic synthesis through a child's dream. Schopenhauer's influence can be discerned most clearly in the dreams of Tolstoy's fictional heroine.

ANNA KARENINA

The principal dreamers in *Anna Karenina* are the two main characters, Anna and Levin. As the heroine draws closer to her tragic death, the hero's quest leads him toward a more fulfilling life. As in *War and Peace*, the opposition between the characters' spiritual progressions is revealed through their dreams. Anna is witness to a series of haunting experiential dreams (*sny*), three of which comprise variations on the same theme. Levin undergoes sudden spiritual manifestations, each of which advances the development of his cherished figurative dreams (*mechty*). Conversely, Anna has no figurative dreams, Levin, no experiential dreams. Minor characters have dreams that contrast, parallel, or synthesize those of the two protagonists. Stiva Oblonsky's "ordinary" dream opens the novel; Aleksei Vronsky's nightmare parallels and reinforces the heroine's; and Serezha's dream moves toward a synthesis of the influences of Anna and Levin.[18]

In the very first chapter of the novel, Anna's brother, Stiva Oblonsky, awakens after a quarrel with Dolly to find himself on the divan in his study. He promptly recalls his dream: a friend of his was giving a dinner party in Darmstadt, which was somehow located in America; food was being served on glass tables, which seemed to be singing "*Il mio tesoro*"; there were little decanters that were also, at the same time, women.[19] Stiva thinks to himself, "Yes, it was nice, very nice. There were many other delightful things that you can't put into words or even express by thoughts when you're awake." (XVIII, 4). Stiva's dream of wine, women, and song reflects the major elements of his life. He is the quintessentially "normal" character in *Anna Karenina* who sleeps soundly and has "healthy" dreams. Yet even his brief reflection upon awakening includes a kernel of Tolstoyan truth: dreams do indeed contain "things" that can be neither articulated nor conveyed by the conscious mind. Only in this one character's dream, however, are these "things" so "delightful."

The dreams of Stiva's sister, on the other hand, are mysterious and haunting; in Schopenhauer's words they are both "vivid in their reality" and "undeniably resemble madness." Anna has four distinct experiential dreams; in three of them a peasant plays the central role.

The first peasants whom the heroine confronts are genuine ones. As her train is arriving at the railway station, she observes peasant workers moving across the tracks, and sees one descending from the train carrying a sack over his shoulder. Then an unfortunate accident occurs: a peasant watchman is run over. In the ensuing confusion, someone asks if he had committed suicide: "What? Threw himself under [the train]?" Anna finds the incident deeply distressing and considers it "a bad omen."

In this brief scene the heroine has encountered peasants who have been drawn from the land to the city to work on the railroad. One man falls victim to "technological progress" almost before her eyes. The anonymous inquiry as to whether he had intended to kill himself, combined with Anna's superstitious reaction, establishes the framework for her own subsequent experiential dreams.

Anna's second encounter with peasants occurs when she experiences a strange state of mind that the author characterizes as "delirium" (*zabyt'e*). She is returning home from Moscow after the unsettling meeting with Vronsky. Sitting in a railway carriage, unable to concentrate on her reading, Anna has a series of vivid erotic sensations, confronting her own sexuality for what seems to be the first time in her life. Then she drifts off into a level of consciousness in which her surroundings are gradually transformed. She even begins to question her own identity: "Am I here, myself? Am I myself or someone else?" She emerges from this trance long enough to realize that a peasant whom she had observed wearing a long nankeen coat was in fact the stoker. Then a bizarre series of dreamlike transformations commences:

> The peasant in the long coat started gnawing at something on the wall; the old woman began stretching her legs the whole length of the carriage, which she filled with a black cloud; then something screeched and clattered in a dreadful manner, as if it was tearing someone to pieces; then a blinding red light appeared, and at last everything was hidden by a wall. (XVIII, 108)

Following the tumultuous events in Moscow and after the heroine's discovery of her sexuality, Anna appears to be losing control over herself. Her strange delirium in the railway carriage is the first instance of irrational forces penetrating into her consciousness. The dreamlike transformations are threatening: the gnawing peasant and the expanding old woman.[20] The images are terrifying: loud noises, bright light, and finally, the wall. Tolstoy is using Anna's delirium as a narrative device to recapitulate the past and to prophesy the future. The violent climax of the passage reflects the watchman's tragic death after the heroine's arrival at the station as well as foreshadows her own suicide at the end of the novel.

Upon recovering her senses, Anna's reaction is extraordinary. Although she feels as if she had "fallen through the floor," the experience strikes her as "amusing," rather than "dreadful." Immediately after her passionate confrontation with Vronsky on the railway platform during the snowstorm, "visions" (*grezy*) return once again to fill the heroine's imagination; but she also finds these "joyful" and "stimulating," rather than "dismal."

While Anna's subconscious images and visions recapitulate and prophesy death, her conscious mind is stubbornly oblivious to that message. Instead, she responds to her delirium with amusement, and to her visions with joy. Sensing that she is on the verge of an exhilarating adventure, she is unaware, except on the deepest level of her being, that it will eventually lead to her demise.

One particular aspect of Anna's new experience, the exploration of her sexuality, is the subject of her first genuine experiential dream. It is the only one in which the figure of the peasant, heretofore encountered both in her life and in her delirium, plays no role. Anna's dream presents what can best be described as her wish-fulfillment fantasy. Almost immediately after the consummation of her affair with Vronsky, she suffers from deep despair and overwhelming guilt. At first she tries to express these emotions in thoughts and words; when this fails, she decides not the think about it at all. Then the author observes that "in her sleep [*vo sne*], when she had no control over her thoughts, her position appeared to her in all of its ugly nakedness" (XVIII, 159). Tolstoy describes the one dream that recurs almost every night. Anna imagines that she is married both to Karenin and to Vronsky at the same time, and that her two husbands are lavishing kisses and caresses on her. "Astonished at what had seemed impossible to her before, she explained to them, laughing, that this was much simpler, and that now they were both satisfied and happy"

(VIII, 159). After relating this idyllic dream-scene, the author explains that "this dream [*snovidenie*], like a nightmare [*koshmar*], oppressed her and she awoke in horror" (XVIII, 159).

Anna's dream provides profound insights into her subconscious, presented within the context of the author's rigid moral framework. The dream-scene reflects the heroine's desire to live in blissful bigamy: Karenin would provide social respectability and security, while Vronsky could offer romantic adventure and sexual fulfillment. In some sense these two "husbands" correspond to the two sides of Anna's personality and confirm an alarming tendency toward "doubleness" that had been increasing since her first encounter with Vronsky. While "thoughts and words" may be incapable of expressing her emotions, the dream embodies her desires in one simple, happy scene.

But Tolstoy's heroine is appalled by her own dream: the "ugly nakedness" of her position "oppresses" and "horrifies" her. Previously, Anna's subconscious delirium in the railway carriage had presented her conscious mind with a series of ominous images prophesying death, but she had reacted with amusement, oblivious to the potential threat. Here, after the consummation of her passion, the heroine's experiential dream offers an idyllic solution to her dilemma, but now her conscious mind is horrified by the thought.

Anna's second experiential dream is the one in which the peasant of her real-life encounters and of her railway carriage delirium reappears. Its significance is underscored by the fact that Vronsky has had the very same dream almost simultaneously. The heroine has been awaiting his return from a week of showing Russian "national amusements" to a foreign prince. Vronsky's late arrival occasions a violent outburst of jealousy followed by a forced reconciliation. Then Anna not only relates, but dramatically reenacts, a dream that, she is convinced, foretells her own death.

In it she imagines herself running into the bedroom to fetch something or find "something" out, only to discover that the "something" is already standing in the corner. It turns around and shows itself to be a little peasant wearing a tangled beard. He is leaning over a sack, fumbling around in it, and muttering in French, "Il faut le battre, le fer, le broyer, le pétrir." Frightened, she wants to wake up; she manages to do so, but only within her dream. When she asks herself what it all means, her former valet explains: "You will die in childbirth." (XVIII, 381). Then the terrified heroine really awakens.

The peasant first encountered at the railway station, and later transformed in her delirium, has now come back to haunt Anna in her experiential dreams. With his tangled beard and a sack over his shoulder, he is a peasant who has forsaken the land to come to the city to work on the railway. His strange words enumerate the steps required to change raw iron into rails. The anomaly, of course, is that the peasant is speaking in French: these urbanized dream-peasants seem to have adopted the speech of their aristocratic masters.[21] Although the peasant's actions and words do not seem to be threatening Anna directly, she "awakens" in fear, only to hear a death sentence pronounced by another (former) peasant, her valet. His menacing words confirm her own superstitions. She finally emerges from the nightmare convinced that her death is imminent. "I shall die," she tells Vronsky, "and I shall deliver both myself and you." Although the truth revealed by the heroine's subconscious is now clearly perceived, the time for decisive action has not yet arrived. Anna's despair is soon dispelled by the quickening of the new baby within her. Vronsky, who has been watching Anna's dramatic reenactment of her dream, dismisses it and her morbid premonition as nonsense; but inasmuch as he had experienced the same dream only a short time before, his voice carries no conviction.

Although Vronsky had first been introduced into the novel as a character who "always enjoyed sound and peaceful sleep," his own dream of the little peasant with a tangled beard precedes Anna's and lends a profound resonance to its recitation. Vronsky had arrived home from his unsettling week with the foreign prince to find Anna's summons. Exhausted by his own ordeal, he lies down for a brief rest. In his presleep ruminations the events of the past week mingle with thoughts of Anna and the peasant-beater who had played such an important role in the recent bear hunt. Vronsky dozes off; upon awakening he recalls the details of his dream. "Yes, the peasant-beater, it seems, small, dirty, with a tangled beard, was bending over doing something and suddenly began to say some strange words in French" (XVIII, 375). Vronsky fails to understand why the dream troubles him so. Rushing off to see Anna, he forgets all about it. But when she acts out her own dream of the little peasant, Vronsky involuntarily recalls his and is filled with horror. Several times he tries to dismiss her account as nonsense; but, having witnessed the same images and undergone similar emotions, even Vronsky perceives the ominous significance of their coincident dreams.

The peasant returns once more, toward the end of the novel, as the subject of what the author describes as Anna's "terrible nightmare" (*koshmar*). When Vronsky fails to come home after a particularly bad quarrel, Anna's thoughts turn morbid. She contemplates suicide as a means of reviving his love for her and as a way of punishing him. Lying in bed in the darkness, she becomes terrified by her own thoughts. She lights a candle and bravely resolves to live on. When she subsequently finds Vronsky fast asleep in his study, she returns to her own bedroom and finally falls asleep. Toward morning she has a dream:

> An old man with a tangled beard was leaning over some iron and doing something, while muttering senseless words in French; and as always in that nightmare (this was what made it so terrible), she felt that this peasant was paying no attention to her, but that he was doing something dreadful to her with the iron. (XIX, 332)

The peasant in Anna's delirium was gnawing on something. In her first dream, he was standing in a corner of her bedroom, fumbling around in a sack, muttering in French. In this nightmare, his actions have a direct impact on her. On the one hand, she feels ignored: he is paying no attention to her whatever. On the other hand, and perhaps somewhat paradoxically, she feels threatened: he is doing something terrible to her. Anna is being simultaneously neglected and victimized by her dream-peasant. Whereas the horror inspired by her first dream had been dispelled by the feeling of new life within her, the terror that she experiences upon awakening from this nightmare cannot be conquered.

From real peasants at the railway station, to transformed peasants in her delirium, dream, and nightmare, this enigmatic figure has haunted Anna, penetrating more deeply into her subconscious. Her reaction to each new manifestation reveals a growing intensity: from superstition at the station, to "amusement" in the carriage, to horror quickly dispelled, and finally, to insurmountable terror.

This haunting dream-peasant has been interpreted by one critic as "a symbol of the remorseless, impersonal power of sex."[22] Indeed, he is certainly connected with this theme. He seems to represent the impersonal, remorseless power of *male* sexuality, a force that simultaneously neglects and victimizes the heroine: part of her is ignored, the other part destroyed by men. But at the same time the dream-peasant is also associated with the theme of death. The incident at the railway station, Anna's violent delirium, the valet's pronouncement, and her own interpretation of the nightmare—all foreshadow her tragic suicide.

At the end of the novel the peasant undergoes one final transformation, when he becomes a real-life figure once again. After Anna boards the train for the last time, she notices a peasant wearing a cap over his tangled hair; he walks past her railway carriage and leans over the wheels. She thinks to herself, "'There is something familiar about that misshapen peasant.' And remembering her dream [*son*], she moved over to the opposite door, trembling with fright" (XIX, 345). At the next station Anna disembarks and promptly receives Vronsky's note. As a freight train approaches, she recalls the little peasant who had been run over on the day she first met Vronsky. With little hesitation she throws herself under the wheels of the oncoming train. "Something huge and relentless struck her on the head and dragged her down. . . . A little peasant muttering something was working on the rails" (XIX, 349).

Anna's startled recognition of the peasant inspecting the wheels, her recollection of the man killed at the station, and her last glimpse of the peasant working on the rails are all images of real peasants, in no way transformed by delirium, dream, or nightmare. Having made its first appearance as a real figure, the image of the peasant returns to reality in its final manifestation. Anna has completed an analogous journey: from life, through delirium, dream, and nightmare, back to reality at the very moment she chooses suicide.

All of Anna's urbanized, alienated peasants have left their traditional pursuits to work on the railway: in forsaking the land, they are doomed to perish. Anna abandons her conventional roles as Karenin's wife and Serezha's mother to become Vronsky's mistress; in rejecting family, she too is condemned to death. The violent imagery of her suicide directly recalls her delirium in the railway carriage. The previously linked images of the train and the peasant here merge into one powerful destructive force; the themes of sex and death, which have also been related, finally combine to destroy the heroine.

The other principal dreamer in the novel, Konstantin Levin, has no experiential dreams in the final version; however, one of Tolstoy's early manuscripts contains the following fragment: "Levin saw Anna on a table and Vronsky with a raised trouser leg, without a hat" (XX, 12). Clearly, at one stage in the creative process, Levin was to have had an erotic dream, not unlike Stiva Oblonsky's, in which his subconscious was to have discerned the sexual bond between the heroine and her lover. But the author abandoned the idea, choosing instead to preserve Levin's sexual innocence.

In the published text, although Levin has no experiential dreams, he has several transcendental "moments" that precede his spiritual enlightment described at the conclusion of the novel. While Anna's unconscious experiential dreams (*sny*) were haunted by alienated peasants, Levin's conscious figurative dreams (*mechty*) serve to document his quest for the meaning of life from traditional, rural peasants.

Levin's first such experience occurs during the mowing scene. As he becomes more accustomed to physical labor, he finds himself with less time for thinking. "He thought of nothing, desired nothing, except not to lag behind and to do his work as well as possible" (XVIII, 265). The suspension of rationality and the physical harmony that it engenders produce "blessed moments" of "unconscious movement":

> The more he mowed, the more often he experienced these minutes of oblivion [*zabyt'e*] when his arms no longer swing the scythe; but the scythe itself made his whole body, full of life and conscious of itself, move after it, as if by magic, without thinking about it. (XVIII, 267)[23]

Levin is transported by this experience of labor from his usual intellectual mode into a new, unfamiliar realm. Work is the cause, oblivion the effect. Tolstoy reports that, after sharing a simple meal with his fellow workers, his hero "fell asleep at once and awoke when the sun touched him"; that is, lying alongside real peasants, Levin enjoys sound dreamless sleep.

The hero's second transcendental moment occurs in the scene on the haystack. He has come to visit his sister's village in order to investigate irregularities in the apportionment of hay. Afterward, sitting on top of a haystack, Levin observes the behavior of a young peasant and his wife. He suddenly becomes aware of their strong, newly awakened love for each other. A little while later, in the song of the peasant women, he is able to identify their genuine joy of living. When, as a consequence, Levin contemplates his own loneliness, physical idleness, and alienation, he considers exchanging his meaningless existence for that of a common laborer. He spends the whole night awake on the haystack, enjoying neither sleep nor dreams; in the morning he "comes to" and attempts to articulate what he had "thought through" and "felt through" during that long night. He decides to renounce his former way of life, including his useless education; instead, he resolves to pursue a pure, simple life in search of inner peace and satisfaction. But Levin is not yet certain how to bring about such a change in himself. As he contemplates the dawn, a "vision" suddenly appears—Kitty riding inside a coach. She and Levin recognize each other, and he realizes instantly that he still loves her and that she will become a necessary part of his solution.

As his participation in peasant labor led to his first "blessed moment" of "oblivion," Levin's observation of peasant love leads to his "vision" and the resolution of his dilemma. In both encounters it is the peasants who teach Levin how to work and how to love through their own example; as Karataev and the "others" instructed Pierre, so Levin's peasants have shown him how to live.

But what of his beloved figurative dreams (*mechty*)? Levin is forced to conclude that they too are nonsense. He rejects his former idealized notions of family life, he grows frustrated with his agricultural pursuits, and he loses interest in his grand schemes to reform the rural order. Although Levin has experienced both work and love, neither can provide him with the ultimate answers to his spiritual quest. The real solution lies elsewhere.

Toward the end of the novel Levin is busy pursuing his search for meaning through reading and conversation. After he rejects philosophy and finds himself contemplating suicide, Levin learns about the existence of a simple peasant who, like Pierre's Karataev, is also named Platon:

At the peasant's words about Platon's living for his soul, righteously, in a godly way, dim but important thoughts crowded into his mind, as if breaking loose from some place where they had been locked up, and all rushing toward one goal, they whirled in his head, dazzling him with their light. (XIX, 376)

The moment of Levin's spiritual illumination has arrived; it too is inspired by peasants, not by their labor or by their love, but by their faith. In one splendid instant Levin achieves unity ("one goal") and enlightenment ("blinding light"). His eyes are lifted toward Prince Andrei's lofty sky and he thanks God for his newfound faith. Now Tolstoy describes the state of mind of this character who has had no experiential dreams, as "if he had just awakened from a dream [*son*]."

Levin's transformation, however, is not to be achieved quite so easily. Just as he had come to reject his previous figurative dreams (*mechty*) of work and love, so too must he reject his "dream" of faith. In the last scene of the novel he stands on the veranda with Kitty, eager to share his "peaceful and joyful" emotions with his beloved wife. But when she disturbs his mood with a trivial domestic detail, he realizes that his new understanding must remain a secret. He had expected to be transformed immediately, but things did not transpire "as he had dreamed" (*mechtal*). Still, Levin's new faith will become the foundation of his life and will give meaning to his existence.

Thus the hero ultimately rejects his third and final figurative dream. His life will not be based on any intellectual conceptions of work, love, or faith. Instead, he has learned the true meaning of each from peasants; now he can cast off all figurative dreams and live his life—working, loving, and believing.

Levin's solution stands as the antithesis of Anna's tragic self-destruction and as a further development of Pierre Bezukhov's spiritual quest. Anna, who had no figurative dream, had hoped to achieve personal happiness through her husband, her son, and ultimately her lover. But she was plagued by menacing experiential dreams and eventually took her own life. In *War and Peace* Pierre had two experiential dreams; at the novel's conclusion he unconsciously synthesized the meaning of both to create his new figurative dream, which would provide direction to Russian society and to the whole world. Levin starts out with figurative dreams of work, love, and faith; through a series of transcendental moments, he learns to discard all such dreams in order to live his life.

Levin contemplates Prince Andrei's lofty sky with reverence, and his peasant-mentor is a reincarnation of Pierre's Platon Karataev. *Anna Karenina*, like *War and Peace*, also contains a dream that moves toward a synthesis of the insights of the two principal dreamers. In the earlier novel Nikolai Bolkonsky, as a result of his dream, was identified as the spiritual heir to both Pierre and Andrei. Anna's young son Serezha also has a dreamlike experience; although it is not as elaborate or as significantly placed as Nikolai's, it nevertheless serves an analogous function in the later novel.

After his mother's departure, Serezha's enthusiasm and affection were gradually being extinguished by his father's cold, severe demeanor. Although Karenin constantly attempted to teach his son about the power of death, Serezha steadfastly maintained his belief that love constituted a stronger force. He stubbornly fails to grasp his father's religious doctrines and his teachers' abstract ideas. On the other hand, Tolstoy writes that Serezha's "soul was yearning for knowledge"; he is continually "learning" from the hall porter, the nurse, the servants, and his tutor, all of them former peasants. These living sources of genuine wisdom are parallel to those from whom Levin has achieved his enlightenment.

Before retiring on the the eve of his ninth birthday, Serezha prays that his mother will visit him the next day. In the ensuing darkness it seems to him that she actually enters his room and stands over him caressing him tenderly. "But then windmills appeared and a knife, and everything became confused" (XIX, 98). The next morning Serezha's wish comes true: Anna comes to visit him. He understands at once both that she is unhappy and that she loves him dearly.

In *War and Peace* Nikolai Bolkonsky had dreamed that he was being carried aloft on cobwebs; that Rostov had reprimanded him for breaking the sealing wax and quill pens; and that his father had returned to be with him. These images closely parallel those in Serezha's dreamlike experience. First he imagines that his mother visits him. Then he sees "windmills"; all that evening he had been building models of them with his tutor, dreaming about one large enough to carry him aloft. Finally, he sees a "knife," like the one with which he absentmindedly scratched the table as he sat waiting for his father, but thinking only about his mother.

In Nikolai's dream the figure of his Uncle Pierre had been transformed into the image of his father, Andrei; the boy awakened with a desperate desire that both men should become proud of him. Serezha's dreamlike experience and the events preceding it indicate that while he, like Levin, is learning about life from peasants, he is also learning about love and suffering from his mother Anna. Like Nikolai's dream in *War and Peace* Serezha's moves toward a synthesis of the experiences of the two main characters and principal dreamers in *Anna Karenina*.

LATE WORKS

The literary dreams in Tolstoy's late works serve very different functions from those in his two major novels.[24] The allegorical dream-vision that forms the conclusion of *The Confession* (1880–82), supposedly based on an actual dream, summarizes in graphic form the author's spiritual crisis and reinforces the inspirational message of this explicitly religious tract.[25] The technique here is similar to that in eighteenth-century works by Radishchev and Novikov. In *Father Sergei* (1890; 1898) the hero's dream about Pashenka and the angel recalls those in Medieval Russian texts, where God's truth was revealed to virtuous men in didactic visions. The heroes' simultaneous dreams in *Master and Man* (1894–95) are similarly allegorical: while the merchant Brekhunov is bargaining in his, the servant Nikita performs his menial duties unquestioningly. When Death summons the master, he finally awakens into spiritual enlightenment.

In "The Dream of a Young Czar" (1894), written after the death of Alexander III and the accession of Nicholas II, Tolstoy devises an allegory on the nature of autocratic power, in which the new monarch beholds the consequences of his political decisions in a dream. "What I Saw in a Dream" (1906) is a parable of moral reconciliation and forgiveness, allegedly based on an incident in the life of Tolstoy's brother Sergei. Finally, in "The Dream" (1909), the conclusion to "Three Days in the Country," Tolstoy expounds on social and political questions relating to peasants and property within the narrative frame of a dream.[26]

In his memoir entitled *Two Years with L. N. Tolstoy*, Nikolai Gusev records the following conversation with the venerable sage:

I asked him if it ever happened that serious thoughts came to him in a dream. "No, I think not," he answered. "It often occurs that what you see in a dream seems serious, but if you consider it when you're awake, then you see that it's all nonsense."[27]

A much younger Tolstoy had maintained that feelings were "truer in a dream," where they were undistorted by the powers of "false reasoning." Indeed, such feelings are explored in great depth in both *War and Peace* and *Anna Karenina*. An older Tolstoy, one who repudiated his own greatest works of imaginative fiction, also rejected the significance of dreams in both life and literature. The "power of reason" applied to what seems to be serious thought in a dream reveals it to be pure "nonsense." In his late works the literary dream ceased to be a technique of psychological characterization, narrative structure, and thematic statement; it becomes instead one more way the author has of making his didactic message tediously explicit.

7. CONCLUSION/SUPERSEDURE

> ... not the psychologists, men of science though they be, have laid bare the deep recesses of the modern soul, but the men of genius who overstepped all frontiers.
>
> Stefan Zweig

From its allegorical and polemic beginnings in Medieval and Classical Russian literature, the dream evolved during the nineteenth century into a fundamental technique of characterization. Literary dreams were used to communicate the most intimate information about the unconscious life, the nonrational side of fictional characters. Inasmuch as they provided the reader with direct access to these characters' innermost thoughts and feelings, dreams came to reveal the underlying psychological motivation and true subjective state of the dreamer. Furthermore literary dreams came to play a significant role in the narrative structure of almost all major nineteenth-century Russian novels. They were able to recapitulate in summary form past events of the fictional plot, as well as to prophesy future developments, including the final resolution of the action. Finally, dreams served to render the author's thematic statements explicit. Some contained the sudden illumination that, when expanded upon during the character's waking life, could lead directly to a discovery of the writer's fundamental truths. Dreams also were used to establish a dichotomy between themselves and real life; characters were forced to negotiate between the two distinct alternatives.

The gradual transformation of the literary dream from a technique of naive allegory has been demonstrated through an analysis of three works selected from Russian literature pre-Pushkin. In "The Island of Bornholm" Karamzin includes the narrator's Gothic dream as a means of making his subjective consciousness the focus of the tale; Zhukovsky discloses his heroine's desires and fears through her nightmare, where the device also plays a role in the narrative structure of the ballad; finally, Sofiya's dream in Griboedov's comedy reveals the complexity of her character, occupies a central place in the course of the action, and establishes a thematic contrast between the heroine's dream and the hero's final awakening.

It is Pushkin who first made extensive use of the literary dream and developed it into a technique capable of expressing his original ideas on the nature of art and life. In his narrative works dreamers abound, and the author draws the crucial distinction between the two kinds of dreams that his characters have. Their subconscious experiential dreams are shown to contain truth since they reveal the dangers inherent in pursuing their conscious figurative dreams. Since this truth is expressed only on the level of the subconscious, these characters continue their pursuit either until they are destroyed or until they learn to keep dreams and life separate. It is only the most admired heroes and heroines, Grinev, Tatyana, and Pushkin-the-narrator, who finally manage to resolve this conflict successfully.

Gogol began by exploring the same dilemma. In his earliest Ukrainian tales the fictional characters arrive at solutions in which life and love prove to be preferable to any dreams. But in his later narrative works, less fortuitous solutions result from the heroes' experiential dreams: Piskarev's decline and death, Ivan Shponka's life-worse-than-death, and Akaky's extraordinary afterlife. Finally, in "The Portrait," Gogol explores the "twilight realms of consciousness" as no other Russian writer had before.

While both Dostoevsky and Tolstoy synthesized the achievements of their predecessors, each author developed the technique in quite diverse ways. In *Crime and Punishment* the distinction drawn by Pushkin between two kinds of dreams reaches its culmination. Raskolnikov's experiential dreams ultimately lead to the renunciation of his figurative dream, thus constituting his first step toward salvation. Dostoevsky continued Gogol's investigation of the subconscious to explore the depths of the human psyche. In *The Brothers Karamazov* the characters' dreams serve to express the emotional state and spiritual achievement of each of the three brothers. Alyosha's religious vision, Dmitry's emotional dream, and Ivan's intellectual nightmare constitute subconscious revelations containing the profound truths that each character must finally acknowledge.

Tolstoy's narrative fiction completed the evolutionary process of the dream from naive allegory to sophisticated literary technique. In his two major novels the protagonists' spiritual progressions are depicted through the juxtaposition of their experiential and/or figurative dreams. In *War and Peace* the dreams of Prince Andrei and Pierre reveal their progress toward their respective states of enlightenment; in *Anna Karenina* the heroine is persecuted by menacing experiential dreams leading eventually to her suicide, while Levin finally learns that all his figurative dreams are deceptive. It is ironic that, in his later, postconversion works, Tolstoy returned to naive allegory, recalling those didactic and satirical dreams and visions of Medieval and Classical Russian texts.

* * *

Toward the end of the nineteenth century, complex historical and literary developments transpired not only in Russia but throughout Europe, which contributed to the decline of the dream as a major technique of narrative fiction. Freud, who credited his poetic and philosophical predecessors with discovering the unconscious, had by now formulated his psychoanalytic system for studying dreams and related phenomena. His theoretical ideas and clinical methods came to exert a powerful influence on creative writers. When they began to ascribe dreams to their fictional characters with a conscious awareness of Freudian concepts, the technique lost its spontaneity and power as a literary device.

Furthermore, there occurred an erosion of the clearly defined boundaries between conscious and subconscious experience. In the nineteenth century, while dreams could appear to be lifelike and life dreamlike, the two realms were always perceived as distinct. However, the advent of the Symbolist movement, with its renewed emphasis on the mysterious and exotic, and, subsequently, of Surrealism, with its vigorous opposition to all rational conventions and restraints, steadily wore away the dividing line between the two realms of consciousness.

150 Conclusion/Supersedure

Two works can serve as representative of the evolution of the dream in twentieth-century Russian fiction. Valery Bryusov, the leader of the Moscow Symbolists, introduces his short story entitled "In the Tower" (1902–7) as a "recorded dream":

> There is no doubt that I dream all this, dreamed it last night. True, I never thought that a dream could be so circumstantial and so consecutive. But none of the events of this dream have any connection with what I am experiencing now or with anything that I can remember. Yet how otherwise can a dream be differentiated from reality except in this way—that it is divorced from the continuous chain of events that occur in our waking hours?[1]

But when this dream is interrupted before the narrator's fate is finally resolved, and he finds himself sitting at a desk recording his vision, "intending to begin the ordinary life of the day," he is struck by a discomforting idea: "What if now I am sleeping and dreaming—and I shall suddenly awake on the straw, in the underground dungeon of the castle?"[2] Bryusov suspects that his "ordinary life" may actually be a dream, and his dream, real life. In Daniil Kharms's surrealist "ministory" entitled "A Dream" (1926) there is no longer any doubt:

> Kalugin fell asleep and dreamed a dream. He was sitting in some bushes, and a militiaman went past the bushes.
>
> Kalugin woke up, scratched his mouth, and fell asleep again, and again he dreamed a dream. He was walking past some bushes, and in the bushes a militiaman was sitting and hiding.
>
> Kalugin woke up, put a newspaper under his head so as not to make the pillow wet with his slobbering, and fell asleep again, and again he dreamed a dream. He was sitting in some bushes, and a militiaman was walking past the bushes.
>
> Kalugin woke up, changed the newspaper, lay down, and again fell asleep. He fell asleep and again he had a dream. He was walking past some bushes, and a militiaman was sitting in the bushes.
>
> At that point Kalugin woke up and decided to sleep no more, but immediately he fell asleep and had a dream. He was sitting behind a militiaman, and some bushes were walking past.
>
> Kalugin shouted and turned over in his bed, but he was no longer able to wake up.

Kalugin slept for four days and nights in a row, and the fifth day he woke up so thin that he had to tie his boots to his feet with twine so that they would not keep falling off.

In the bakery, where Kalugin always bought wheat bread, they didn't recognize him and slipped him bread that was half rye.

The Sanitary Commission inspected the apartment house and saw Kalugin, and declared him to be unsanitary and good for nothing, and ordered the apartment cooperative to throw Kalugin out with the trash.

They folded Kalugin in two and threw him out with the trash.[3]

In addition to the impact of Freud and to the erosion of clear boundaries, the nature of European narrative prose itself was also evolving. In order to give literary expression to this merging of conscious and subconscious experience, writers began to place the reader inside the consciousness of their characters; the conventional figure of the narrator, through whose eyes all previous literary dreams had been related, started to disappear. Other "modes of subjectivity"[4] were emerging as preeminent in modern fiction, particularly the "stream of consciousness." The phrase, first used by William James in his *Principles of Psychology* (1890) to characterize the unbroken flow of thought and awareness in the waking state, has since been adopted by critics to describe all the diverse techniques used by modern writers to represent the state and process of a character's mind in which sense perceptions mingle with thoughts, fragments, memories, feelings and associations.

One of the principal techniques of stream of consciousness fiction is the "interior monologue." Although in current usage this term is often interchangeable with *stream of consciousness*, some critics have suggested that *interior monologue* be reserved for those occasions when the author tries to reproduce the course and rhythm of consciousness exactly as it occurs in a character's mind—with little or no intrusion by the author. The use of this technique can be traced back at least as far as Sterne's *Tristram Shandy*. Isolated examples can also be found in nineteenth-century narrative works by Dostoevsky and Tolstoy: Raskolnikov's extended meditations on his crime, Myshkin's deeply introspective moments preceding his epileptic seizures, and Anna Karenina's desperate contemplation of suicide. The technique seems to have been identified and the term coined in 1856 by the Russian critic N. G. Chernyshevsky in his perceptive essay on Tolstoy's "Sevastopol Stories." Referring to what struck him as an innovative way for conveying what he called the hero's "dialectic of mind," Chernyshevsky invented the phrase *interior monologue* (*vnutrennii monolog*).[5] It was only during the early part of the twentieth century that Russian writers began to experiment extensively with this technique; the Symbolist Andrei Bely was one of the first to do so; his autobiographical novel *Kotik Letaev* (1915–16) comprises an extended exploration of the various possibilities of interior monologue.

The dream did not entirely disappear from later twentieth-century Russian literature. In short stories by Bunin, Babel, Nabokov, and Kazakov, in novels by Remizov, Pasternak, and Maksimov, fictional characters continued to fall asleep and to witness imaginative night visions.[6] But as a device for psychological characterization, narrative structure, and thematic statement the dream was superseded by other, more innovative techniques of modern fiction. Nevertheless, the literary dreams created by Pushkin, Gogol, Dostoevsky, and Tolstoy continue to move and persuade us in their unique way—enriching both the reader and the novels in which they appear.

APPENDIX OF LITERARY DREAMS*

N. M. KARAMZIN
"The Island of Bornholm"
Narrator's Dream

I dreamed that all the suits of armor hanging on the wall were changed into knights and that these knights came toward me with unsheathed swords. With furious expressions they said: "Unfortunate man! How dare you come to our island? Do sailors not pale at the sight of its granite shores? How dare you enter the terrible sanctuary of this castle? Does not its horror resound in all its surroundings? Does not the traveller turn back from its awesome towers? Impudent man! Die for your pernicious curiosity!" Swords clanged over me, blows rained down on my chest, but suddenly everything disappeared. I awoke, but in another minute I fell asleep again. Then a new dream disturbed my spirit. I dreamed that terrible thunder resounded in the castle, iron gates crashed, windows shook, the floor trembled and a horrible winged monster which I am unable to describe, flew toward my bed with roaring and hissing sounds. The dream vanished. . . .   *Izbrannye sochineniya*, Moscow–Leningrad, 1964, 1:669).

V. A. ZHUKOVSKY
"Svetlana"
Heroine's Dream

    Resting on her elbows,
      Svetlana hardly breathes . . .
    Now . . . lightly at the locked door
      She hears someone knocking;
    Timidly she glances into the mirror
      Over her shoulders,

---

*Translations by the author unless otherwise noted. Bracketed numbers precede different dreams by the same character. Bracketed letters indicate different scenes of the same dream.

Someone, it seems, is staring
   With bright eyes . . .
Her breathing stops out of fear.
Suddenly she catches the sound
   Of a quiet, light whisper:
"I am here, my fair beauty;
The heavens have been calmed,
   Your grumbling has been heard!"

She glances around . . . her beloved
   Extends his arms toward her.
"Joy, light of my life,
   There is no parting us.
Let us go! The priest is already waiting
   In the church with the deacon and the sextons;
The choir is singing a wedding song;
   The church is lit with candles.
She replied with a tender glance;
They set out across the courtyard
   Through the wooden gates;
The sleigh awaits them at the gates;
The horses chafe impatiently
   At their silken reins.

They mounted . . . the horses gallop off;
   They breathe smoke from their nostrils;
From their hooves a snowstorm
   Rises over the sleigh.
They gallop . . . all around is barren;
   Svetlana looks out at the steppe:
Around the moon is a ring of mist,
   The meadows are just a glimmer.
Her prophetic heart trembles;
The maiden asks timidly:
   "Why have you fallen silent, my dear?"
Not a word in answer to her:
He glances at the moonlight,
   Pale and mournful.

The horses fly across the hills,
   They trample the deep snow . . .
There to the side a lonely church
   Appears;

A gust of wind opens its doors;
   A crowd of people stands in the church;
The bright light of the chandelier
   Grows dim in the incense;
A black coffin stands in the center,
And the priest says in a drawl:
   "Be thou taken unto the grave!"
The maiden shakes even more;
The horses fly by; her friend is silent,
   Pale and mournful.

Suddenly a blizzard surrounds them,
   Snow falls in large flakes;
A black raven, whistling,
Hovers over the sleigh;
   The raven screams: Misfortune!
   The horses hurry
And sentiently look into the dark distance,
   Shaking their manes;
A light is shimmering in the field;
A peaceful shelter appears,
   A little hut covered with snow.
The bold horses fly faster,
   Straight toward it, raising the snow
   With their friendly flight.

Here they are . . . and suddenly,
   Horses, sleigh, and bridegroom
Disappear from sight,
   As if they'd never existed.
Alone, in the darkness,
   Abandoned by her friend,
The maiden stands in a dreadful place,
Surrounded by snowstorms and blizzards.
There's no way to return home . . .
She sees a light in the hut:
   She makes the sign of the cross,
And with a prayer she knocks at the door . . .
The door shakes . . . creaks . . .
   And quietly opens.

What's in there? . . . A coffin stands in the hut, covered
   With a white pall.

The savior's icon stands at its feet,
   A candle before the icon.
Oh, Svetlana! What's the matter?
   Whose dwelling have you entered?
The silent inhabitant of this
   Deserted hut is terrifying.
She enters trembling, in tears;
She prostrates herself before the icon
   And prays to the Savior.
And with a cross in her hand,
She timidly hides
   Under the saints' icons in the corner.

All is quiet . . . the storm abates . . .
   The candle flickers faintly,
Now it sheds its trembling light,
   Then it goes dark again . . .
All is wrapped in deep, deadly sleep,
   A horrible silence . . .
Hark, Svetlana! . . . in the quiet,
   A light fluttering . . .
She looks: into the corner toward her,
A snow-white dove flies,
   With bright eyes,
Quietly fluttering,
And quietly comes to rest on her breast,
   Enfolding her in its wings.

Everything becomes silent once again . . .
   Then Svetlana notices
That under the white canvas
   The corpse is stirring.
The shroud falls off; the corpse
   (His countenance darker than night)
Becomes completely visible—a crown on his forehead,
   His eyes shut tight.
Suddenly, a moan emerges from his closed mouth;
He tries to unfold his
   Cold arms.
And what about the maiden? She trembles . . .
Her end is near . . . but the
   White dove is vigilant.

He flutters and spreads out
   His graceful wings;
He takes flight and lands on the corpse's chest . . .
   Deprived of all his strength,
Moaning, he gnashes his
   Teeth terribly,
And casts a glance at the maiden
   With his awful eyes . . .
Again the pallor on his lips,
By the whites of his eyes
   Death becomes apparent.
Behold, Svetlana . . . Oh, Creator!
Her beloved friend—is a corpse!
   Ah! . . . and she awoke.

[Stanzas 6–15]
Sobranie sochinenii, Moscow–Leningrad, 1959, 2:20–23)

A. S. GRIBOEDOV
Woe from Wit
Sofiya's Dream

Now . . . you see . . . at first
A flowery meadow; and I was searching
   For an herb,
Which one, I can't remember now that I'm awake.
Suddenly, a nice man, one of those whom
   We see once and feel as if we've always known him,
Appeared along side me; ingratiating and clever,
But timid . . . you know, a man who was born in poverty . . .

Then everything vanished: meadow and sky.
We're in a dark room. To complete the wondrous scene,
   The floor opened up—and you emerged
   Pale as death, with all your hair standing on end!
   Then the doors were flung open with a loud noise
   By something—neither man nor beast;
They separated us—and tortured the man who
   Was sitting with me.
He seems dearer to me than any treasures,
I want to go to him—you drag me off with you.

Shouting, roaring, laughing, and whistling of
Monsters accompany us!
He shouts after us!
I awoke.

[act 1, scene 4, lines 174–97]
Sochineniya v stikhakh, Leningrad, 1967, 74–75)

A. S. PUSHKIN

Boris Godunov

Grigory's Dream

I dreamed that a steep staircase
Led me up a tower; from the top
All of Moscow appeared to me like an anthill;
Below, people were swarming in the square
And pointing up at me, laughing;
And I became ashamed and frightened—
And, falling headlong, I awoke. . . .

[scene 5]
Polnoe sobranie sochinenii, Moscow–Leningrad,
1937–59, 7:19)

"The Snowstorm"

Marya Gavrilovna's Dream

First she dreamed that at the very moment when she was getting seated in the sleigh in order to drive to her wedding, her father stopped her, dragged her with agonizing speed across the snow, and hurled her into a dark, bottomless dungeon . . . and she plunged headlong with an indescribable sinking heart; then she saw Vladimir, lying on the grass, pale, bloodied. Dying, he implored her in a piercing voice to make haste and marry him. . . . (8:78).

"The Coffin Maker"

Adriyan Prokhorov's Dream

The room was full of corpses. The moon, shining through the windows, lit up their yellow and blue faces, sunken mouths, dark, half-closed eyes and protruding noses. . . . With horror Adriyan recognized all the people whom he had buried, and, in the guest who entered together with him, he recognized the brigadier buried in pouring rain. All of them, men and women, surrounded the coffin maker, bowing and greeting him, except for one poor fellow, recently buried free of charge, who, aware of and embarrassed by his tattered clothes, did not approach, but stood humbly in the corner. The others were all dressed decently: women in caps and ribbons, officials in uniforms but with unshaven beards, merchants in festive caftans. "You see, Prokhorov," stated the brigadier, speaking for the entire honored assembly, "we have all risen to accept your invitation; only those who are no longer able, or who have fallen to pieces completely, and those of whom there remain only bones without flesh—have remained at home. But even one of these could not resist—he so wanted to be here with you. . . ." At this moment a small skeleton pushed its way through the crowd and approached Adriyan. His skull smiled affectionately at the coffin maker. Shreds of bright green and red cloth and ancient linen hung on him here and there, as from a pole, and the bones of his legs rattled in large jackboots, like pestles in mortars. "You don't recognize me, Prokhorov," said the skeleton. "Don't you remember the retired Sergeant of the Guard, Petr Petrovich Kurilkin, the very same one to whom you sold your first coffin in 1799—a pine one which you said was oak?" With these words the corpse stretched out its arms for a bony embrace; but Adriyan, gathering his strength, shouted and pushed him away. Petr Petrovich reeled back, fell down, and crumbled to pieces. Among the corpses a rumbling of indignation arose; everyone stood up for the honor of their comrade; they importuned Adriyan with abuse and threats, and the poor host, deafened by their shouts and almost crushed, lost his presence of mind, himself fell upon the bones of the retired Sergeant of the Guard, and lost consciousness (8:93–94).

"The Queen of Spades"

Germann's Dreams
Quoted in the text, pp. 49–51.

The Captain's Daughter

Grinev's Dream
I dreamed that the storm was still raging and that we were still wandering about in the snowy wilderness. . . . Suddenly I saw a gate and drove into the courtyard of our estate. My first thought was one of danger—that my father would be angry for my involuntary return to the paternal home and he would consider it deliberate disobedience. With a feeling of uneasiness I jumped out of the sleigh and saw that my mother was coming out to meet me on the porch with a look of deep sadness. "Quietly," she says to me, "your father is ill, lying near death, and he wishes to take leave of you." Struck with fear, I follow her into the bedroom. I observe that the room is dimly lit; people with sad faces are standing around the bed. I approach it

quietly, my mother lifts the curtain and says: "Andrei Petrovich, Petrusha has come; he returned when he learned of your illness; give him your blessing." I go down onto my knees and fix my eyes on the sick man. What's this? . . . Instead of my father there is a peasant with a black beard lying in his bed, looking up at me cheerfully. In astonishment I turn to my mother and say to her: "What does this mean? This is not father. Why should I ask this peasant for his blessing?" "It's all the same, Petrusha," my mother answers, "this is your proxy father; kiss his hand and let him bless you . . ." I do not agree. Then the peasant jumps up out of bed, seizes an axe from behind his back, and begins swinging it in all directions. I want to flee . . . but am not able to; the room is filled with dead bodies; I stumble against them and slip in pools of blood. The terrible peasant calls to me tenderly saying: "Don't be afraid, come and ask my blessing." Horror and bewilderment overcome me . . . At that moment I awoke [ch.2] (8:289).

Eugene Onegin

Tatyana's Dream. (Roman numerals refer to stanzas in the original.)*

XI. And Tatyana dreams a wonder-filled dream. She dreams that she is walking across a snow-covered clearing, surrounded by sad mist. Ahead of her, in the snowdrifts, a torrent, boiling, dark, hoary, not bound by winter, roars and billows with its waters. Two poles held together by a block of ice have been thrown across the torrent as a shaky, dangerous bridge. And before the roaring abyss, full of misgivings, she stops.

XII. Tatyana complains about the brook as one complains about a vexing separation. She can see no one who might stretch out a hand to her from the other side. But suddenly a snowdrift stirs and who appears from under it? A large shaggy bear. Tatyana cries "Ah!" and he roars and stretches out his paw to her, sharp claws and all. Steeling herself, she leans on it with her trembling little hand, and with timid steps she makes her way across the brook. She walks on . . . and what does she see? The bear follows her.

XIII. Not daring to look back, she accelerates her pace, but she can't in any way elude the shaggy lackey. Grunting, the odious bear presses on. There is a wood before them. The pines, in their sullen beauty, stand motionless. All their branches are weighted down with snow. The rays of night's luminaries shine through the tops of bare aspens, birches, lindens. There is no road. Bushes and ravines have all been drifted over by a blizzard and are buried deep in snow.

XIV. Into the woods goes Tatyana. The bear follows her. The soft snow is up to her knees. A long twig suddenly catches her by the neck; another tears her

*Translated by Nicholas Fersen, Williams College.

golden earrings forcibly out of her ears. Her wet slipper sinks into the crumbly snow and comes off her charming little foot. She drops her kerchief and has no time to pick it up. She is afraid. She hears the bear behind her and is too modest to raise the hem of her dress with a trembling hand. She runs, he keeps after her, and she has no strength left to run any further.

XV. She falls into the snow. Nimbly the bear picks her up and carries her. She feels nothing, she submits, she doesn't stir, she doesn't breathe. He rushes along a forest trail with her. Suddenly, among the trees, appears a humble hut. All is wilderness around. Solitary, it is buried in the snow. A window is brightly lit and there is noise and shouting in that hut. The bear announces: "My friend is here: go warm yourself a bit in the house!" And he goes straight into the hall and deposits her on the threshold.

XVI. Tatyana comes to her senses, looks around. . . . The bear is no longer there. She is in a hall. Behind the door she can hear shouting and the tinkle of glasses, as at some important funeral. Seeing not a drop of sense in this, she peeks secretly through a crack, and what does she see? Monsters sit all around a table. One has horns and a dog's face, another has a rooster's head, and here's a witch with a goat's beard, and here's a skeleton, prim and proud. Over there a dwarf with a small tail and also a creature half-crane, half-cat.

XVII. But more frightening, more astonishing still: a crayfish astride a spider, a skull in a red bonnet spinning atop a goose's neck; a windmill dances squatting down, flapping and clattering its wings. Barking, guffaws, singing, whistling, clapping, human speech, and equine hoofbeats! But what did Tatyana think when among the guests she recognized the one she loved, the one she fears—the hero of our novel! Onegin sits at the table and stealthily looks through the door.

XIX. And she is frightened. Hastily she attempts to flee. Impossible. Thrashing about impatiently she wants to scream, but can't. Eugene pushes the door open and the maiden appears before the eyes of those ghosts from hell. Wild laughter rings out savagely. All eyes, hooves, crooked trunks, tufted tails, fangs, mustaches, bloody tongues, horns, bony fingers—all point at her and they all scream: "Mine! Mine!"

XX. "Mine!" says Eugene fiercely and the whole gang suddenly vanishes. In the frosty darkness the young maiden is now left alone with him. Gently Onegin draws Tatyana into a corner and stretches her out on a rickety bench and puts his hands on her shoulder. Suddenly Olga walks in, followed by Lensky. Lights go on. Onegin raises his fist and his eyes wander wildly and he berates the uninvited guests. Tatyana lies, more dead than alive. . . .

XXI. The argument gets louder, louder. Suddenly Eugene grabs a long knife and Lensky is smitten in a second. Shadows thicken awesomely. An unbearable scream resounds . . . the hut shudders . . . and Tanya awakens in terror . . . [ch.5, stanzas 11–21] (6:101–7).

Onegin's Dream*
XXXVII. And gradually he falls into a somnolence of thoughts and feelings, and before him his imagination deals out its motley hand of faro. First he sees a youth motionless as though asleep on melting snow, and hears a voice, "Well? He is dead." Then he sees forgotten enemies, slanderers, and malicious cowards, and a swarm of fair young deceivers and a circle of contemptible companions. Then again a country house and by the window she sits . . . forever she! . . .   [ch. 8, stanza 37] (6:183–84).

N.V. GOGOL
"Gants Kyukhelgarten"
Luiza's Dream

> I dreamed: I was in a dark desert,
> Surrounded by mist and woods.
> And in the swampy meadow
> There was no dry land at all.
> A heavy odor: marshy, boggy;
> If I took a step, there was an abyss below me:
> I am afraid to move a foot;
> And suddenly, it became so painful,
> So painful, I can hardly say . . .
> From nowhere Gants appeared—wild, strange—
> With blood flowing, streaming from a wound,
> Suddenly he began to weep over me,
> But instead of tears, there flowed streams
> Of turbid water . . .
> I awoke.

[scene 10]
(*Polnoe sobranie sochinenii*, Moscow, 1937–52, 1:83)

"Ivan Fyodorovich Shponka and His Auntie"
Shponka's Dream

First he dreamed that everything was whirling noisily around him; he was running and running, as fast as his legs could carry him. He was at his last

*Translated by Nicholas Fersen, Williams College.

gasp. Suddenly someone caught him by the ear. "Ouch! Who is it?" "It's me, your wife!" a voice resounded. And suddenly, he woke up. Then he imagined that he was already married, that everything in their little house was so peculiar, so strange: a double bed stood in his room instead of a single one. His wife was sitting on a chair. He felt strange; he didn't know how to approach her, what to say to her; and then he noticed that she had the face of a goose. Inadvertently turning aside, he saw another wife, also with the face of a goose. Turning to another side, there was a third wife. Behind him, still another wife. He panicked and ran out into the garden, but out there it was hot. He took off his hat and there was a wife sitting in it. Beads of sweat ran down his face. He put his hand in his pocket for his handkerchief, and there was a wife in his pocket, too. He took a wad of cotton out of his ear, and there was a wife there too. Then he suddenly began hopping on one leg and his Auntie, looking at him, said with a dignified air, "Yes, you must hop now, because you are a married man." He went toward her, but his Aunt was no longer his Aunt, but a belfry. And he felt that someone was dragging him by a rope up the belfry. "Who's dragging me?" he asked plaintively. "It's me, your wife. I am dragging you because you are a bell." No, I'm *not* a bell. I am Ivan Fyodorovich!" he cried. "Yes, you *are* a bell," said the colonel of his [former] infantry regiment, who just happened to be passing by. Then he suddenly dreamed that his wife was not a person at all, but some kind of woolen material; and that he went into a shop in Mogilev. "What sort of material would you like?" asked the shopkeeper. "You had better have some wife, that's the latest thing. It wears very well. Everyone's having coats made from it nowadays." The shopkeeper measured and cut off a wife. Ivan Fyodorovich put her under his arm and went off to a Jewish tailor. "No," said the Jew, "this is poor material. No one has coats made from it anymore."

Ivan Fyodorovich woke up terrified . . .   [ch. 5] (1:307–8).

"Nevsky Prospect"

Piskarev's Three Dreams

[1] The door opened and a footman in rich livery entered. Rich livery had never appeared before in his lonely room, let alone at such an unusual time. . . . He was perplexed and looked at the footman with impatient curiosity.

"That lady," the footman said with a courteous bow, "whom you visited a few hours ago, asks to see you and has sent her carriage to fetch you."

Piskarev stood in silent amazement: "Carriage, a footman in livery!. . . . No, there must be some mistake . . ." "My dear sir," he said timidly, "you must have come to the wrong place. No doubt the lady sent you to fetch someone else, and not me."

"No sir, I have made no mistake. Did you not accompany a lady on foot to a house on Liteiny Prospect, to a room on the fourth floor?"

"Yes, I did."

"Then please come quickly, the lady definitely wishes to see you and asks that you come straight to her house."

Piskarev ran down the stairs. There really was a carriage standing in the courtyard. He took a seat in it, the doors slammed shut, the pavement stones rumbled noisily under the wheels and hooves—and soon a lighted panorama of houses with bright signs passed by the carriage windows. All along the way Piskarev pondered, but he was unable to explain the adventure. Her own house, a carriage, a footman in rich livery—he was unable to reconcile all of this with a room on the fourth floor, dusty windows, and a piano out of tune.

The carriage stopped in front of a brightly lit entrance, and at once he was struck by a row of carriages, the talk of coachmen, brightly lit windows, and the sound of music. The footman in rich livery helped him out of the carriage and politely escorted him into a hall with marble columns, with a doorman decked in gold, scattered with cloaks and fur-coats, and with a bright lamp. An ethereal staircase with dazzling railings, fragrant with perfumes, led upstairs. He was already on it, already entering the first room, frightened and drawing away at first from the enormous crowd. The extraordinary diversity of faces completely bewildered him; it seemed as if some demon had cut up the whole world into a multitude of different pieces and then mixed all these pieces together without sense or order. The gleaming shoulders of women and black tail-coats, chandeliers, lamps, airy floating gauzes, ethereal ribbons, and the fat double-bass looking out from behind the railings of the magnificent gallery—everything seemed so overwhelming to him. . . .

But one lady stood out among all the rest, dressed more elegantly and dazzlingly than the others. An inexpressible, most subtle taste was expressed in her entire apparel, and yet it seemed as if she had taken no trouble at all over it, as if it came naturally, of its own accord. She looked and then refrained from looking at the surrounding crowd of spectators; she lowered her lovely, long eyelashes indifferently, and the dazzling whiteness of her face became even more blinding when a light shadow fell across her ravishing brow as she bent her head.

Piskarev exerted all his strength to separate the crowd and get a closer look at her; but, to his great annoyance, some huge head with dark curly hair kept getting in his way; moreover the crowd pressed against him so that he dared not move forward or backward, fearing that he might somehow shove a Privy Councillor. But then he made his way forward and glanced down at his apparel, wanting to be sure that everything was in order. Heavenly Father, what's this? He was wearing a coat spotted with paint: in his hasty departure he forgot to change into appropriate clothing. He blushed to the roots of his hair, lowered his head, wanted to escape, but there was nowhere to flee: court chamberlains in bright suits formed an impenetrable wall behind him. He wished that he were as far away as possible from the beautiful lady with the lovely brows and eyelashes. He raised his eyes fearfully to see if she were looking at him. Oh God, she was standing in front of him . . . But what's this? What's this? "It is she!" he exclaimed almost at the top of his voice. Indeed, it was she, the very one whom he met on Nevsky Prospect and whom he followed home.

Meanwhile she raised her eyelashes and looked at everyone with her bright eyes. "Oh, my goodness, how lovely she is," was all he could utter with bated breath. Her eyes roamed around; all the men were vying with each other for her attention; but with weariness and boredom she soon turned away from them and her eyes met Piskarev's. Oh, good heavens! What paradise! Lord, give me strength to endure this! His life could not contain such joy; it threatened to annihilate his soul. She made a sign, not with her hand, nor with an inclination of her head—no: this sign was expressed by her striking eyes in such a subtle imperceptible manner, that no one could see it; but he saw it and understood it. The dancing lasted a long time; the languid music seemed to fade and die away, and then it burst forth again, shrieked and thundered; finally—it was over. She sat down, her breast heaving under a light cloud of gauze; her hand (Oh Lord, what a wonderful hand!) dropped into her lap, crushed the ethereal dress beneath it, and the dress seemed to breathe with the music; its light lilac color made the brilliant whiteness of her lovely hand even more apparent. He only wanted to touch it—nothing more! No other desires—they would be impertinent . . . He stood behind the chair near her, not daring to speak, not daring to breathe.

"Were you feeling bored?" she asked. "I was also bored. I sense that you hate me," she added, lowering her long eyelashes.

"Hate you! Me? I . . .," Piskarev completely taken aback, was about to say, and probably would have said, a lot of very confused things, but at that moment a court chamberlain approached with a beautifully curled tuft of hair, and began spouting witty and pleasant observations. He rather charmingly displayed a row of nice teeth and every witty remark he made drove a sharp nail into Piskarev's heart. Fortunately, some stranger finally turned to the court chamberlain with a question.

"How unbearable this is!" she said, raising her heavenly eyes to him. "I will sit down at the other end of the room; come there!"

She slipped through the crowd and disappeared. Like a madman he shoved the crowd aside and was there at once.

So, it was she; she was sitting like a czarina, better than all the others, lovelier than all the others, and her eyes were searching for him.

"You are here," she said quietly. "I will be frank with you: the circumstances of our meeting must seem strange. Did you really imagine that I could belong to that despised class of creatures among whom you first encountered me? My actions seem strange to you, but I shall tell you a secret. Will you be in a position," she asked, looking him straight in the eye, "never to betray it?"

"Oh yes, I will, I will, I will!"

But just at that moment a rather elderly man approached her and began conversing in a language which Piskarev did not understand, and he offered her his arm. She looked at Piskarev with an imploring glance and gave him a sign—to remain there and await her return; but in a burst of impatience he was unable to obey any commands, even those which she uttered. He set out after her, but the crowds separated them. He could no longer see the lilac dress; he passed from room to room in agitation, shoving unmercifully everyone he met; but in all of the rooms there sat important people plunged into deep silence, playing games of whist. In one corner of a room several elderly people were arguing about the superiority of military service over civil service. In another, people in magnificent tail-coats were casting aspersions on the voluminous labors of a hard-working poet. Piskarev realized that one elderly gentleman with a distinguished look had button-holed him and was presenting for his opinion one of his very judicious observations, but he rudely pushed him aside, not even noticing that he was wearing a rather important order around his neck. He ran into another room—she wasn't there either. Into a third—not there. "Where was she? Give her to me! Oh, I can't go on living without another look at her! I must hear what she wanted to tell me." But all his searching was in vain. Agitated, exhausted, he remained in his corner and looked at the crowd; but then his straining eyes began to see everything in an unclear form . . .   (3:22–27).

[2] Oh God, what joy! It was she! Once again it was she! But in a completely different guise. Oh, she was lovely sitting near the window of a bright little country house. Her attire was simplicity itself—such as that in which only the thought of a poet clothes itself. And her coiffure . . . Oh Lord, how simple it was and how it suited her! A small kerchief was thrown lightly around her graceful neck; everything about her was modest, everything revealed a secret, inexplicable sense of taste. How sweet her graceful walk! How musical the sounds of her footsteps and her plain dress! How lovely her arm, encircled by a bracelet of hair. With tears in her eyes, she says: "Do not despise

me; I am not the sort of woman whom you take me for. Look at me, look closely and ask: can I really be capable of doing what you think?" "Oh, no, no! let anyone who thinks so, let anyone. . . ." (3:29–30).

[3] He dreamed of his studio. He was so happy; with such enjoyment he sat with palette in hand! And she was there, too! She was already his wife. She sat along side of him, resting her lovely elbows on the back of his chair and looking at his work. Her languid, tired eyes expressed the burden of blissfulness; everything in the room breathed of paradise; it was so right, so neat. Oh Lord, she leaned her lovely little head against his chest. . . . (3:30).

F. M. DOSTOEVSKY
Crime and Punishment
Raskolnikov's Five Dreams

[1] He dreamed about his childhood, back in his little town. He was about seven years old and on one holiday, toward evening, he was walking with his father outside the town. It was a grey, stifling day; the place was exactly as he remembered it, although it was much less vivid in his memory than it appeared in his dream. The little town stood apart, as if on an open hand with no trees around it; somewhere very far away, at the edge of the horizon, there stood a dark little wood. Several paces past the last garden of the town there stood a tavern, a large tavern which always produced the most unpleasant impressions on him, even fear, when he went past on a walk with his father. There was always such a crowd there; they shouted, guffawed, cursed, sang so horribly and hoarsely, and they brawled frequently; there were always such drunken and terrible types loitering around outside the tavern . . . encountering them, he would press closer to his father and would tremble. Along side of the tavern was a road, a cart-track, always dusty, and the dust on it was always so black. The road went on, winding, and turned toward the right after about 300 paces to the town cemetery. In the midst of the cemetery there was a stone church with a green cupola; twice a year he went there with his father and mother to attend vespers, when a requiem was sung for his grandmother who died a long time ago and whom he had never seen. On these occasions they always took with them wrapped in a napkin a white dish of rice boiled with sugar and raisins with a cross of raisins on the top. He loved this church and its ancient icons, mostly without frames, and the old priest with his trembling head. Next to his grandmother's grave on which there stood a tombstone, was the small grave of his younger brother, who died when he was only six months old, whom he had never known and could not even remember.

But he had been told that he had a little brother, and every time that he visited the cemetery, he made the sign of the cross over the grave religiously and respectfully, bowed and kissed it. Now he dreamed that he and his father are walking along the road toward the cemetery and they are passing by the tavern; he holds his father by the hand and glances at the tavern. A particular circumstance attracts his attention: this time it seemed to be a special occasion: there was a crowd of townsfolk, peasant women and their husbands and all sorts of rabble. They were all drunk, singing songs. Next to the tavern porch there stood a cart, but it was a strange cart. It was one of those large carts to which are harnessed large dray horses, which transport goods and wine barrels. He always loved to look at those huge dray horses, with their long manes, their heavy hooves moving along serenely at a measured pace and pulling behind them some huge mountainous load, not straining in the least, as if it were easier to pull a loaded cart than an unloaded one. But now, a strange thing occurred: to such a large cart there was harnessed a peasant's small, skinny, dun-colored nag, one of those, he had seen it often, who would strain under a large load of firewood or hay, especially if the cart got stuck in the mud or mire; on such an occasion, the peasants would always whip them so mercilessly, so mercilessly, sometimes even across their face and eyes, and he would always feel so sorry, so sorry to see this, that he would almost cry; and his mother would lead him away from the window. But suddenly it became very noisy: some very large, very drunken peasants in red and blue shirts, with coats thrown over their shoulders, came out of the tavern shouting, singing and playing balalaikas. "Get on, everybody get on!" Just then there was a burst of laughter and shouting.

"That old nag can't pull a thing!"

"Hey, Mikolka, are you out of your mind or something? To harness that old mare to such a cart?"

"That old nag must be at least twenty years old, lads!"

"Get on, I'll take all of you!" shouts Mikolka again, jumping into the cart himself; he takes the reins and stands up straight in the front of the cart. "Matvei has taken the bay horse away," he shouts from the cart, "and this old mare, lads, is just breaking my heart: if it kills her, it doesn't matter; she's not earning her keep. Get on, I say! I'll make her gallop! She'll gallop alright!" And he takes the whip in hand, preparing to beat the nag with delight.

"So get on then!" laughs the crowd. "You hear, she'll gallop alright."

"She hasn't galloped in the last ten years."

"She will today!"

"Have no pity, lads, let each take a whip, get ready."

"That's it! Hit her!"

Everyone climbs into Mikolka's cart laughing and joking. Six people climbed on, and there was room for more. They took on one fat ruddy peasant woman. She was wearing a red cotton frock, a head-dress trimmed with beads, and had clogs on her feet; she was cracking nuts and laughing. The crowd around was also laughing. Indeed, how could one help from laughing: such a sorry mare supposed to gallop with such a heavy load! Two lads in the cart took up their whips to help Mikolka. There was a roar of "Gee up!" The nag pulled with all of her strength, but she could scarcely budge at all, let alone gallop; she merely scraped her hooves, grunted, and flinched from the blows of three whips showering down upon her like hail. The laughter in the cart and in the crowd doubled, but Mikolka got angry and in a fury whipped the mare with faster strokes, as if he really expected her to gallop.

"Let me come too, lads!" shouts one lad from the crowd who was attracted by the spectacle.

"Get on! Everyone get on!" shouts Mikolka, "she'll take you all. I'll whip her!" And he lashes, lashes, and in his fury he no longer knows what he's doing.

"Papa, papa," the child cries to his father, "papa, what are they doing? Papa, they are beating the poor horse!"

"Let's go away, let's go," says the father, "they're drunk, playing pranks, they're fools: let's go, don't look!" And he wants to lead him away, but the child tears himself from his father's arms and, unaware of what he is doing, runs to the horse. But the poor creature was in a bad way. She was panting, continually stopping, then pulling again, almost falling.

"Beat her to death!" cries Mikolka, "that's what it's come to. I'll thrash her!"

"Why are you wearing a cross; you're more like a devil!" cries one old man from the crowd.

"How can you imagine that such a horse could pull that load," adds another.

"You'll kill her!" cries a third.

"Keep away! It's my property! I'll do what I want. Get on, some more of you. Everyone get on! I want her to gallop!"

Suddenly there was a burst of laughter that drowned out everything else: the mare could not endure the faster blows and she began to kick feebly. Even the old man could not keep from laughing. Indeed, such a decrepit mare still kicking!

Two lads from the crowd picked up whips and ran to the horse to beat her from the sides. Each ran from his own side.

"Across her face, whip her across the eyes, the eyes!" shouts Mikolka.

"A song, lads!" shouts someone from the cart, and everyone joined in. They sang a drunken song, shook a tambourine, whistled with the chorus. The peasant woman was still cracking nuts and laughing.

The child runs toward the horse, runs around front, sees how they are beating her across the eyes, across her very eyes! He weeps. His heart rises up within him and tears begin to flow. One of those doing the beating whips him across the face; he doesn't feel it, he wrings his hands, shouts, and hurls himself at a grey-haired old man with a grey beard who was shaking his head and disapproving of the entire business. One peasant woman takes him by the hand and wants to lead him away; but he breaks away and runs to the horse again. She was almost at her last gasp, but once again began kicking.

"You devil, you!" screams Mikolka in a fury. He throws his whip aside, bends over and drags a long, heavy shaft out from the bottom of his cart, takes one end into his hands and with some effort swings it over the old nag.

"It will crush her!" shouts the crowd.

"He will kill her!"

"It's my property!" shouts Mikolka, and with all his might he lets the shaft fall. A heavy thud resounds.

"Whip her, whip her! Why did you stop!" shout voices from the crowd.

And Mikolka swings a second time, and another heavy blow falls onto the back of the unfortunate nag. Her hind quarters sink down, but she keeps on tugging and jerking, jerking with all her last strength in various directions in order to get away; but from all sides six whips rain down upon her, and the shaft is lifted up again, and falls for a third time, then a fourth, with a rhythmic swing. Mikolka was furious that he was unable to kill her with a single blow.

"She's a tough one!" shouted someone in the crowd.

"This time she'll fall for sure, lads, this is her end!" shouted another spectator.

"Get an axe! Finish her off at one go," shouted a third.

"Hey, may you be bitten by mosquitoes! Watch out!" shrieked Mikolka furiously; he throws down the shaft, bends over into the cart again and drags out an iron crowbar. "Look out!" he cries and with all his strength he crashes it down onto his poor horse. The blow was a crushing one; the mare staggered, sank down, wanted to stand, but the crowbar once again came down with such force on her back and she fell to the earth as if all four of her legs had been cut out from under her at once.

"Finish her off!" shouts Mikolka and jumps down from the cart, quite beside himself. Several lads, also drunk and red-faced, seize whatever they can—whips, sticks, the shaft—and they run toward the dying mare.

Mikolka stands to the side and begins to beat her back at random with the crowbar. The nag stretched out her muzzle, drew a deep breath, and died.

"You finished her off!" shouts the crowd.

"And she still didn't gallop!"

"It's my property!" shouts Mikolka, with the crowbar in his hands and with bloodshot eyes. He stood as if regretting that there was nothing more to beat.

"Well, for sure there's no cross on you!" cry out many voices from the crowd now.

But the poor little boy was quite beside himself. With a shriek he pushes his way through the crowd toward the nag, he embraces her dead, bloody muzzle and kisses her, kisses her eyes, lips . . . Then he suddenly springs up and in a rage hurls himself with his little fists against Mikolka. At this moment his father, who had been pursuing him for a long time, seizes him and finally leads him away from the crowd.

"Let's go, let's go," he says to him, "let's go home."

"Papa! Why did they . . . kill . . . the poor horse?" he sobs, but his breathing was labored and the words were wrenched from his tightened chest in screams.

"They are drunk, they are playing pranks, it's not our business, let's go!" says his father. He embraces his father, but his chest is tightly constricted. He wants to catch his breath, to cry out, and he awakens   [pt. 1, ch. 5] (*Polnoe sobranie sochinenii*, Leningrad, 1972–, 6:46–49).

[2] Quoted in text p. 98.

[3] He awoke at dusk as the result of a horrible scream. God, what a scream it was! He had never before seen or heard such unnatural sounds, such howling and wailing, gnashing of teeth, tears, blows, and curses. He could not imagine such ferocity, such frenzy. In horror he raised himself and sat up on his bed, all the time trembling and agonizing. But the struggling, wailing, and cursing became stronger and stronger. Suddenly, to his great astonishment, he discerned the voice of his landlady. She was howling, shrieking, and wailing, emitting words so hurriedly and hastily, that it was impossible to understand anything; she was imploring someone about something—of course, to stop beating her, because she was being beaten mercilessly on the stairs. The voice of the person giving her the beating became so horrible with rage and fury; he was already hoarse, but nevertheless kept on saying something, also quickly, indistinctly, hastily, and stuttering. Suddenly Raskolnikov shuddered like a leaf: he recognized that voice: it was the voice of Ilya Petrovich. Ilya Petrovich is here and he is beating the landlady! He is kicking her, banging her head against the stairs—it was clear, the sounds,

the wailing and the blows convinced him. What's happened? Has the world been turned upside down? He heard a crowd gathering on each landing of the stairway, he heard voices, exclamations; he heard how they climbed the stairs, knocked, slammed doors, dispersed. "What is it for, what for . . . and how is it possible," he repeated, seriously thinking that he had gone completely mad. But no, he heard it too clearly! But then, if that was so, they would come for him next, "because . . . it must be on account of . . . because of yesterday's . . . Oh, Lord!" He wanted to fasten the doorlock, but he could not lift up his hand . . . and it would have been useless! Fear overwhelmed his soul like ice, tortured him, numbed him. But finally the whole uproar, which had continued for at least ten minutes, gradually began to subside. The landlady moaned and groaned; Ilya Petrovich kept on threatening and cursing. . . . But finally it seems that even he became silent, he was no longer audible. "Has he really gone? Oh, Lord!" Yes, the landlady was leaving now; still moaning and wailing . . . and her door slammed shut . . . Now the people are dispersing from the stairs and returning to their own apartments—they are exclaiming, arguing, calling to one another; their speech first rises to a screech, then falls to a whisper. There must have been a lot of them; the whole house must have come out. "But, God, it is really all possible? And why, why did he come here?"   [pt. 2, ch. 2] (6:90–91).

[4] He drifted into sleep; it seemed strange to him that he didn't remember how he could have turned up on the street. It was already late evening. Twilight was deepening, the full moon was shining brighter and brighter; but the air was somehow very stuffy. Crowds of people were walking along the streets; craftsmen and working men were returning to their homes, others were out for a stroll; the air smelled of lime, dust, stagnant water. Roskolnikov was gloomy and worried: he remembered very well that he had left home with some intention, that he had to hurry up and do something, but what it was, he had forgotten. Suddenly he stopped and noticed that on the other side of the street, on the sidewalk, stood a man waving to him. He crossed the street toward him, but suddenly this man turned around and walked away indifferently, lowering his head, not turning around, and not giving any indication that he had summoned him. "Enough of this, did he call me?" wondered Raskolnikov, and began to follow him. Before he had gone ten paces, he suddenly recognized him and became frightened: it was that bourgeois, wearing the same clothes and with the same stooped posture. Raskolnikov walked along at a distance; his heart was thumping; they turned into an alley—he still didn't turn around. "Does he know that I am following him?", wondered Raskolnikov. The bourgeois entered the gates of a large house. Raskolnikov went up to the gates quickly and began looking: would he glance back and call him? Indeed, after passing through the

Appendix of Literary Dreams 173

gateway and coming out into the courtyard, he suddenly turned around and seemed to beckon to him again. Raskolnikov went through the gateway too, but the bourgeois was no longer in the courtyard. He must have turned into the first stairway. Raskolnikov raced after him. Indeed, two flights above, he heard someone's measured, unhurried footsteps. It was strange, this staircase seemed familiar. There was a window on the first floor: moonlight was shining through the glass mournfully and mysteriously; here's the second floor. Oh! It was the same apartment in which the painters were working . . . How come he didn't realize that at once? The footsteps of the man ahead died away. "He must have stopped or be hiding somewhere." Here's the third floor; should he go further? How quiet it was, even frightening. . . . But he went on. The noise of his own footsteps frightened and alarmed him. Oh God, how dark it was! The bourgeois must be hiding in some corner. Ah! the door to an apartment stood open onto the landing; he thought a bit and entered. It was very dark and empty in the entrance hall, there was not a soul, as if everything had been removed: quietly, on tip-toe, he went into the living room; the whole room was brightly enveloped in moonlight; every thing was as it was before: chairs, mirror, yellow sofa, and framed pictures. The huge, round, copper-red moon looked directly into the windows. "This stillness is because of the moon," thought Raskolnikov, "it must be posing riddles now." He stood and waited, waited a long time, and the quieter the moon was, the louder his heart thumped—it even began to hurt. And stillness prevailed. Suddenly he heard a momentary dry crackling, as if a twig had broken, and then everything went silent again. An awakened fly suddenly flew against the windowpane and began buzzing plaintively. At this moment in the corner, between the small wardrobe and the window, he discerned what seemed to be a cloak hanging on the wall. "Why is there a cloak?" he wondered, "it wasn't there before." He approached quietly and realized that someone seemed to be hiding behind the cloak. Carefully he drew back the cloak with his hand and saw a chair standing there, and on the chair in the corner sat the old woman, all huddled up and holding her head in such a way that he could not see her face—but it was she. He stood over her. "She is afraid," he thought, quietly withdrawing the axe from its loop; he struck the old woman over the head once and then again. But it was strange: she didn't even stir under the blows, it was as if she were made of wood. He became afraid, bent over, and began to look closely at her; she bent her head even lower. He crouched all the way down to the floor and then looked up into her face; he took one look and he grew numb; the old woman was sitting there and laughing—she was overcome by quiet, inaudible laughter, trying with all her strength to make sure that he didn't hear her. Suddenly it seemed to him that the door to her bedroom was opening slightly and that there too someone was laughing and whispering. Madness overcame him: with all his might he began to strike the old woman on the head, but with each blow of the axe, the laughter and whispering from the bedroom sounded stronger and louder, and the old woman was shaking with mirth. He tried to flee, but the entire entrance hall was already full of people, the doors onto the landing were open, and on the landing, on the staircase and below—there stood a crowd of people, head to head, everyone looking, but everyone was quiet, all waiting, all silent! His heart was constricted, his feet would not move, they became rooted to the spot. He wanted to cry out and—he awoke   [pt. 3, ch. 6] (6:212–14).

[5] During his illness he dreamed that the whole world was condemned to fall victim of some terrible, previously unknown pestilence which was moving out of the depths of Asia toward Europe. Everyone would perish, except for a chosen few, very few. Some kind of new trichina had appeared, microscopic organisms which settled in human bodies. But these organisms were creatures endowed with intelligence and will. People who were affected immediately became possessed and insane. But never, never did these people consider themselves so intelligent and so infallible in the truth, as when they were infected. Never did they consider their pronouncements, their scientific conclusions, their moral convictions and beliefs more infallible. Whole populations, whole towns and nations became infected and went insane. Everyone was anxious, no one understood each other, each one thought that truth resided in him alone, and, regarding all others, suffered, beat his chest, wept and wrung his hands. They didn't know whom and how to make judgments, they couldn't agree on what constituted good and evil. They did not know whom to condemn, whom to acquit. People killed each other in senseless rage. They assembled whole armies against each other, but when these armies were on the march, they suddenly began to fight among themselves; the ranks disintegrated, the soldiers fell on one another, stabbed and cut each other, bit and ate each other. In towns the alarm sounded all day long: they summoned everyone, but who and why they were called, no one knew, and everyone was anxious. They abandoned the most ordinary trades because everyone proposed his own thoughts and suggestions, and they were unable to agree; agriculture was abandoned. In some places people formed into groups, agreed on something together, and swore not to disband—but immediately they began to do something quite different from what they themselves had previously proposed. They began to accuse each other, to fight and to slaughter each other. Conflagrations began, famine followed. Everything and everyone perished. The pestilence grew and advanced further and further. Only a few people in the whole world could be saved, these were pure and chosen, destined to found a new race of people and a new life, to

renew and purify the earth; but no one had ever seen these people, no one had ever heard their words or their voices [epilogue, ch. 2] (6:491–20).

Svidrigaylov's Dream
[a] He was already dozing off: his feverish trembling had subsided; suddenly something seemed to be running underneath the blanket along his arm and leg. He shuddered. "Damn it all, I bet it's a mouse!" he thought, "all because I left the veal on the table . . ." He had no desire to unwrap himself, get up and shiver, but once again something unpleasant suddenly came up against his leg; he tore the blanket off and lit a candle. Trembling with a feverish chill, he bent over to examine the bed—there was nothing there. He shook out the blanket and suddenly a mouse scampered out onto the sheet. He tried to catch it, but the mouse did not jump off the bed, but darted back and forth in zigzags, slipped out of his fingers, ran across his hand, and suddenly plunged underneath the pillow; he threw the pillow down, but he felt at once that something jumped onto his chest and was running across his body, down his back, under his shirt. He began to tremble nervously and awoke. . . .

[b] He imagined a charming landscape; it was a bright, warm, almost hot day, a holiday—Whit Sunday. There was a rich, luxurious country cottage in the English style, completely overgrown with fragrant flowerbeds, surrounded by flowery borders going around the house; the porch was entwined with climbing plants and surrounded by beds of roses; there was a light, cool staircase, covered with a luxurious carpet, and banked with rare flowers in Chinese vases. He noticed particularly the bouquets of delicate white narcissus in vases filled with water on the windows; the flowers were leaning on their bright green, long, thick stems, emitting a strong aromatic fragrance. He didn't want to leave them, but he climbed the staircase and entered a large, high room, and once again there were flowers everywhere—on the windows, near the doors opening onto the terrace, and on the terrace itself. The floors were strewn with freshly cut grass, the windows were open and a fresh, light, cool breeze was blowing into the room; the birds were chirping under the windows, and in the middle of the room, on tables covered with white satin shrouds, there stood a coffin. This coffin was lined with white silk and bordered with a thick white frill. Wreaths of flowers surrounded it on all sides. A young girl was lying amidst the flowers, she was wearing a white tulle dress; her hands were folded and pressed against her breast—as if they were chiselled out of marble. But her loosened hair, her fair blonde hair, was wet; a garland of roses was on her head. The stern and already fixed profile of her face also seemed to have been chiselled out of marble, but the smile on her pale lips was full of some unchildlike, infinite

grief and great pain. Svidrigaylov knew this girl; there was no icon and no lit candle standing near the coffin, and no prayers could be heard. This girl was a suicide by drowning. She was only fourteen, but her heart had been broken and had destroyed itself, ashamed of the insult which had so horrified and amazed this young childish consciousness, had overwhelmed her angelic pure soul with undeserved shame, and had torn from her a last cry of despair, unregarded, but boldly shrieked into the dark night, into the blackness, the cold, damp thaw, when the wind was howling.

[c] He fastened the window, walked away from it, lit a candle, pulled on his vest and coat, put on his hat and went out into the corridor with a candle in order to find the tattered waiter who was sleeping somewhere in a little room among all sorts of trash and candle ends, to settle the bill for his room and to leave the hotel. "This is the very best moment, I couldn't choose a better one."

He walked a long time down the long, narrow corridor without finding anyone, and was about to shout out loud, when suddenly in a dark corner, between an old wardrobe and the door, he discerned some strange object, something which seemed alive. He leaned over with his candle and noticed that it was a child—a little girl age five, no more, in a soaking wet dress, as damp as a dishrag, shivering and crying. She seemed not to be afraid of Svidrigaylov, but looked at him with dull wonder from her large black eyes, and from time to time she burst into sobs, like a child who has been crying for a long time, but who had already stopped and even been consoled, but not quite, and suddenly bursts into sobs again. The little girl's face was pale and exhausted; she was numb from the cold. "But how did she get here? She must have hidden here and not slept the whole night." He began to question her. The girl suddenly came to life and very quickly began to babble something to him in her childish language. There was something about "mommy" and "how mommy will be angry," and about some cup which was broken. The little girl talked on without stopping; somehow he was able to figure out that she was an unloved child whose mother was a cook and constantly drunk; probably she worked in that very hotel, and she frightened and beat the child; that the girl had broken her mother's cup and was so scared that she had run away that very evening; she had probably hidden for a long time somewhere in the courtyard in the pouring rain; finally, she had crept in here, hidden behind the wardrobe, and sat in the corner the whole night—crying, trembling from the damp and the darkness and from the fear that she would receive a beating for all of this. He picked her up, carried her into his room, sat her on the bed, and began to undress her. The worn shoes on her bare feet were as wet as if she'd sat in a puddle the whole night. After he undressed her, he put her to bed, covered her, and wrapped her up from head to foot in a blanket. She fell asleep at once. When he finished all this, he relapsed into gloomy thoughts once again.

"Now I've gotten myself all involved!" he thought suddenly with a heavy, malicious feeling. "What nonsense!" He picked up his candle in annoyance to go out and find that waiter no matter what and to get out of there as soon as possible. "Oh, the little girl!" he thought swearing an oath; just as he was opening the door; he returned to have another look at her, to see whether or not she was asleep. He lifted up the blanket carefully. The little girl was sleeping soundly and peacefully. She had gotten warm under the blanket, and her color had already returned to her pale cheeks. But a strange thing: this color seemed to be brighter and stronger than the ordinary rosiness of childhood. "It's a feverish blush," Svidrigaylov thought, but it was more like a flush from wine, as if she'd been given a whole glass to drink. Her scarlet lips were aglow, burning or what? It suddenly seemed to him that her long black eyelashes were fluttering and winking, as if they were about to open, and from under them looked a sly, sharp, somehow unchildlike eye, as if the little girl were not asleep, and only pretending. Yes, indeed it was so: her lips were parting into a smile; the ends of her lips were quivering, as if still restrained. But now she stopped restraining herself; now it was laughter, obvious laughter; something impudent and inviting shines forth in her very unchildlike face; it was corruption, the face of a courtesan, the impudent face of a mercenary French harlot. Now she's no longer hiding; both her eyes open wide: they envelop him with a fiery and shameless look, they beckon him, laughing . . . There was something infinitely disgusting and offensive in that laughter, in those eyes, in all of the nastiness in the child's face. "What! A five-year old!" whispered Svidrigaylov in genuine horror. "This . . . what on earth is this?" But now she was turning her glowing face toward him, stretching out her arms . . . "Ah, accursed girl!" Svidrigaylov shouted in horror, raising his hand as if to strike her . . . But at this moment he awoke   [pt. 6, ch.6] (6:390–93).

The Brothers Karamazov

Alyosha's Dream

"And the third day there was a marriage in Cana of Galilee," read Father Paisiy, "And the mother of Jesus was there; and both Jesus and His disciples were called to the marriage."

"Marriage? What's that? . . . A marriage, . . ." flew like a whirlwind through Alyosha's mind; "she is happy too . . . she drove off to a feast . . . No, she didn't take the knife, she didn't take the knife . . . That was only a "tragic" phrase. Well, one must forgive tragic phrases, absolutely. Tragic phrases comfort the soul . . . without them grief would be too difficult for people to bear. Rakitin has gone off to the alleyway. When Rakitin broods on his insults, he always goes off to an alleyway . . . But the road—the road is large, straight, bright, crystal-clear, and the sun is at its end . . . Ah? what's being read?"

". . . And when they wanted wine, the mother of Jesus saith unto Him: 'They have no wine,'" Alyosha heard.

"Oh yes, I missed that, but I didn't want to miss it; I love this part: it's Cana of Galilee, the first miracle . . . Ah, that miracle; ah, that fine miracle! Christ visited men's joy, not their grief; the first time He enacted a miracle, He helped their joy. . . . "He who loves men, loves their joy also." He was constantly repeating that; it was one of his principal thoughts. Without joy life itself is impossible, says Mitya . . . yes, Mitya . . . Everything that is true and beautiful, is always full of forgiveness—he used to say that, too. . . .

"Jesus saith unto her: 'Woman, what has it to do with thee or me? Mine hour is not yet come.' His mother saith unto the servants: 'Whatsoever he saith unto you, do it.'"

"Do it . . . Joy, joy of some poor people, very poor people . . . Well of course poor people, if they didn't even have enough wine for a wedding. Historians write that at that time in the whole area around the Lake of Gennesaret were living the poorest people that can possibly be imagined. And another great heart of another great creature who was there, His mother, also knew that He had come not only to make His great terrible sacrifice. She knew that His heart was open even to the simple, innocent merrymaking of some obscure, very obscure and artless beings, who had affectionately summoned Him to their poor marriage. "Mine hour is not yet come," He says with a quiet smile (He must have smiled to her gently) . . . And indeed, was it only to make wine plentiful at poor weddings that He had come down to earth? But He did go and He did as she asked him. . . . Ah, he's reading again."

"Jesus saith unto them, 'Fill the pots with water.' And they filled them to the brim.

"And he saith unto them, 'Draw out now and bear unto the governor of the feast.' And they bare it.

"When the ruler of the feast had tasted the water that was made into wine, and knew not whence it was; [but the servants which drew the water knew] the governor of the feast called the bridegroom.

"And he saith unto him: 'Every man at the beginning doth set forth good wine; and when men have well drunk, that which is worse; but thou hast kept the good wine until now.'"

"But what's this, what's this? Why is the room becoming larger . . . Ah, yes, it's the marriage, the wedding . . . yes, of course. Here are the guests, here sit the young people, and the merry crowd and . . . where is the wise governor of the feast? But who is this? Who? Once again the room becomes larger . . . Who is standing up there from behind the big table? What . . . Is he here, too? But he's in the coffin . . . but he's here, too . . . he stood up, he sees me, he's coming over here . . . Oh, Lord!"

Yes, he moved toward him, toward him, a thin little old man with tiny wrinkles on his face; he was joyful and laughing quietly. There was no longer a coffin; he was wearing the same clothes as he did yesterday when he was sitting with them. His face was open, his eyes, shining. How can this be, how can he be here at the feast, called to the marriage of Cana of Galilee?

"My dear, I was called too, called and summoned," a quiet voice said above him. "Why did you hide here so that I couldn't see you . . . come and join us, too."

It was his voice, the voice of the Elder Zosima . . . And how couldn't it be he, if he calls? The Elder raised Alyosha by the hand; he rose from his knees.

"Let us rejoice," continued the thin old man, "we are drinking new wine, the wine of a new, great joy; you see how many guests there are? Here's the bride and groom, here's the wise governor of the feast; he is tasting the new wine. Why are you standing in awe of me? I gave away an onion, and I am here too. And many here have given away an onion each, only one little onion . . . What are our deeds? And you, my quiet boy, my gentle boy, today you too knew how to give an onion to a hungry woman. Begin your work, my dear boy, my gentle boy . . . And do you see our Sun, do you see Him?"

"I am afraid . . . I dare not look," whispered Alyosha.

"Do not fear Him. He is terrible in His greatness before us, awesome in His eminence, but He is infinitely merciful; out of love He made Himself like unto us and He rejoices with us. He changes water into wine so that the joy of the guests may not be interrupted, and He awaits new guests, He summons new ones constantly forever and ever. Here they are bringing new wine, do you see, they are bringing the vessels . . ."

Something was glowing in Alyosha's heart, something suddenly filled it up until it ached, tears of escstasy burst forth out of his soul . . . He stretched out his hands, cried out, and awoke   [bk. VII, ch. 4] (14:326–27).

Dmitry's Dream

He was driving somewhere out in the steppes, where he had been stationed a long time ago, and a peasant was driving him in a cart with a pair of horses through the slush. Mitya felt cold; it was early November and snow was falling in large wet flakes; as soon at it hit the ground, it melted immediately. The peasant drove along quickly, boldly snapping his whip; he had a long, fair beard. He wasn't an old man—perhaps fifty years old, wearing a grey peasant's smock. And there was a village not far off, he could make out the very black huts, and half of the huts had been burned down, there were only charred beams sticking up. And along the road leading out of the village, there were standing lots of peasant women, a whole row, all thin and wan, with brownish faces. There was especially one at the edge, such a bony woman, tall, about forty years old, but perhaps only twenty, with a long, thin face; and in her arms there was a child crying; her breasts must have been so dried up that there wasn't a drop of milk in them. And the babe was crying, crying, holding out his bare little arms, with his little fist blue from the cold.

"Why are they crying? What are they crying for?" asks Mitya, as he flew past them quickly.

"It's the babe," the driver answers him, "it's the babe crying." And Mitya is struck by the fact that he said it in his own way, in the peasant way, "babe" and not "baby." He likes the peasant's calling it a babe: it seemed as if there was more pity in it.

"But why is it crying?" Mitya persisted, like a fool. "Why are its little hands bare, why don't they wrap it up?"

"The babe had gotten chilled, its little clothes are frozen and they don't provide any warmth."

"But why is it so? Why?" foolish Mitya still persisted.

"Why they are poor people, burned out; they have no bread; they are begging because they've been burned out."

"No, no." Mitya still seemed not to understand, "tell me: why are those poor mothers standing there, why are the people poor, why is the babe poor, why is the steppe barren, why don't they hug each other, kiss each other, why don't they sing songs of joy, why are they so dark from black misery, why don't they feed the babe?"

And he felt that although his questions were unreasonable and senseless, still he wanted to ask them and he had to ask them in just that way. And he felt also that a feeling of sweet tenderness was rising up in his heart, one that he had never experienced before, and that he wanted to weep, he wanted to do something for everyone so that the babe would no longer cry, so that the black dried-up mother of the baby would no longer cry, so that no one would shed any more tears from this moment forth, and he wanted to do all this at once, at once, without delay, in spite of all obstacles, with all the Karamazov recklessness.

"And I am with you too, I shall not leave you, I will go with you for your whole life," next to him he hears Grushenka's kind words, full of emotion. And his whole heart was glowing and aspiring toward some light, and he longed to live and live, to go on and on, toward some new beckoning light, and quickly, quickly, now, at once!   [bk. IX, ch. 8] (14:456).

Appendix of Literary Dreams 181

Ivan's Dream
See *The Brothers Karamazov*, translated by Constance Garnett, revised by Ralph E. Matlaw. (New York, 1976), 601–17, bk. XI, ch. 9, "The Devil. Ivan Fyodorovich's Nightmare" (15:69–85).

L. N. TOLSTOY
War and Peace

Prince Andrei's Two Dreams
[1] "What's this? Am I falling? My legs are giving way," he thought and fell onto his back. He opened his eyes, hoping to see how the battle between the French and the artillerymen would end, wanting to know if the red-haired artilleryman would be killed or not, and if the cannon would be captured or saved. But he didn't see anything. Above him there was no longer anything except the sky—the lofty sky, not clear, but immeasurably lofty, with grey clouds floating quietly across it. "How quiet, peaceful and solemn, not at all as it was when I was running," thought Prince Andrei, "not like when we were running, shouting, and fighting; not at all like when the Frenchman and artilleryman with furious and frightened faces were struggling for the ramrod; in a very different way these clouds are floating across this lofty, infinite sky. How is it that I have never seen this lofty sky before? And how happy I am that I have come to know it at last. Yes, all is vanity, all is falsehood, except for this infinite sky. There is nothing, nothing but this. But even this does not exist, there is nothing except quiet and peace. And thank God! . . . (*Polnoe sobranie sochinenii*, Moscow, 1928–58, 9:344).

"*Voilà une belle mort*," said Napoleon, looking at Bolkonsky.
Prince Andrei understood that this was said about him and that it was Napoleon who said it. He heard how the person who said these words was called sire. But he heard these words as if he were hearing the buzzing of a fly. Not only was he uninterested in them, but he didn't even notice them, and he forgot them immediately. His head was burning, he felt that he was bleeding to death, and above him he saw the distant, lofty, and eternal sky. He knew that this was Napoleon, his hero, but at this moment Napoleon seemed to him a small, insignificant creature in comparison to what was occurring now between his soul and this lofty, infinite sky with clouds running across it. At that moment he didn't care at all who was standing over him or what was said about him; he was simply glad that people had stopped over him and only wished that these people would help him and bring him back to life, which seemed so beautiful to him, because now he understood it in a different way. He collected all his strength to move and make some sound.

182   Appendix of Literary Dreams

Feebly he moved his leg and made a weak, sickly groan which inspired his own pity. . . . (9:356–57).

In spite of the fact that five minutes earlier Prince Andrei could say a few words to the soldiers who were transporting him, now, fixing his eyes directly on Napoleon, he was silent. . . . At that moment all of the interests which occupied Napoleon seemed so insignificant to him, his hero himself seemed so trivial to him, with his trivial vanity and joy of victory, in comparison with the lofty, just, and good sky which he saw and understood; he was unable to answer him.

Indeed everything seemed so futile and insignificant compared to that stern, solemn train of thought which was aroused in him by his weakness from loss of blood, suffering, and the nearness of death. Looking into Napoleon's eyes, Prince Andrei thought about the insignificance of greatness, about the insignificance of life, the meaning of which no one could understand, and about the even greater insignificance of death, the meaning of which no one alive could understand or explain. . . . (9:358–59).

The stretchers moved on. At every jolt he felt once again unendurable pain; his feverish condition intensified and he began to be delirious. Visions of his father, wife, sister, and future son, and the tenderness which he experienced on the eve of the battle, the figure of the small, insignificant Napoleon, and above all of this the lofty sky—all this formed the main subjects of his feverish imagination.

He imagined the quiet life and peaceful family happiness of Bald Hills. He was enjoying this happiness when suddenly there appeared the small Napoleon with his unsympathetic, limited outlook, reflecting happiness based on the unhappiness of others; there began doubts and torment; only the sky promised peace. Toward morning all of these dreams mixed and flowed together into the chaos and darkness of unconsciousness and oblivion. . . . [bk. III, ch. 13] (9:359–60).

[2] He dreamed that he was lying in the same room in which he really was lying, but that he was not wounded, but quite well. Many different people, all insignificant and apathetic, appeared before Prince Andrei. He was talking with them, arguing about something unnecessary. They are preparing to go off somewhere. Prince Andrei dimly recollects that all of this is insignificant and that he has other, more important concerns, but he continues talking, surprising them with his empty, witty words. Little by little, unnoticed, all of these people begin to disappear, and everything becomes focused on one question—the closed door. He gets up and goes to the door to bolt and lock it. *Everything* depends on whether or not he has time to lock it. He

moves in haste, but his feet do not budge, and he knows that he will not have time to lock the door; nevertheless he strains all of his powers. And an agonizing fear overcomes him. And this fear is the fear of death: *it* is standing behind the door. But at the same time that he is weakly and clumsily crawling toward the door, this terrible something, pushing from the other side, was already breaking its way in. Something not human—death—was breaking down the door, and he had to restrain it. He seizes the door, exerts his last efforts—it was no longer possible to lock it—now just to hold it back; but his efforts were weak, clumsy, and the door, pushed by that horrible something, opens and then closes again.

Once again it pushed in from outside. His last superhuman efforts are in vain, and both halves of the door open silently. *It* entered, and it is *death*. And Prince Andrei died.

But at the very moment that he died, Prince Andrei remembered that he was asleep, and at the very moment that he died, having made a great effort, he awoke.

"Yes, it was death! I died and I woke up. Yes, death is an awakening!" [bk. XII, ch. 4] (12:63–64).

Pierre Bezukhov's Two Dreams

[1] "To be a soldier, just a soldier!" thought Pierre as he fell asleep. "To enter into this communal life with all one's being, to be imbued with what makes them what they are. But how to cast off from oneself all that superfluous, diabolical burden of one's outer man? At one time I could have done it. I could have run away from my father, as I wanted to. Or I could have been sent to be a soldier after the duel with Dolokhov." And in Pierre's imagination there flashed the dinner at the club at which he challenged Dolokhov, and also his benefactor at Torzhok. And now Pierre imagines a solemn meeting of the lodge. The meeting takes place at the English Club. And someone familiar, near and dear to him, sits at the end of the table. Yes it's he! It's his benefactor. "But didn't he die?" wondered Pierre. "Yes, he died; but I didn't know that he's still alive. I was so sorry that he died, and I am so glad that he is alive once again!" On one side of the table sat Anatole, Dolokhov, Nesvitzky, Denisov and others like them (in his dream this category of people was just as cleverly defined in Pierre's soul, as was the category of people whom he called "they"), and these people, Anatole and Dolokhov, were shouting loudly and singing; but from behind their shouting the voice of the benefactor could be heard, speaking incessantly, and the sound of his words was just as significant and uninterrupted as the booming on the battlefield, but it was pleasant and comforting. Pierre did not understand what the benefactor was saying, but he knew (in his dream this category of thought was

also clear) that the benefactor was talking about goodness and about the possibility of becoming what *they* [the "others"] were. And from all sides *they*, with their simple, kind, solid faces, surrounded the benefactor. But although they were good, they did not look at Pierre, they did not know him. Pierre wanted to attract their attention and to speak. He stood up, but at that very moment his legs grew cold and became bare.

He felt ashamed, and covered up his legs from which his coat had actually slipped. For a moment arranging his coat, Pierre opened his eyes and saw the same roofs, posts, yard—but now it was all bluish, lit up, and glittering with dew or frost.

"It is growing light," thought Pierre. "But that's not important. I must hear out and understand the words of my benefactor." He covered himself again with his coat, but now neither his lodge meeting nor his benefactor was there. There were only thoughts, clearly expressed in words, thoughts which someone was uttering or which Pierre himself formulated.

Remembering these thoughts afterwards, in spite of the fact that they evoked by the impressions of that day, Pierre was convinced that someone outside of him had said them to him. It seemed to him that he never would have been in a position to think and express these thoughts in such a way when awake.

"War is the most difficult subordination of man's freedom to the law of God," said the voice. "Simplicity is submission to God, you cannot escape from Him. And *they* are simple. *They* do not talk, but act. A spoken word is silver, but an unspoken one is golden. Man can be master of nothing, while he fears death. And he who does not fear it, possesses all. If there were no suffering, man would not know his limitations, would not know himself. The most difficult thing (Pierre continued to think and hear in his dream) is to be able to unite in your soul the meaning of everything." "To unite everything?" Pierre said to himself. "No, not to unite. It is impossible to unite thoughts, but to *harness* all these thoughts—that's what's needed! Yes, one must harness, one must harness!" he repeated to himself with internal rapture, feeling that only with these words could he express what he wanted to express, and could he solve the problems which tormented him.

"Yes, one must harness, it's time to harness."

"One must harness, it's time to harness, your excellency! Your excellency," a voice repeated, "one must harness, it's time to harness . . ."

This was the voice of the groom waking Pierre. . . .   [bk. XI, ch. 6] (11:293–94).

[2] He slept again as he had at Mozhaysk after the battle of Borodino.

Once again events of reality merged with dreams and again someone, he himself or someone else, spoke thoughts to him, and even those same thoughts which had been spoken to him at Mozhaysk.

"Life is everything. Life is God. Everything changes and moves, and this movement is God. And while there is life, there is joy in consciousness of divinity. To love life, to love God. It is more difficult and more blessed than all else to love this life in one's sufferings, in one's innocent sufferings."

"Karataev!" came into Pierre's mind.

And suddenly Pierre vividly saw his long forgotten gentle old tutor who had given Pierre geography lessons in Switzerland. "Wait," said the old man. And he showed Pierre a globe. The globe was alive—a pulsating sphere without fixed dimensions. The entire surface of the sphere consisted of drops pressed together closely. And these drops were moving constantly, changing places, first merging into one, then dividing into many. Each drop tried to spread out, to occupy as much space as possible, but the others, trying to do the same, compressed it, sometimes destroyed it, sometimes merged with it.

"That is life," said the old tutor.

"How simple and clear it is," thought Pierre. "Why didn't I know this before?"

In the middle is God, and each drop tries to spread out in order to reflect Him to the greatest extent. And it grows, merges, is compressed, and destroyed on the surface, sinks into the depths and emerges again. Here he is, Karataev, now he has spread out and disappeared. "*Vous avez compris, mon enfant,*" said the tutor.

"*Vous avez compris, sacré nom,*" cried a voice and Pierre awoke [bk. XIV, ch. 3] (12:158–59).

Nikolai Rostov's Two Dreams

[1] He dozed off for a moment, but in that short interval of unconsciousness he dreamed about a large number of things: he saw his mother and her large white hand, he saw Sonya's thin shoulders, Natasha's eyes and laughter, and Denisov with his voice and mustache, and Telyanin and the whole affair with Telyanin and Bogdanych. That whole affair was the same thing as this soldier with the shrill voice, and it was that affair and that soldier that were so agonizingly, incessantly pulling, pressing, and dragging his arm in one direction. He tried to move away from them but they did not let go of his shoulder even for a moment. It wouldn't have hurt, it would have been fine, if only they wouldn't pull it; but it was impossible to get away from them.

He opened his eyes and looked up [bk. II, ch. 16] (9:243).

[2] That same night Rostov was with a platoon on skirmishing duty in front of Bagration's detachment. His hussars were stationed along the line in pairs; he himself rode along the line trying to master the sleepiness which kept coming over him. Behind him one could see an enormous space with the campfires of our army burning dimly in the mist; in front of him was

misty darkness. Try as he did to look into this misty distance, he could see nothing: first something appeared grey, then it seemed that something appeared black; then it seemed that some lights flickered where the enemy should have been; then it occurred to him that this was only flashing in his own eyes. His eyes kept closing and in his imagination there appeared first his sovereign, then Denisov, then Moscow memories, and he quickly opened his eyes again; he saw in front of him the head and ears of the horse on which he was seated, sometimes the black figures of the hussars, when he was only about six paces away from them, and in the distance, still the same misty darkness. "Why not? It's very possible," thought Rostov, "that the sovereign, meeting me, would give me a commission, as he would to any officer, and he would say, 'Ride and find out what's out there!' Many men have related how completely by chance he came to know an officer and attached him to himself. What if he were to attach me to himself! Oh, how I would protect him, how I would tell him the whole truth, how I would expose his deceivers!" And Rostov, in order to imagine vividly his love and devotion to the sovereign, imagined to himself an enemy or deceitful German, whom he would not only kill with delight, but whom he would beat across the face in front of his sovereign. Suddenly a distant cry awoke Rostov. He shuddered and opened his eyes.

"Where am I? Yes, in the line; pass and watchword—*shaft, Olmütz*. What a nuisance that tomorrow our squadron will be in reserve," he thought. "I will request action. This may be my one chance to see the sovereign. Yes, it's not long now until the guard changes. I'll ride around once more and when I return I'll go to the general and ask him." He readjusted himself in his saddle and touched his horse to ride once more around his hussars. It seemed lighter to him. To the left he saw a sloping incline lit up, and opposite, a black mound which seemed as steep as a wall. On this mound there was a white spot which Rostov couldn't make out: was it a meadow in the forest, lit up by the moon, remaining snow, or some white houses. It even seemed to him that something was moving across this white spot. "It has to be snow—this spot; spot—*une tache*," thought Rostov. "There now, it's not a *tache*."

"Natasha, sister, black eyes. Na . . . tashka. (Won't she be surprised when I tell her that I've seen the sovereign!) Natashka . . . take my sabretache . . ." "Keep right, your honor, there are bushes over here," said the voice of a hussar, past whom Rostov, dozing off, had ridden. Rostov suddenly raised his head which had dropped almost to the horse's mane and stopped next to the hussar. Youthful, childish sleep was overcoming him gradually. "Yes, now, what was I thinking? I don't want to forget. How will I speak to the sovereign? No, not that—that's tomorrow. Yes, yes! Natashka, sabretache, to sabre, to sabre us—whom? The hussars. Ah, the hussars and mustaches . . . Along Tverskaya Street rode a hussar with a mustache; I thought about him too, opposite Gurev's house . . . The old man Gurev . . . Hey, a fine lad Denisov! Yes, that's all nonsense. The main thing now is that the sovereign is here. How he looked at me, and how he wanted to say something, but he didn't dare . . . No, it was I who didn't dare. But that's nonsense, and the main thing is not to forget the important thing that I was thinking. Natashka, sabretache, to sabre, to sabre them—yes, yes, yes. That's good." And his head once again fell forward onto the horse's neck. Suddenly it seemed to him that someone was shooting at him. "What? What? What! Cut them down! What?" said Rostov, waking up   [bk. III, ch. 12] (9:324–26).

Petya Rostov's Dream
Petya should have known that he was in the forest, with Denisov's band, less than a mile from the road, that he was sitting on a wagon captured from the French, near which horses were tethered, that sitting near him was the Cossack Likhachev who was sharpening his sabre, that the large black spot to the right was the guard's hut, and the bright red spot below on the left was a dying campfire, that the man who came for a cup was a hussar who wanted to drink; but he didn't know and didn't want to know anything about all this. He was in a magical kingdom in which nothing resembled reality. Perhaps the large black spot really was a guard's hut, but perhaps it was a cave which led to the depths of the earth. Perhaps the red spot was a fire, but perhaps it was the eye of an enormous monster. Perhaps he really was sitting on a wagon, but perhaps instead of sitting on a wagon, he was on a very tall tower from which, if he fell, he would have to fall a whole day, a whole month, before reaching the earth, and perhaps he'd never reach it. Perhaps it was only the Cossack Likhachev sitting next to the wagon, and perhaps it was the best, bravest, most wonderful, most outstanding man on earth, whom no one knows. Perhaps it was a hussar who passed by looking for water and went back to the hollow, but perhaps he disappeared from sight, vanished altogether and no longer existed.

Whatever Petya saw now, nothing would have surprised him. He was in a magical kindgom in which everything was possible.

He looked at the sky. And the sky was as magical as the earth. The sky was clearing and over the tops of the trees clouds were floating by quickly, as if uncovering the stars. Sometimes it seemed that the sky was clearing and there appeared clear black sky. Sometimes it seemed that these black spots were little clouds. Sometimes it seemed that the sky was lifting way, way up overhead; sometimes the sky was sinking way down, so that one could touch it with one's hand.

Petya began to close his eyes and he swayed a little. Drops fell. Quiet talk was heard. The horses neighed and jostled each other. Someone was snoring . . .

"Ozhig, zhig, ozhig, zhig," whistled the sabre against the whetstone. And suddenly Petya heard a harmonious musical orchestra playing some unknown, sweetly solemn hymn. Petya was as musical as Natasha and more so than Nikolai, but never studied music and didn't think about music; thus the themes which came into his head so unexpectedly were particularly new and pleasant to him. The music became more and more audible. The melody grew, passed from one instrument to another. What emerged was a fugue, although Petya hadn't the least conception of what a fugue was. Each instrument, first resembling a violin, then a horn, but better and purer than violins and horns, each instrument played its part, and before finishing the melody, was merged with another, beginning almost the same, and with a third and a fourth, and all merged into one and then became separate again and once more merged, first into something solemnly ecclesiastical, then into something dazzlingly brilliant and triumphant.

"Ah, yes, but I'm dreaming," Petya said to himself lurching forward. "It's in my ears. But perhaps it's my own music. There it is again. Play on, my music! Well! . . ."

He closed his eyes. And from all sides, as if out of the distance, sounds fluttered, began to grow harmonious, separate, merge, and again join into the same sweet, solemn hymn. "Ah, this is simply wonderful! As much as I like and just as I like," said Petya to himself. He tried to conduct this enormous orchestra.

"Now softer, softer, die away." And the sounds obeyed him. "Now fuller, brighter. More, more joyful." And from unknown depths there arose increasingly triumphant sounds. "Now voices join in!" ordered Petya. And at first from afar came the men's voices and then the women's. The voices grew, grew in harmonious triumphant strength. Petya feared and rejoiced to hear their extraordinary beauty.

Their song mingled with the triumphant, victorious march, and the drops fell, and the sabre whistled vzhig, zhig, zhig . . . and the horses jostled each other again and neighed, not disturbing the choir, but entering into it.

Petya didn't know how long it continued: he was enjoying himself, all the while wondering at his own enjoyment and feeling sorry that there was no one to share it with. Likhachev's kindly voice awoke him.   [bk. XIV, ch. 2] (12:146–48).

Nikolai Bolkosky's Dream
He dreamed that he and Pierre were wearing helmets, just like those depicted in his edition of Plutarch. He and Uncle Pierre were marching at the

head of a huge army. The army consisted of white sloping lines which filled the air like cobwebs which float about in autumn and which Dessalles called *le fil de la Vierge*. In front was glory, similar to these threads, but only somewhat thicker. They, he and Pierre, were carried lightly and joyously, closer and closer to their goal. Suddenly the threads which were moving them began to slacken and become entangled; it became difficult to move. And Uncle Nikolai Ilich [Rostov] stood before them in a stern and threatening pose.

"Did you do this?" he said, pointing at the broken sealing wax and quill pens. "I loved you, but Arakcheev has given me orders, and I will kill the first one who advances." Nikolenka glanced up at Pierre; but it wasn't Pierre any longer. Pierre was his father, Prince Andrei, and his father was without image or form, but he was there; seeing him, Nikolenka felt faint out of love: he felt weak, limp, formless. His father caressed him and pitied him. But Uncle Nikolai Ilich moved closer and closer toward them. Horror seized Nikolenka and he awoke. [first epilogue, ch. 4] (12:294).

Anna Karenina

Stiva Oblonsky's Dream

Yes! Alabin was giving a dinner in Darmstadt; no, not in Darmstadt, but somewhere in America. Yes, but Darmstadt was in America. Yes, Alabin was giving a dinner on glass tables, yes, and the tables were singing: *Il mio tesoro*, not *Il mio tesoro*, but something better; and some small decanters, but they were also women. . . . [pt. I, ch. 1] (18:4).

Anna's Three Dreams

[1] One dream occurred to her almost every night. She dreamed that both men were her husbands, that both were lavishing caresses on her. Aleksei Aleksandrovich [Karenin] was weeping, kissing her hands, and saying "How nice it is now!" And Aleksei Vronsky was there too, and he was also her husband. And astonished at what had seemed impossible to her before, she explained to them, laughing, that this was much simpler and that now they were both satisfied and happy   [pt. II, ch. 11] (18:159).

[2] "Yes, a dream," she said. "I dreamed it long ago. I dreamed that I ran into my bedroom to fetch something or to find out something; you know how it happens in a dream," she said, opening her eyes wide in horror. "And in the bedroom, in the corner, was standing something.

"And this something turned around, and I saw that it was a little peasant with a tangled beard, small and horrible. I wanted to flee, but he bent over a sack and was fumbling around in it. . . ."

She showed how he was fumbling around in the sack. Horror was on her face. And Vronsky, remembering his dream, felt the same horror filling his soul.

"He was fumbling and muttering in French, very quickly, and you know, rolling his 'r's': *Il faut le battre le fer, le broyer, le pétrir.* . . ." And I wanted to wake up from that terror, and I awoke, but I awoke in my dream. And I began to ask myself what it all meant. And Kornei says to me, 'In childbirth, you will die in childbirth, ma'am.' And then I awoke" [pt. IV, ch. 3] (18:380–81).

[3] quoted in text, p. 139.

Vronsky's Dream
"What horrors I dreamed. Yes, yes, the peasant-beater, it seems, small, dirty, with a tangled beard, was bending over doing something and suddenly began to say some strange words in French. Yes, that was all there was in the dream," he said to himself, "but why did it seem so terrible?" [pt. IV, ch. 2] (18:375).

Serezha's Dream
When the candle had been taken away, Serezha heard and felt his mother. She was standing over him and caressing him with a loving gaze. But then windmills appeared, and a knife, and everything became confused, and he fell asleep   [pt. V, ch. 27] (19:98).

NOTES

Chapter 1. Dreams in Life and Literature
1. S. T. Coleridge, quoted in H. G. Schenck, *The Mind of the European Romantics* (London, 1966), 8.
2. Erich Fromm, *The Forgotten Language: An Introduction to the Understanding of Dreams, Fairy Tales and Myths* (New York, 1951), 24.
3. E. Kiester, Jr., "Images of the Night: The Physiological Roots of Dreaming," *Science 80*, 1 (May/June 1980), 36.
4. Ibid.
5. L. Lévy-Bruhl, *Primitive Mentality* (New York, 1923), 101.
6. See E. R. Dodds, *The Greeks and the Irrational* (Berkeley, Calif., 1973), 102–42, and D. Coxhead and S. Hiller, *Dreams, Visions of the Night* (New York, 1976), 5–7.
7. Homer, *The Odyssey*, trans. E. V. Rieu (New York, 1977), 302.
8. Virgil, *The Aeneid: A Verse Translation*, trans. Rolfe Humphries (New York, 1951), 175.
9. See Coxhead and Hiller, *Dreams*, 7–8.
10. See M. Weidhorn, *Dreams in Seventeenth-Century English Literature* (The Hague, 1970), 15.
11. G. Chaucer, *The Canterbury Tales*, trans. by Nevill Coghill (New York, 1977), 181–96.
12. D. Traversi, *An Approach to Shakespeare: Henry VI to Twelfth Night* (London, 1968), 1, 51. See also M. Garber, *Dreams in Shakespeare* (New Haven, Conn., 1974).
13. E. Cassirer, *The Philosophy of the Enlightenment* (Boston, 1951), 5.
14. Schenck, *The Mind*, 3.
15. F. M. Dostoevsky, *Notes from Underground* (New York, 1960), 25.
16. See Czeslaw Milosz, "Dostoevsky and Swedenborg," *Slavic Review*, 34 (June 1975), 302–18.
17. See R. Darnton, *Mesmerism and the End of the Enlightenment in France* (Cambridge, Mass., 1968), and Maria M. Tatar, *Spellbound: Studies on Mesmerism and Literature* (Princeton, N.J., 1978).
18. L. L. Whyte, *The Unconscious before Freud* (New York, 1960), 114.
19. Ibid., 115.
20. Albert Beguin, *L'Ame romantique et le rêve* (Marseille, 1937), 1, 106–7.
21. Whyte, *The Unconscious*, 119.
22. Quoted in Raymond de Becker, *The Understanding of Dreams: And Their Influence on the History of Man* (New York, 1968), 91.
23. See Beguin, *L'Ame romantique*, 1, 185–227.

24. Ibid., 228–67.
25. C. G. Carus, *Psyche: Zur Entwicklungsgeschichte der Seele* (Pforzheim, 1846), 1.
26. Ibid., 220.
27. See H. W. Hewett-Thayer, *Hoffmann: Author of the Tales* (Princeton, N.J., 1948), 181–82.
28. See Alethea Hayter, *Opium and the Romantic Imagination* (Berkeley, Calif., 1968), 67–83.
29. Quoted in S. Fraiburg, "Kafka and the Dream," in *Art and Psychoanalysis*, ed. W. Phillips (New York, 1957), 32.
30. Quoted in Schenck, *The Mind*, 8.
31. E. M. Forster, *Aspects of the Novel* (London, 1974), 58.
32. A. A. Mendilow, *Time and the Novel* (New York, 1972), 202.
33. Simon O. Lesser, *Fiction and the Unconscious* (New York, 1962), 60.
34. George Devereux, *Dreams in Greek Tragedy: An Ethno-Psycho-Analytical Study* (Berkeley, Calif., 1976), ix.
35. Elizabeth Dalton, *Unconscious Structure in "The Idiot": A Study in Literature and Psychology* (Princeton, N.J., 1979), 154.
36. Quoted in L. Trilling, "Freud and Literature," in *The Liberal Imagination* (New York, 1953), 44.
37. S. Freud, *The Interpretation of Dreams*, trans. A. A. Brill (New York, 1913), 81.
38. Ibid., 81 n.
39. Ibid., my italics.
40. Eventually Freud turned to literary texts for the light they shed on the psyche of the author: "Another path led from the investigation of dreams to the analysis of works of imagination and ultimately to the analysis of their creators—writers and artists themselves." Freud, "On the History of the Psychoanalytic Movement," in *Standard Edition of the Complete Psychological Works*, ed. James Strachey, (London, 1953–74), 14, 36. See also Lesser, *Fiction*, 17ff.
41. S. Freud, *Delusion and Dream, and Other Essays*, ed. Philip Rieff (Boston, Mass., 1956), 62.
42. Ibid., 25.
43. Ibid., 96–97, my italics.
44. Ibid., introduction by P. Rieff, 7.
45. C. J. Jung, "The Practical Use of Dream-Analysis," in *Dreams*, trans. R. F. C. Hull (Princeton, N.J., 1974), 95.
46. Ibid., 90.
47. Jung, "On the Nature of Dreams," in *Dreams*, 69.
48. Jung, "Psychology and Literature," in *The Spirit in Man, Art and Literature*, trans. R. F. C. Hull (Princeton, N.J., 1966), 104, my italics.
49. Ibid., 88–91.
50. Jung, "*Ulysses*: A Monologue," in *The Spirit*, 123.
51. R. B. Lower, "On Raskol'nikov's Dreams in Dostoevsky's *Crime and*

Punishment," Journal of the American Psychoanalytic Association, 17 (July 1969), 742.

52. Dalton, *Unconscious Structure*, 13.
53. Ibid., 101.
54. Freud, *Delusion and Dream*, 28.
55. The Appendix contains translations of the principal dreams discussed in this book (except for those quoted in full within the text).
56. The chapter entitled "Oblomov's Dream," the so-called embryo of the novel, was published separately in 1849. Although called a "dream," it is really much closer to a "prose poem" or "illustrative flashback" that illuminates the hero's upbringing and his environment. See Richard Freeborn, *The Rise of the Russian Novel* (Cambridge, 1973), 150, and A. and S. Lyngstad, *Ivan Goncharov* (New York, 1971), 79.
57. On dreams in Turgenev, see A. Remizov, *Tourgueniev: Poète du rêve* (Paris, 1933), and E. Kagan-Kans, *Hamlet and Don Quixote: Turgenev's Ambivalent Vision* (The Hague, 1975), 121–36.
58. Chekhov became fascinated by Grigorovich's tale "Karelin's Dream" (1887). See G. Struve, "On Chekhov's Craftmanship: The Anatomy of a Story," *Slavic Review*, 20 (October 1961) 466–71; see also K. Kramer, *The Chameleon and the Dream: The Image of Reality in Čexov's Stories* (The Hague, 1970), 76–92.

Chapter 2. Allegory and Polemic Pre-Pushkin

1. N. Frye, *The Anatomy of Criticism* (New York, 1966), 90.
2. Num. 12:6, King James Version.
3. V. Peretts, *Slovo o polku Igorevim* (Kiev, 1926), 243.
4. Saint John Climacus, *The Ladder of Divine Ascent* (London, 1959), 64–65. A modern version of the same belief is expressed in N. V. Rozhdestvensky's treatise *Prophetic Dreams (Veshchie sny)* (St. Petersburg, 1897), 9: "To believe in dreams, to be controlled by their directives in one's actions, is as unreasonable as chasing after the wind."
5. Josephus Flavius, *The Great Roman-Jewish War: A.D. 66–70* trans. William Whiston (New York, 1960), 32.
6. *La prise de Jérusalem de Joseph le Juif*, 2 vols. ed. V. Istrin (Paris, 1934–38), 1:48. See also, N. A. Meshchersky, *Istoriya Iudeiskoi voiny Iosifa Flaviya v drevnerusskom perevode* (Moscow-Leningrad, 1958), 479.
7. Quoted in Peretts, *Slovo*, 239.
8. *Letopisets Pereyaslavlya Suzdal'skago*, ed. M. A. Obolensky, (Moscow, 1851), 11.
9. *The Penguin Book of Russian Verse*, ed. D. Obolensky (Baltimore, Md., 1962), 10–11.
10. See Peretts, *Slovo*, 238–65 and N. K. Gudzy, *History of Early Russian Literature* (New York, 1949), 165. Also: E. V. Barsov, *Slovo o polku Igoreve kak khudozhestvennyi pamyatnik kievskoi druzhinnoi Rusi*, (1887), 2:38–44;

D. Ainalov, "Son Svyatoslava v *Slove o polku Igoreve*", in *Izvestiya po russkomu yazyku i slovesnosti*, 1, no. 2 (Leningrad, 1928), 477–82; D. S. Likhachev and L. A. Dmitriev, *Slovo o polku Igoreve i pamyatniki kulikovskogo tsikla* (Moscow-Leningrad, 1966), 79; and D. S. Likhachev, "*Slovo o polku Igoreve" i kul'tura ego vremeni* (Leningrad, 1968), 229–34.

11. This example was called to my attention by Professor William Mills Todd, Stanford University.

12. Earlier in the same petition Avvakum refers to the *Tale of the Novgorod White Cowl*; that text might well have supplied him with this vision, since it contains a graphic description of the plagues visited upon Constantine for his lack of faith.

13. Later in the same series, Novikov records another dream, which contains satirical references to various religious and social issues. He concludes with the following statement:

Simple Russian folk place a great deal of faith in dreams and foretell their own future well-being or misfortune by means of them. But since they often make mistakes, I do not seek an interpretation from the folk; instead I humbly request that you inquire as to whether there can be found some elucidation . . . in any books that interpret dreams according to the signs of the Zodiac. Or perhaps my dream was a result of my own views concerning good and evil acts.

14. See Roger B. Anderson, *N. M. Karamzin's Prose: The Teller in the Tale* (Houston, Tex., 1974), 132.

15. Cf. Karamzin's letter to Dmitriev of 2 May 1800: "I have become completely immersed in Russian history; when I sleep, I dream of Nikon and Nestor."

16. This source was suggested by V. E. Vatsuro, in "Literaturno-filosofskaya problematika povesti Karamzina 'Ostrov Borngol'm'" in *Derzhavin i Karamzin v literaturnom dvizhenii XVIII-nachala XIX veka*, *XVIII vek*, (Leningrad, 1969), 8:190–209.

17. Ibid., 200–1.

18. See Michael R. Katz, *The Literary Ballad in Early Nineteenth-Century Russian Literature* (Oxford, 1976), 56–59.

19. Manuscript No. 286; 1, 78, 10, State Public Library, Leningrad.

20. Ibid.

21. See Ts. S. Vol'pe's introduction, in V. A. Zhukovsky, *Stikhotvoreniya*, (Leningrad, 1960), 1:xvii.

22. In a letter from Persia dated 7 November 1820, presumably addressed to A. A. Shakhovskoi, Griboedov recorded a dream that has often been said to contain the embryo of the plot of *Woe from Wit*. For the text of the letter, see A. S. Griboedov, *Sochineniya*, 2 vols. (Moscow, 1971), 2:212–13; for a discussion, see *A. S. Griboedov v russkoi kritike*, ed. A. M. Gordin (Moscow, 1958), 382–3, and *N. K. Piksanov, Tvorcheskaya istoriya "Gorya ot uma"* (Moscow, 1971), 82–83. Jean Bonamour, *A. S. Griboedov et la vie littéraire de son temps* (Paris, 1965), 223, cites evidence of work on the play dating as far back as 1812. A comparison of Griboedov's dream with the plot of *Woe from Wit*

reveals parallels as well as discrepancies and provides an interesting reflection of the characters and events of the comedy.
23. Griboedov, *Sochineniya*, 2:239.
24. Gordin, A. S. *Griboedov*, 40–41.
25. D. S. Mirsky, *A History of Russian Literature from Its Beginnings to 1900* (New York, 1958), 116.
26. Gerald Janeček, "A Defense of Sof'ja in *Woe from Wit*," *Slavic and East European Journal*, 21, no. 3 (1977), 318–31.
27. In act 1, scene 9, Famusov notes that Sofiya "whispered" this line; in the next scene, however, he says that she "said it aloud." See Piksanov, *Tvorcheskaya istoriya*, 276.
28. Gordin, A. S. *Griboedov*, 175–76.
29. Piksanov, *Tvorcheskaya istoriya*, 270–78. See also Bonamour, 253–54.
30. R. E. Matlaw, "The Dream in *Yevgeniy Onegin*, with a Note on *Gore ot uma*," *Slavonic and East European Review*, 37, (1959), 500–3.
31. I. Medvedeva makes the unlikely argument that Sofiya's dream is evidence of her "Russian soul" inasmuch as it is supposedly based on a Russian folktale. See *Gore ot uma A. S. Griboedova*, published with G. P. Makogonenko, "*Evgenii Onegin A. S. Pushkina* (Moscow, 1971), 11–13.
32. See B. Malnick, "The Theory and Practice of Russian Drama in the Early Nineteenth Century," *Slavonic and East European Review*, 34 (1955), 12–14.
33. See David Welsh, *Russian Comedy: 1765–1823* (The Hague, 1966), 89–93.
34. A. S. Griboedov, *Sochineniya v stikhakh* (Leningrad, 1967), 475.

Chapter 3. Pushkin's "Dreams vs. Life"

1. D. C. Čiževsky, *Evgenij Onegin, A Novel in Verse* (Cambridge, Mass., 1953), 258.
2. All references are to A. S. Pushkin, *Polnoe sobranie sochinenii*, 17 vols. (Moscow-Leningrad, 1937–59), hereafter abbreviated as *PSS*.
3. M. O. Gershenzon, *Stat'i o Pushkine* (Moscow, 1926), 97.
4. A. S. Griboedov, *Sochineniya v stikhakh* (Leningrad, 1967), 375.
5. The critic M. V. Dobuzhinsky, in an unpublished article entitled "On Pushkin's Drawings" (1937), described several "demonic scenes" that were sketched by Pushkin at various times. One is contained in the manuscript of *Boris Godunov* on the same page as Grigory's phrase "diabolical dream"; it depicts strange demons—one, an "elbow-shaped insect full of despair," another, "all huddled up and bristly," like a "trembling, spherical ball." (The article is in the possession of Professor Gleb Struve, University of California, Berkeley.)
6. Cf. *menya mutil, menya vela, na menya ukazyval; mne snilos', mne stanovilos', mne snilsya.*
7. The verb (*probuzhdal*) is in the imperfective aspect to remind us that

Grigory's dream is repeated. Cf. the perfective finality of the heroine's awakening in Zhukovsky's *Svetlana*: "Akh! i probudilas'."

8. "... vrag/Moi slabyi son mechtan'yami smushchaet...", Pushkin, *PSS*, 8:283.

9. The motifs of the "evil monk" and Grigory-as-"dreamer" (*mechtatel'*) both originate in Karamzin's history. See *Istoriya gosudarstva rossiiskago* (St. Petersburg, 1892), 11:75.

10. V. G. Belinsky, *Polnoe sobranie sochinenii*, 13 vols. (Moscow, 1953–59), 7:529.

11. Gershenzon, *Stat'i*, 102.

12. Mikhail Bakhtin interprets this dream as an image of the "carnival imposter-king" who is being subjected to the "discrowning ridicule" of the folk on the public square. See *Problems of Dostoevsky's Poetics*, trans. R. W. Rotsel (Ann Arbor, Mich., 1973), 141.

13. See J. L. I. Fennell, *Nineteenth-Century Russian Literature* (Berkeley, Calif., 1973), 57.

14. Gershenzon unfortunately bases his discussion on a misreading of the epigraph. He cites it as, "The prophetic dream [*son*] portends sorrow," and then interprets the dream as "prophetic." The line, correctly quoted by Pushkin, comes from an earlier, but published, version of Zhukovsky's "Svetlana," and actually reads, "The prophetic moan [*ston*] portends sorrow." N. Ya. Berkovsky maintains that "The Snowstorm" is a polemic with Washington Irving's "The Spectre Bridegroom," translated into Russian as early as 1825. As Irving quotes Bürger's "Lenore," so Pushkin quotes Zhukovsky's "Svetlana." See "O povestyakh Belkina" in *Stat'i o literature* (Moscow-Leningrad, 1962), 289–94, as well as D. Bethea and S. Davydov, "Pushkin's Saturnine Cupid: The Poetics of Parody in *The Tales of Belkin*," *Publications of the Modern Language Association*, 96, no. 1 (1981) 1, 8–21.

15. J. van der Eng argues that Shakespeare and Scott share a Romantic conception of the gravedigger, i.e., a witty character in a macabre profession. Pushkin, on the other hand, rejects this image, and returns to a more classical portrait inasmuch as Adriyan's character corresponds more closely to his profession. See "Les récits de Belkin," in *The Tales of Belkin* by A. S. Pushkin (The Hague, 1968), 35.

16. S. G. Bocharov suggests that with Tryukhina's death, Adriyan's dream (*mechta*) has been fulfilled in his dream (*son*), since he had been hoping to make some money on the funeral arrangements. See "O smysle 'Grobovshchika,'" *Kontekst 1973* (Moscow, 1974), 216.

17. See Bethea and Davydov, "Pushkin's Saturnine Cupid" for an imaginative "literary" interpretation of *The Tales of Belkin* in general, and of Adriyan's dream in particular.

18. J. T. Shaw, "The 'Conclusion' of Pushkin's *Queen of Spades*," in *Studies in Russian and Polish Literature in Honor of W. Lednicki*, ed. Z. Folejewski, *et al.* (The Hague, 1962), 114–26.

19. F. M. Dostoevsky, *Pis'ma* (Moscow, 1959), 4: 178.

20. V. Shklovsky, *Zametki o proze Pushkina* (Moscow, 1937), 66. This view

is echoed by C. E. Passage in *The Russian Hoffmannists* (The Hague, 1963), 135n. While noting its Hoffmannesque quality, Passage failed to discover the exact source. V. Setchkarev in his review of Passage, (*Slavic and East European Journal*, 8, no. 1 [1964] 72–76) locates the source of one image (*grandiflor*) in two specific tales of Hoffmann.

21. N. W. Ingham suggests a source for Germann's first dream in Hoffmann's *Spielerglück*, when Menars first conceives of the possibility of becoming rich overnight. See *E. T. A. Hoffmann's Reception in Russia* (Würzburg, 1974), 135.

22. G. A. Gukovsky, *Pushkin i problemy realisticheskogo stilya* (Moscow, 1957), 341–43. (Cf. Gogol's "The Portrait.")

23. M. P. Alekseev, *Pushkin, Svravnitel'no-istoricheskie issledovaniya* (Leningrad, 1972), 102–3. See also Darnton, *Mesmerism*, and Tatar, *Spellbound*.

24. Ingham, *Reception*, 138.

25. The epigraph to this chapter, which refers to a vision seen by the affable Baroness von B., is the only mention of Emanuel Swedenborg in Pushkin's work, but it has never been located. It was probably invented by him and is used to suggest that mystical "visions" were as fashionable as experiments with Mesmer's "magnetism."

26. Shaw, in "The 'Conclusion' of Pushkin's *Queen of Spades*, interprets this dream as "prophetic," inasmuch as its images (the flower, Gothic portals, and spider) suggest the fatal outcome of the story, including Germann's loss at cards. Nathan Rosen counters Shaw, asserting that the dream is "causative," representing a repressed force, Germann's guilt for the death of the countess; it is this force that drives him to mistake the queen for an ace in the final scene. By an elaborate analysis of visual similarities and auditory puns, Rosen posits a series of equations to explain how the spider becomes identified with the queen of spades (and the countess) and thus occasions Germann's error. According to Rosen, it is Germann's unconscious need for self-punishment that determines the nature of his fatal mistake at the card table. Shaw's conclusion seems more logical, in spite of Rosen's imaginative analysis. The psychologizing about Germann's guilt as a result of the countess' death and his unconscious need for self-punishment seems unnecessarily far-fetched and un-Pushkinian. See N. Rosen, "The Magic Cards in *The Queen of Spades*," *Slavic and East European Journal*, 19, no. 3 (1975),255–75.

27. Pushkin refers to Pugachev and his men both as *nevedomaya sila* and *nevedomye lyudi*.

28. Gershenzon argues that the first part (Grinev's return home and his father's illness) is the result of the hero's remorse after his spree in Simbirsk, while the second part reveals his intuitive perception of Pugachev's strength and foreshadows both the bloodbath and the offer of protection. Blagoi extends Gershenzon's interpretation, seeing the dream as a prophecy of the entire relationship between Grinev and Pugachev, which he views as the internal theme of the work. See D. D. Blagoi, *Masterstvo Pushkina* (Moscow, 1955), 252.

29. Caryl Emerson, employing a semi-Freudian/semi-Bakhtinian ap-

proach, concludes that the father is not an Oedipal figure, but rather a "carnivalized" image. See "Grinev's Dream: The Captain's Daughter and a Father's Blessing," *Slavic Review*, 40, no. 1 (1981), 60–76.

30. Pugachev is also the peasants' "proxy father." Pushkin's "Remarks on the Rebellion" record a conversation with an old Ural peasant: "Tell me. . . how was Pugachev your proxy father?"—"For you, he was Pugachev," the old man replied, "but for me he was the great sovereign, Peter Fedorovich." Pushkin, *PSS*, 9:373.

31. Pugachev draws a parallel between himself and the other famous Russian usurper, Grigory Otrepev; he is thus connected to the historical theme in *Boris Godunov*.

32. Masha's intercession with Catherine parallels the Grinev-Pugachev relationship. See Yu. M. Lotman, "Ideinaya struktura *Kapitanskoi dochki*" in *Pushkinskii sbornik*, ed. E. A. Maimin (Pskov, 1962), 17.

33. V. F. Miller, *Pushkin kak poet-etnograf* (Moscow, 1899), 45; V. F. Botsyanovsky, "Nezamechennoe u Pushkina," *Vestnik literatury* (1921), 3, 6–7; N. L. Brodsky, *Evgenii Onegin—Roman A. S. Pushkina* (Moscow, 1957), 239–41; Čiževsky, *Onegin*, 258–60; Gukovsky, *Pushkin*, 214–17; A. L. Slonimsky, *Masterstvo Pushkina* (Moscow, 1959), 354–58; L. N. Stilman, "Problemy literaturnykh zhanrov: traditsii v *Evgenii Onegine* Pushkina. K voprosu perekhoda ot romantizma k realizmu," *American Contributions to the Fourth International Congress of Slavists* (The Hague, 1958), 321–67; Stanley Mitchell, "Tatiana's Reading," *Forum for Modern Language Studies*, 4 (January 1968), 1–21; W. M. Todd, "*Eugene Onegin*: Life's Novel," in *Literature and Society in Imperial Russia: 1800–1914*, ed. W. M. Todd (Stanford, Calif., 1978), 203–35.

34. M. P. Samarin, "Iz marginalii k *Evgeniyu Oneginu*," *Naukovi zapiski naukogo-doslidchoi katedri istorii ukrainskoi kul'turi*, 6 (1927), 313; Matlaw, "The Dream," 495–96; D. D. Blagoi, *Sotsiologiya tvorchestva Pushkina* (Moscow, 1929), 107; E. Tangl, "Tatjanas Traum," *Zeitschrift für slavische Philologie*, 25 (1956), 239–41; V. Nabokov, *Eugene Onegin, A Novel in Verse, by A. S. Pushkin* (New York, 1964), 2:503.

35. Gershenzon, *Stat'i*, 105–8; E. Wilson, "In Honor of Pushkin," in *The Triple Thinkers, Ten Essays on Literature* (New York, 1938), 61–62; Čiževsky, *Onegin*, 258; Ludolf Müller, "Tatjanas Traum," *Die Welt der Slaven*, 7 (1962), 389; R. A. Gregg, "Tat'yana's Two Dreams," *Slavic and East European Review*, 48 (1970), 492–505.

36. Other sources of images are the dreams in Richardson's *Clarissa Harlowe* (the heroines's dream in letter 39 of vol. 2; Lovelace's in letter 48 of vol. 7); and in Goethe's *Die Leiden des jungen Werthers* (the hero's dreams in the letters of 21 August and 14 December). See Todd, "*Onegin*," 214–17.

37. The English excerpts from *Eugene Onegin* are adapted from Nicholas Fersen's (Williams College) unpublished prose translation.

38. Here novel (*roman*) is significantly *not* rhymed with deceit (*obman*).

39. Nabokov, *Onegin*, III, 227–8.

40. Todd, *"Onegin,"* 217–18.
41. In one early manuscript this phrase reads: "Or interpreted dreams" (*Ili tolkovannye sny*). This suggests a parallel to Tatyana's search in Martin Zadeka.
42. Olga is aptly described by the Russian proverb "[She] slept a lot but saw little in [her] dream."

Chapter 4. Gogol's "Mixed Vegetable Salad"

1. V. Bryusov, "Ispepelennyi," *Vesy*, 4 (1901), 119.
2. A. Remizov, *Ogon' veshchey* (Paris, 1954), 24.
3. L. J. Kent adopts a psychoanalytic approach to Gogol's literary dreams in *The Subconscious in Gogol' and Dostoevskij and its Antecedents*; W. W. Rowe in *Through Gogol's Looking Glass: Reverse Vision, False Focus, and Precarious Logic* (New York, 1976) treats the dreams as an example of Gogolian "reverse vision."
4. All references are to N. G. Gogol, *Polnoe sobranie sochinenii*, 14 vols. (Moscow, 1940–52), hereafter abbreviated as *PSS*.
5. See F. C. Driessen, *Gogol as a Short Story Writer* (The Hague, 1965), 103, and V. Setchkarev, *Gogol: His Life and Works*, trans. Robert Kramer (New York, 1965), 113.
6. See D. Magarshack, *Gogol: A Life* (New York, 1957), 118.
7. See Chapter 6 "Early Works," on Tolstoy's autobiographical tale, "A History of Yesterday."
8. See J. M. Holquist, "The Devil in Mufti," *Publications of the Modern Language Association*, 82 (October 1967), 355.
9. Richard Peace, who "psychologizes" Katerina's dreams, argues the contrary. He maintains that it *is* she who desires her father: "There is more than a suggestion that, subconsciously at least, Katerina bears the guilt of the 'ultimate wickedness.'" See *The Enigma of Gogol* (Cambridge, 1981), 16–24.
10. See the Freudian interpretations of I. D. Yermakov, *Ocherki po analizu tvorchestva N. V. Gogolya* (Moscow-Petrograd, 1924), 78–98; A. L. Bem, "Dramatizatsiya breda," in *O Dostoevskom: Sbornik statei* (Prague, 1929), 1:112; Driessen, *Gogol*, 103ff.; Kent, *The Subconscious*, 66.
11. Akaky's overcoat has been interpreted by some critics as his substitute "wife"; there are indeed similarities between "Ivan Shponka" and "The Overcoat": Akaky accompanies Petrovich to the shop and buy cloth for his new coat; they purchase "good material"; and the tailor himself admits that, "You can't find better cloth."
12. Driessen, in *Gogol*, describes Shponka's dream as a "wild fantastic dance" that reflects the hero's obsession with women (114); Kent, in *The Subconscious*, argues that the dream transforms Shponka into Gogol's first "downtrodden hero" with a sensitive soul (71–73); Rowe in *Through Gogol's Looking Glass* maintains that "if Shponka's dream is construed as a Gogolian prophetic nightmare, he does eventually marry Storchenko's sister—with

some rather startling and uncomfortable results (59)." Simon Karlinsky in *The Sexual Labyrinth of Nikolai Gogol* (Cambridge, Mass., 1976) argues that "the dream itself, totally Freudian and genuinely surrealistic, is a quantum jump of Gogol's imagination into the remote future" (46). Peace in *The Enigma of Gogol* labels it "a nightmare full of symbols equated with wives, such as to gladden the heart of any critic with a Freudian bent" (16).

13. See Karlinsky, *The Sexual Labyrinth*, 47.
14. Quoted in W. Kayser, *The Grotesque in Art and Literature* (Bloomington, Ind., 1963), 21–22.
15. Abram Tertz (Andrei Sinyavsky), *V teni Gogolya* (London, 1975), 161.
16. See Rowe, *Through Gogol's Looking Glass*, 136–37.

Chapter 5. Dostoevsky's "Variations and Nuances"

1. A. G. Dostoevskaya, *Vospominaniya*, ed. L. P. Grossman (Moscow-Leningrad, 1925), 45. Cf. Dostoevsky's letter to his wife from Ems in July, 1874: "I keep on having bad dreams [*sny*].... You know that long ago I was compelled into believing in them" (*Pis'ma*, Moscow-Leningrad, 1928–34, 3:330).
2. R. L. Jackson, *The Art of Dostoevsky: Deliriums and Nocturnes* (Princeton, N.J., 1981), 293–94.
3. Janko Lavrin, *Dostoevsky and His Creation: A Psycho-Critical Study* (London, 1920), 46.
4. Bakhtin, *Problems of Dostoevsky's Poetics*, 123. See also pp. 140–42 on Dostoevsky's use of the "crisis dream."
5. All references are to F. M. Dostoevsky, *Polnoe sobranie sochinenii* (Leningrad, 1972–   ), hereafter abbreviated as *PSS*.
6. George Gibian, "C. G. Carus' *Psyche* and Dostoevsky," *American Slavic and East European Review*, 14 (1955), 371–82. Regarding the subject of dreams, Gibian observes in a final footnote, "Dreams as revelations of the unconscious are also apposite in this connection, although their use by Dostoevsky is too large a subject to broach here and would require independent treatment."
7. Robin F. Miller suggests that here the narrator's thoughts are indistinguishable from the hero's and that this passage could be read as Myshkin's own interior monologue. See her *Dostoevsky and The Idiot: Author, Narrator, and Reader* (Cambridge, Mass., 1981), 138.
8. Jackson, *The Art of Dostoevsky*, 291.
9. Dostoevsky, *Pis'ma*, I, 87.
10. W. J. Leatherbarrow, "Pushkin and the Early Dostoevsky," *Modern Language Review*, 74 no. 2 (1979), 373.
11. J. Frank, *Dostoevsky: The Seeds of Revolt, 1821–1849* (Princeton, N.J., 1976), 314–17.
12. Konstantin Mochulsky, *Dostoevsky. His Life and Work* (Princeton, N.J., 1967), 67.

13. Leatherbarrow, "Dostoevsky's Treatment of the Theme of Romantic Dreaming in 'Khozyayka' and 'Belyye nochi,'" *Modern Language Review*, 69, no. 3 (1974), 591.
14. Dostoevsky, *Pis'ma*, IV, 178.
15. L. J. Kent, *The Subconscious*, 112.
16. This distinction was pointed out by J. T. Shaw in "Raskol'nikov's Dreams," *Slavic and East European Journal*, 17 (1973), 131–32.
17. In the notebooks for the novel Dostoevsky refers to another of the hero's dreams: Raskolnikov "sees Porfiry in a dream. N.B. Disgusting, humiliating, childish dream about how Porfiry is tracking him." See *The Notebooks for Crime and Punishment*, ed. E. Wasiolek (Chicago, 1967), 203.
18. See Jackson, *The Art of Dostoevsky*, 198–202 for an illuminating discussion of the philosophical "pro and contra" that underlies this dream.
19. See N. M. Chirkov, *O stile Dostoevskogo* (Moscow, 1963), 161–2.
20. See G. Gibian, "Traditional Symbolism in *Crime and Punishment*," in Dostoevsky, *Crime and Punishment* (New York, 1964), 581.
21. Shaw, "Raskol'nikov's Dreams," 133.
22. Bakhtin notes the "typical carnival combination" in this dream and connects it to the Pretender's dream in Pushkin's *Boris Godunov* and to the Countess's wink in "The Queen of Spades." See *Problems of Dostoevsky's Poetics*, 140–42.
23. See D. M. Fiene, "Raskol'nikov and Abraham: A Further Contribution to a Defense of the Epilogue of *Crime and Punishment*," *International Dostoevsky Society Bulletin*, 9 (1979), 32–35.
24. A fragment included in Dostoevsky's notebooks for *The Idiot* contains a plan for a historical novel entitled "The Emperor"; it begins with the following passage:

A cellar, darkness, a young man; he doesn't know how to speak. Ivan Antonovich, a youth of about twenty. A description of the nature of this man. He develops all by himself; fantastic pictures and images, dreams [*sny*], a maiden (in a dream [*vo sne*]). His notions of everything; a tremendous imagination, mice, a cat, a dog. (PSS IX, 113).

25. See Alexis Guédroitz, "Son i bred u Dostoevskogo," *Transactions of the Association of Russian-American Scholars in the USA*, 14 (1981), 215–16, and Miller, *Dostoevsky and The Idiot*, 140.
26. See Dalton, *Unconscious Structure*, 152–58 for a bizarre psychoanalytic interpretation of Ippolit's "anxiety dream."
27. In "The Dream of a Ridiculous Man" (1877) Dostoevsky's suicidal hero is transported to the very same Greek archipelago where he beholds a similar utopia. In this variation the hero corrupts mankind by introducing passion, jealousy, cruelty, and shame, as well as slavery, religion, and suffering. Upon awakening, the hero is transformed, resolved to preach the truth and share his insights. See M. Holquist, *Dostoevsky and the Novel* (Princeton, N.J., 1977), 161–64, and Jackson, *The Art of Dostoevsky*, 290–94.
28. Dostoevsky, *Pis'ma*, 4:114.

29. Victor Terras in *A Karamazov Companion: Commentary on the Genesis, Language, and Style of Dostoevsky's Novel* (Madison, Wis., 1981), 273–74 pursues this "joy" (*radost*') as the principal leitmotif of the chapter.

30. Mark G. Pomar, "Aleša Karamazov's Epiphany: A Reading of 'Cana of Galilee,'" *Slavic and East European Journal*, 27 (1983), 47–56.

31. *The Notebooks for The Brothers Karamazov*, ed. E. Wasiolek (Chicago, 1971), 170.

32. Terras in *A Karamazov Companion*, 334, observes that the woman's brownish, elongated face is an iconographic image.

33. R. Sewall, "The Tragic World of the Karamazovs," in *Tragic Themes in Western Literature*, ed. C. Brooks (New Haven, Conn., 1955), 113–14.

34. The most intriguing experiential dream belonging to a minor character is Liza's "amusing dream" related to Alyosha in the chapter entitled "Little Demon." The dreamer imagines that she is alone at night surrounded by devils (*cherti*) who threaten to seize her. When she crosses herself, the devils retreat. When she blasphemes, they advance; she crosses herself again, and they retreat. Liza's dream restates the fundamental motif of the novel: the struggle between faith and doubt. It also foreshadows Ivan's dream, where the conflict is dramatized on an even grander scale. And finally it further undermines the theme of the "innocence of little children."

35. Bakhtin characterizes this phenomenon as "the complete dialogization of Ivan's consciousness." See *Problems of Dostoevsky's Poetics*, 185.

36. Dostoevsky, *Pis'ma*, 4:190.

37. Quoted in H. Troyat, *Tolstoy* (New York, 1967), 486.

38. L. N. Tolstoy, *Polnoe sobranie sochinenii* (Moscow, 1928–58), 89:229.

Chapter 6. Tolstoy's "Truer Feelings"

1. L. N. Tolstoy, *Sobranie sochinenii*, 20 vols. (Moscow, 1965), 19:77. All subsequent references are to L. N. Tolstoy, *Polnoe sobranie sochinenii*, 20 vols. (Moscow, 1928–58), hereafter abbreviated as *PSS*.

2. M. Gorky, *Reminiscences of Tolstoy, Chekhov and Andreyev* (New York, 1959), 22.

3. Ibid., 23.

4. Nikolai's dream is absent from an early version of this scene; Tolstoy's manuscript contains merely a series of events:

12 August 1833—It was a fine day. Ivan Karlovich [*sic*] woke us as usual at 7:30. . . . At 7:30 we got up, got dressed, and as usual, went with Karl Ivanovich to exchange greetings downstairs. (*PSS*, 1:108)

5. Cf. N. Gusev, "About dreams in general, L. N. thinks that they are formed at the moment of awakening," *Dva goda s L. N. Tolstym* (Moscow, 1928), 86.

6. See I. R. Eiges, "Iz tvorcheskoi istorii rasskaza 'Al'bert' L. Tolstogo," *Iskusstvo* (1928), kn. 1–2; and B. M. Eikhenbaum, *Lev Tolstoi*, 3 vols. (Leningrad, 1928), 1:327–8.

7. The second version amplifies the conclusion with the following:

I cast shame away from myself and wept over past, irretrievable happiness, over the impossibility of future happiness, over someone else's happiness. . . . But in these tears there was contained happiness of the present. (*PSS*, 7:118)

8. The only exception is Marya Bolkonskaya, who is said to have a hidden figurative dream (*mechta*); she longs to leave her family, home, and worldly cares to become a simple, devout pilgrim. But when she looks closely at her father and nephew, her resolve weakens and she abandons her dream.

9. See the final paragraphs in this section on *War and Peace*.

10. Tolstoy also recounts three experiential dreams (*sny*) from Pierre's diary that are in fact allegorical depictions of the hero's passions. The manuscript version of one of these contains the following erotic passage:

There are exquisite drawings on the pages— amorous adventures of the soul with its beloved—I see a beautiful depiction of a maiden in transparent clothes with a transparent body—floating up to the clouds—I know that it is the youngest Countess Rostova [Natasha], and that this depiction is from the 'Song of Songs.' And I know that I am wrong in looking at the pictures. (*PSS*, 13:713)

11. An additional dream was rejected even in the manuscript:

. . . and some kind of beasts, having caught him. He ran away from them, they seized him, he ran toward the water, to a pond, fell into it, the water covered over his head, and he died. But as soon as he had died. . . . (*PSS*, 14:350)

12. In one early manuscript Tolstoy also ascribed his prose poem "Dream" (see above, "Early Works") to Nikolai Rostov (*PSS*, 13:498–99).

13. See John Bayley, *Tolstoy and the Novel* (London, 1966), 135–36.

14. Marianna Torgovnick, *Closure in the Novel* (Princeton, N.J., 1981) 67.

15. Quoted in Sigrid McLaughlin, "Tolstoy and Schopenhauer," *California Slavic Studies*, 5 (1970), 199.

16. See B. M. Eikhenbaum, "Tolstoi i Shopengauer," *Literaturnyi sovremennik*, 11 (1935), 134–49.

17. A. Schopenhauer, "Essay on Spirit Seeing," in *Parerga and Paralipomena*, trans. E. F. J. Payne, (Oxford, 1974), 1:265.

18. The only other female character in *Anna Karenina* who has any dreams is Kitty. During the time that she is under Varenka's influence, she is said to possess "secret dreams" (*mechty*) to help the poor and unfortunate. See n. 8 above.

19. In the earliest version of this scene there was no dream whatever. For its evolution, see *PSS*, 20:79–80, 86, 93.

20. Sydney Schultze in *The Structure of Anna Karenina* (Ann Arbor, Mich., 1982), 124–25, suggests that the image of the old woman stretching her legs represents Anna's precognition of childbirth pains as well as the author's close linkage of childbirth to death.

21. Schultze, ibid., 123–24, argues convincingly that the use of French is clarified only when Anna throws herself under the train. Just before she leaves the carriage she overhears a conversation in which a woman declares in French: "Reason has been given to man to enable him to escape from what disturbs him." Tolstoy notes: "These words seemed to answer Anna's thought."

22. E. Wasiolek, *Tolstoy's Major Fiction* (Chicago, 1978), 153.
23. Note the use of *zabyt'e*: Levin's "oblivion," but Anna's "delirium" (above).
24. See also the dreamlike transformations in Nekhlyudov's presleep meditation in *Resurrection* (*PSS*, 32:203).
25. Gusev defines the importance of this dream in his memoir, *Dva goda s L. N. Tolstym*:

In this dream he imagined in graphic form everything that he had experienced during his crisis—beginning with his first doubts and ending with the bright and joyous escape from the difficult and agonizing predicament in which he found himself after his long and anxious search. (86)

26. An entry in Tolstoy's diary for 22 October 1909 records the actual dream on which the work is based. "Now it is midnight. I had a wonderful dream in which I spoke heatedly about H[enry] George. I want to write it down" (*PSS*, 38:445).
27. Gusev, *Dva goda s L. N. Tolstym*, 86.

Chapter 7. Conclusion/Supersedure

1. V. Bryusov, *The Republic of the Southern Cross and Other Stories* (London, 1918), 155.
2. Ibid., 162.
3. D. Kharms and A. Vvedensky, *Russia's Lost Literature of the Absurd*, ed. G. Gibian (New York, 1974), 72–73.
4. Leon Edel, *The Modern Psychological Novel* (New York, 1964), v.
5. Gleb Struve, "Monologue intérieur: The Origins of the Formula and the First Statement of its Possibilities," *Publications of the Modern Language Association*, 69 (1954), 1101–11; see also Edel, *The Modern Psychological Novel*, 147–53.
6. See S. Aronian, "The Dream as a Literary Device in the Novels and Short Stories of Aleksej Remizov," unpublished dissertation (Yale University, 1971).

SELECTED BIBLIOGRAPHY

The bibliography includes primary sources followed by a list of secondary sources arranged under separate headings: General Works, Russian Literature Pre-Pushkin, Pushkin, Gogol, Dostoevsky, and Tolstoy.

Primary Sources

Dostoevsky, F. M. *Polnoe sobranie sochinenii.* Vols. 1– . Leningrad, 1972– .
Gogol, N. G. *Polnoe sobranie sochinenii.* Vols. 1–14. Moscow, 1937–52.
Griboedov, A. S. *Sochineniya v stikhakh.* Leningrad, 1967.
Karamzin, N. M. *Izbrannye sochineniya.* Vols. 1–2. Moscow-Leningrad, 1964.
Pushkin, A. S. *Polnoe sobranie sochinenii.* Vols. 1–17. Moscow-Leningrad, 1937–59.
Tolstoy, L. N. *Polnoe sobranie sochinenii.* Vols. 1–90. Moscow, 1928–58.
Zhukovsky, V. A. *Sobranie sochinenii.* Vols. 1–4. Moscow-Leningrad, 1959.

Secondary Sources

General Works

Alexandrian, Sarane. *Le Surréalisme et le rêve.* Paris, 1974.
Alter, Robert. *Partial Magic: The Novel as a Self-conscious Genre.* Berkeley, Calif., 1975.
Becker, Raymond de. *The Understanding of Dreams: And Their Influence on the History of Man.* New York, 1968.
Beguin, Albert. *L'Ame romantique et le rêve.* 2 vols, Marseille, 1937.
Bergson, Henri Louis. *The World of Dreams.* New York, 1958.
Besançon, Alain. "Fonction du rêve dans le roman russe." In *Entretiens sur le grand siècle russe et ses prolongements,* edited by Alain Besançon and V. Weidle. Paris, 1971, 263–97.
Bousquet, Jacques. *Les Themes du rêve dans la littérature romantique.* Paris, 1964.
Callois, Roger. *The Dream Adventure.* New York, 1963.
Carus, C. G. *Psyche: Zur Entwicklungsgeschichte der Seele.* Pforzheim, 1846.
Cohn, Dorrit. *Transparent Minds: Narrative Modes for Presenting Consciousness in Fiction.* Princeton, N.J., 1978.
Crews, Frederick. *Out of My System: Psychoanalysis, Ideology and Critical Method.* New York, 1975.
Darnton, R. *Mesmerism and the End of Enlightenment in France.* Cambridge, Mass., 1968.

Selected Bibliography

Devereux, George. *Dreams in Greek Tragedy: An Ethno-Psycho-Analytical Study*. Berkeley, Calif., 1976.
Edel, Leon. *The Modern Psychological Novel*. New York, 1964.
———. *The Stuff of Dreams: Experiments in Literary Psychology*. New York, 1982.
Ellenberger, Henri F. *The Discovery of the Unconscious: The History and Evolution of Dynamic Psychiatry*. New York, 1970.
Freud, S. *Delusion and Dream, and Other Essays*. Ed. Philip Rieff. Boston, 1956.
———. *The Interpretation of Dreams*. Trans. A. A. Brill. New York, 1913.
Friedman, Melvin. *Stream of Consciousness*. New Haven, Conn., 1955.
Fromm, Erich. *The Forgotten Language: An Introduction to the Understanding of Dreams, Fairy Tales and Myths*. New York, 1951.
Gibian, George, ed. *Russia's Lost Literature of the Absurd. A Literary Discovery: Selected Works of Daniil Kharms and Alexander Vvendensky*. Ithaca, N.Y., 1971.
Gudzy, N. K. *History of Early Russian Literature*. New York, 1949.
Hall, C. S., and Lind, R. E. *Dreams, Life and Literature: A Study of Franz Kafka*. Chapel Hill, N.C., 1970.
Hardy, Barbara. *Tellers and Listeners: The Narrative Imagination*. London, 1975.
Hayter, Alethea. *Opium and the Romantic Imagination*. Berkeley, Calif., 1968.
Hill, Brian. *Such Stuff as Dreams*. London, 1967.
Hoffman, F. *Freudianism and the Literary Mind*. New York, 1959.
Humphrey, R. *Stream of Consciousness in the Modern Novel*. Berkeley, Calif., 1954.
Jung, C. *Modern Man in Search of a Soul*, Trans. W. S. Dell and C. F. Baynes. New York, 1968.
———. *Symbols of Transformation*. Trans. R. F. C. Hull. Princeton, N.J., 1968.
Lesser, Simon O. *Fiction and the Unconscious*. New York, 1962.
Mendilow, A. A. *Time and the Novel*. New York, 1972.
Meyerhoff, Hans. *Time in Literature*. Berkeley, Calif., 1960.
Porter, Lawrence M. *The Literary Dream in French Romanticism: A Psychoanalytic Interpretation*. Detroit, Mich., 1979.
Ratcliff, A. J. J. *A History of Dreams*. Boston, Mass., 1923.
Remizov, Aleksei. *Ogon' veshchei: Sny i predson'e*. Paris, 1954.
———. *Le monde des rêves*. Paris, 1949.
Schenk, H. G. *The Mind of the European Romantics*. London, 1966.
Scholes, Robert, and Kellogg, Robert. *The Nature of Narrative*. New York, 1966.
Schubert, G. H. von. *Die Symbolik des Traumes*. Bamberg, 1814.
Stragnell, G. "The Dream in Russian Literature." *Psychoanalytic Review*, 8 (July 1921), 225–51.
Strakhov, I. V. *Psikhologicheskii analiz v literaturnom tvorchestve*. Saratov, 1975.

Struve, Gleb. "Monologue intérieur: The Origins of the Formula and the First Statement of its Possibilities." *Publications of the Modern Language Association*, 69 (1954), 1101–11.
Tatar, Maria M. *Spellbound: Studies on Mesmerism and Literature*. Princeton, N.J., 1978.
Trilling, L. *The Liberal Imagination*. New York, 1953.
Vogelsang-Davydov, Olga. *Der Traum als lexikalisches Element in Prosa und Dichtung der russischen Romantik: ein Beitrag zur Theorie des sprachlichen Feldes*. Munich, 1968.
Whyte, L. L. *The Unconscious before Freud*. New York, 1960.
Woods, Ralph L., ed. *The World of Dreams: An Anthology*. New York, 1947.
Ziolkowski, Theodore. *Disenchanted Images: A Literary Iconology*. Princeton, N.J., 1977.

Russian Literature Pre-Pushkin

Anderson, Roger B. *N. M. Karamzin's Prose: The Teller in the Tale*. Houston, Tex., 1974.
Bonamour, Jean. *A. S. Griboedov et la vie littéraire de son temps*. Paris, 1965.
Cross, A. G. *N. M. Karamzin: A Study of His Literary Career*. Carbondale, Ill., 1971.
Janeček, Gerald. "A Defense of Sof'ya in *Woe from Wit*." *Slavic and East European Journal*. 21, no. 3 (1977), 318–31.
Katz, Michael R. *The Literary Ballad in Early Nineteenth-Century Russian Literature*. Oxford, 1976.
Kochetova, N. *N. M. Karamzin*. Boston, Mass., 1975.
Malnick, B. "The Theory and Practice of Russian Drama in the Early Nineteenth Century." *Slavonic and East European Review*, 34 (1955), 10–33.
Medvedeva, I. *Gore ot uma A. S. Griboedova*. Published with G. P. Makogonenko, *Evgenii Onegin A. S. Pushkina*. Moscow, 1971, pp. 5–100.
Nebel, N. M. *N. M. Karamzin: A Russian Sentimentalist*. The Hague, 1967.
Neuhauser, R. "Karamzin's Spiritual Crisis of 1793 and 1794." In *Essays on Karamzin: Russian Man-of-Letters, Political Thinker, Historian, 1766–1826*. Edited by J. L. Black. The Hague, 1975, pp. 56–74.
Piksanov, N. K. *Tvorcheskaya istoria 'Gorya ot uma.'* Moscow, 1971.
Vatsuro, V. E. "Literaturno-filosofskaya problematika povesti Karamzina 'Ostrov Borngol'm.'" In *Derzhavin i Karamzin v literaturnom dvizhenii XVIII-nachala XIX veka, XVIII vek*. Leningrad, 1969, 8:190–209.
Welsh, David J. *Russian Comedy: 1765–1823*. The Hague, 1966.

Pushkin

Berkovsky, N. Ya. "O povestyakh Belkina." In *Stat'i o literature*. Moscow-Leningrad, 1962.
Bethea, D., and Davydov, S. "Pushkin's Saturnine Cupid: The Poetics of Parody in *The Tales of Belkin*." *Publications of the Modern Language Association*, 96, no. 1 (1981) 8–21.

Bocharov, S. G. "O smysle 'Grobovshchika.'" *Kontekst 1973*. Moscow, 1974, 196–230.
Brodsky, N. L. *Evgenii Onegin—Roman A. S. Pushkina*. Moscow, 1957.
Čiževsky, D. C. *Evgenij Onegin, A Novel in Verse*. Cambridge, Mass., 1953.
Emerson, Caryl. "Grinev's Dream: The Captain's Daughter and a Father's Blessing." *Slavic Review* 40, no. 1 (1981), 60–76.
Eng, J. van der, ed. *Tales of Belkin by A. S. Pushkin*. The Hague, 1968.
Gershenzon, M. O. *Stat'i o Pushkine*. Moscow, 1926.
Gibian, George. "Love by the Book: Pushkin, Stendhal, Flaubert." *Comparative Literature*, 3 (Spring 1956), 97–109.
Gregg, R. A. "Tat'yana's Two Dreams." *Slavic and East European Review*, 48 (1970), 492–505.
Gukovsky, G. A. *Pushkin i problemy realisticheskogo stilya*. Moscow, 1957.
Lotman, Yu. M. "Ideinaya struktura *Kapitanskoi dochki*." In *Pushkinskii sbornik*, edited by E. A. Maimin. Pskov, 1962, 3–20.
Matlaw, R. E. "The Dream in Yevgeniy Onegin." *Slavonic and East European Review*, 37 (1959), 487–503.
Miller, V. F. *Pushkin kak poet-etnograf*. Moscow, 1899.
Mitchell, Stanley. "Tatiana's Reading." *Forum for Modern Language Studies*, 4 (January 1968), 1–21.
Müller, Ludolf. "Tatjanas Traum." *Die Welt der Slaven*, 7 (1962), 387–74.
Nabokov, V. *Eugene Onegin, A Novel in Verse, by A. S. Pushkin*. Vols. 1–4. New York, 1964.
Nesaule, Valda. "Tatiana's Dream in Puškin's *Evgenij Onegin*." *Indiana Slavic Studies*, 4 (1967), 119–24.
Remizov, Alexei. "Six rêves de Pouchkine." In *Trajectoire du rêve*. Paris, 1938.
Rosen, N. "The Magic Cards in *The Queen of Spades*." *Slavic and East European Journal*, 19, no. 3 (1975), 255–75.
Samarin, M. P. "Iz marginalii k *Evgeniyu Oneginu*." *Nauvoki zapiski naukogodoslidchoi katedri istorii ukrainskoi kul'turi*, 6 (1927), 307–14.
Shaw, J. T. "The 'Conclusion' of Pushkin's *Queen of Spades*." In *Studies in Russian and Polish Literature in Honor of W. Lednicki*, ed. Z. Folejewski, *et al*. The Hague, 1962, 114–26.
Shklovsky, V. *Zametki o proze Pushkina*. Moscow, 1937.
Slonimsky, A. *Masterstvo Pushkina*. Moscow, 1959.
Stilman, L. N. "Problemy literaturnykh zhanrov i traditsii v *Evgenii Onegine* Pushkina. K voprosu perekhoda ot romantizma k realizmu." In *American Contributions to the Fourth International Congress of Slavists*. The Hague, 1958, 321–67.
Tangl, E. "Tatjanas Traum." *Zeitschrift für slavische Philologie*, 25 (1956), 230–60.
Todd, W. M. "*Eugene Onegin*: Life's Novel." In *Literature and Society in Imperial Russia: 1800–1914*, edited by W. M. Todd. Stanford, Calif., 1978.
Wilson, Edmund. "In Honor of Pushkin." In *The Triple Thinkers, Ten Essays on Literature*. New York, 1938.

Gogol

Ermakov, I. D. *Ocherki po analizu tvorchestva N.V. Gogolya: Organichnost' proizvedenii Gogolya.* Moscow-Petrograd, 1924.
Fanger, Donald. *The Creation of Nikolai Gogol.* Cambridge, Mass., 1979.
Holquist, J. M. "The Devil in Mufti." *Publications of the Modern Language Association,* 82 (October 1967), 352–62.
Hughes, Olga. "The Apparent and the Real in Gogol's Nevskij Propekt." *California Slavic Studies,* 8 (1975), 77–91.
Karlinsky, Simon. *The Sexual Labyrinth of Nikolai Gogol.* Cambridge, Mass., 1976.
McLean, Hugh. "Gogol and the Whirling Telescope." In *Russia: Essays in History and Literature,* edited by L. H. Legters. Leiden, 1972, 79–99.
———. "Gogol's Retreat from Love: Towards an Interpretation of Mirgorod." In *American Contributions to the Fourth International Congress of Slavists.* The Hague, 1958, 225–45.
Maguire, Robert A., ed. *Gogol from the Twentieth Century: Eleven Essays.* Princeton, N.J., 1974.
Peace, Richard. *The Enigma of Gogol.* Cambridge, 1981.
Rowe, W. W. *Through Gogol's Looking Glass: Reverse Vision, False Focus, and Precarious Logic.* New York, 1976.
Tertz, Abram (Sinyavsky, Andrei). *V teni Gogolya.* London, 1975.
Vinogradov, V. V. *Evolyutsiya russkogo naturalizma: Gogol' i Dostoevsky.* Leningrad, 1929.

Dostoevsky

Al'tman, M. "Videnie Germanna. Pushkin i Dostoevsky." *Slavia,* 9 (1930), 792–800.
Bakhtin, Mikhail. *Problems of Dostoevsky's Poetics.* Trans. R. W. Rotsel. Ann Arbor, Mich., 1973.
Bem, A. L. *O Dostoevskom: Sbornik statei.* Vols. 1–3. Prague, 1929–36.
Chirkov, N. M. *O stile Dostoevskogo.* Moscow, 1963.
Dalton, Elizabeth. *Unconscious Structure in "The Idiot": A Study in Literature and Psychology.* Princeton, N.J., 1979.
Gibian, George, "C. G. Carus' *Psyche* and Dostoevsky." *American Slavic and East-European Review,* 14 (1955), 371–82.
Guédroitz, Alexis. "Son i bred u Dostoevskogo," *Transactions of the Association of Russian-American Scholars in the USA,* 14 (1981) 214–30.
Holquist, Michael. *Dostoevsky and the Novel.* Princeton, N.J., 1977.
Jackson, R. L. *The Art of Dostoevsky: Deliriums and Nocturnes.* Princeton, N.J., 1981.
Kanser, Mark. "The Vision of Father Zossima from *The Brothers Karamazov.*" *American Imago,* 8 (December 1951), 329–35.
Kent, L. J. *The Subconscious in Gogol' and Dostoevskij and its Antecedents.* The Hague, 1969.
Kiremidjian, D. "Crime and Punishment: Matricide and the Women Question." *American Imago,* 33 (Winter, 1976), 403–33.

Kravchenko, Maria. *Dostoevsky and the Psychologists*. Amsterdam, 1978.
Laing, R. D. *Self and Others*. London, 1971.
Lavrin, Janko. *Dostoevsky and His Creation: A Psycho-Critical Study*. London, 1920.
Leatherbarrow, W. J. "Dostoevsky's Treatment of the Theme of Romantic Dreaming in 'Khozyayka' and 'Belyye nochi.'" *Modern Language Review*, 69, no. 3 (1974), 584–95.
———. "Pushkin and the Early Dostoevsky." *Modern Language Review*, 74, no. 2 (1979), 368–85.
Miller, Robin F. *Dostoevsky and The Idiot: Author, Narrator, and Reader*. Cambridge, Mass., 1981.
Milosz, Czeslaw. "Dostoevsky and Swedenborg." *Slavic Review*, 34 (June 1975), 302–18.
Mortimer, Ruth. "Dostoevsky and the Dream." *Modern Philology*, 54 (November, 1956), 106–16.
Pachmuss, Temira. *F. M. Dostoevsky: Dualism and Synthesis of the Human Soul*. Carbondale, Ill., 1963.
———. "The Technique of Dream-Logic in the Works of Dostoevskij." *Slavic and East European Journal*, 18 (1960), 220–42.
Rahv, Philip. "Dostoevsky in Crime and Punishment." *Partisan Review*, 27 (Summer 1960), 393–425.
Rosen, Nathan. "Style and Structure in *The Brothers Karamazov*." *Russian Literature Triquarterly*, 1 (1971), 352–65.
Rowe, William W. *Dostoevsky: Child and Man in His Works*. New York, 1968.
Shaw, J. T. "Raskol'nikov's Dreams." *Slavic and East European Journal*, 17 (1973), 131–45.
Shchennikov, G. K. "Funktsii snov v romanakh Dostoevskogo." *Uchennye zapiski Ural'skogo universiteta imeni A. M. Gor'kogo*." Vyp. 16, "Russkaya literatura 1870–90-ykh godov," Sbornik 3, no. 99. Sverdlovsk, 1970.
Smith, S. Stephenson, and Isotoff, Andrei. "The Abnormal from Within: Dostoevsky." *Psychoanalytic Review*, 22 (October 1935), 361–91.
Snodgrass, W. D. "Crime and Punishment: The Tenor of Part One." *Hudson Review*, 13 (1960), 202–53.
Terras, Victor. *A Karamazov Companion: Commentary on the Genesis, Language, and Style of Dostoevsky's Novel*. Madison, Wis., 1981.
Wasiolek, E. "Raskol'nikov's Motives: Love and Murder." *American Imago*, 31 (Fall, 1974), 252–69.
Wilson, Raymond J. III. "Raskol'nikov's Dream in *Crime and Punishment*." *Literature and Psychology*, 26, no. 4 (1976), 159–66.

Tolstoy

Eikhenbaum, B. M. *Lev Tolstoi, Semidesyatye gody*. Leningrad, 1974.
———. *Molodoi Tolstoi*. Petersburg and Berlin, 1922.
———. "Tolstoi i Shopengauer." *Literaturnyi sovremennik*, 11 (1935), 134–49.
Ermolaev, H. "Bog Andreya i Bog P'yera." *Transactions of the Association of Russian-American Scholars in the USA*, 11 (1978), 174–82.

Konick, Willis. "A Little Peasant Mutters at the Rails: The Function of the Dream in *Anna Karenina*." Unpublished paper, 1976.

Krugovoi, G. "P'yer Bezukhov i Platon Karataev: Puti k pravednosti v 'Voine i mire'." *Transactions of the Association of Russian-American Scholars in the USA*, 11 (1978), 138–53.

Lee, C. N. "Dreams and Daydreams in the Early Fiction of L. N. Tolstoy." *American Contributions to the Seventh International Congress of Slavists*. The Hague, 1973, 2:373–92.

McLaughlin, Sigrid. "Tolstoy and Schopenhauer." *California Slavic Studies*, 5 (1970) 187–248.

Merezhkovsky, D. S. *L. Tolstoy i Dostoevsky*. St. Petersburg, 1902–4.

Schultze, Sydney. *The Structure of Anna Karenina*. Ann Arbor, Mich., 1982.

Torgovnick, Marianna. *Closure in the Novel*. Princeton, N.J., 1981.

Wasiolek, E. *Tolstoy's Major Fiction*. Chicago, 1978.

INDEX

Aleksandriya, 18
Alekseev, M. P., 50
Antiochus, Saint, *Prologues*, 17
Aquinas, Saint Thomas, 4
Aristotle, "On Divination in Sleep," 3; "On Dreams," 3
Artimedorus, *Oneirocritica*, 3
Avvakum, 20–21, 194n

Bakhtin, M., 85, 196n, 201n, 202n
Belinsky, V., 31, 44
Bely, Andrei, *Kotik Letaev*, 152
Bible, 3–4, 16–17
Blagoi, D. D., 54
Botsyanovsky, V. F., 54
Brodsky, N. L., 54, 55
Bryusov, V., 66; "In the Tower," 150
Bürger, G. A., "Lenore," 25, 196n
Byron, 57; "The Dream," 8

Carus, C. G., *Psyche: On the History of the Development of the Soul*, 7–8, 10, 37, 86, 133
Chaucer, Geoffrey, "Nun's Priest's Tale," 4
Chekhov, A. P., 15, 193n
Chernyshevsky, N. G., 152; *What is to be Done?*, 15
Chet'i Minei, 17
Chronicles, 19
Čiževsky, D., 37, 54, 55
Coleridge, S. T., 1; "Kubla Khan," 8

Dalton, E., 9, 13–14
Dante, *Divine Comedy*, 4
De Quincey, Thomas, 8, 78
Devereux, G., 9
Dobuzhinsky, M. V., 195
Dostoevsky, F. M., 49, 84–116, 133, 148–49, 151
  Adolescent, 92, 105, 107–9, 115
  Brothers Karamazov, 105, 109–16, 149, 177–81, 202n
  Crime and Punishment, 95–104, 105, 106, 107, 109, 111, 112, 115, 148, 167–77, 201n
  Double, 88–90, 91, 104
  "Dream of a Ridiculous Man," 201n
  "How Dangerous to Indulge in Vainglorious Dreams," 90–91
  Idiot, 86–87, 105–7, 200n, 201n
  Landlady, 93–94, 95, 105
  Mr. Prokharchin, 91–93, 105
  Netochka Nezvanova, 94–95, 105
  Notes from Underground, 5–6
  Poor Folk, 83, 88
  Possessed, 105, 107, 108, 115
Dürer, Albrecht, 76

Forster, E. M., 9
Freud, Sigmund, 10–11, 12, 13, 14, 85, 149, 151; "Delusion and Dream," 11, 14; *Interpretation of Dreams*, 10–11; "On the History of the Psychoanalytic Movement," 192n
Fromm, Erich, 1
Frye, Northrop, 16

Gershenzon, M. O., 40, 44, 55, 196n
Gibian, G., 86, 200n
Goethe, J. W. von, *Die Leiden des jungen Werthers*, 56, 198n
Gogol, N. V., 66–83, 148
  "Christmas Eve," 71
  Dead Souls, 66, 80–81
  Gants Kyukhelgarten, 65, 68–70, 83, 162
  Government Inspector, 66, 81
  "Ivan Shponka," 70, 72–76, 79, 82, 88, 90, 162–63, 199–200n
  "Lost Letter," 71
  "May Night," 70, 71
  "Nevsky Prospect," 76–79, 80, 163–67
  "Nose," 80, 88
  "Overcoat," 79–80, 88, 90, 199n
  "Portrait," 67, 68, 81–83
  "Taras Bulba," 80

214 Index

Gogol, N. V. (*continued*)
  "Terrible Vengeance," 67–68, 70,
  71–72, 80, 93, 199n
  "Vii," 80
Goncharov, I. A., *Oblomov*, 15, 193n
Gorky, Maksim, 118
Gregg, R., 55
Gregory the Great, 4
Griboedov, A. S., 28–35; *Woe from Wit*,
  28–35, 36, 42, 48, 55, 59, 69, 148,
  157–58, 194–95n
Gukovsky, G. A., 50, 54
Gusev, N., 145–46, 202n, 204n

Hamann, J. G., 6–7
Herder, J. G., 7
Hippocrates, *On Regimen*, 3
Hoffmann, E. T. A., 8, 78, 86, 88, 197n
Homer, *The Odyssey*, 3

Ingham, N. W., 50
Irving, Washington, "The Spectre
  Bridegroom," 196n

Jackson, R. L., 84, 88
James, William, *Principles of Psychology*,
  151
Jensen, Wilhelm, *Gradiva*, 11
Josephus, Flavius, *History of the Jewish
  Wars*, 18
Jung, Carl Gustav, 11–13, 85; "Psychology and Literature," 13

Karamzin, N. M., 22–24, 194n, 196n;
  "The Island of Bornholm," 22–24, 26,
  27, 32, 34, 36, 148, 153
Kent, L. J., 9
Kharms, Daniil, "A Dream," 150–51

Lamb, Charles, 8
Lavrin, Janko, 84–85
Lermontov, M. Yu., "Shtoss," 15
Lévy-Bruhl, L., 2
Lichtenberg, G. C., 6
Lower, R. B., 13

Matlaw, R. E., 32, 54, 55
Mesmer, Franz Anton, 6
Miller, V. F., 54
Milton, John, *Paradise Lost*, 4–5

Mirsky, D. S., 29
Mitchell, S., 54
Mochulsky, K., 92
Müller, L., 55

Nabokov, V., 55, 59
Napoleon, 57
de Nerval, Gerard, *Aurélia*, 8
Nodier, Charles, 8
Novikov, N. I., "News from Helicon,"
  21; *The Painter*, 21, 194n

Odoevsky, V. F., *Russian Nights*, 15

Piksanov, N. K., 31–32
Plato, *The Timaeus*, 3
Pogodin, M. P., *Martha the Mayoress*, 46
Porter, L., 9
Pushkin, A. S., 28–29, 37–65, 148
  Boris Godunov, 36, 42–46, 50, 65, 89,
    158, 198n, 201n
  "Bridegroom," 39, 41–42
  Captain's Daughter, 51–54, 65, 119,
    159–60, 197n, 198n
  "Coffin Maker," 47–48, 59, 65, 92,
    158–59, 196n
  Eugene Onegin, 28, 29, 34, 36, 54–64,
    65, 66, 69, 74, 78, 83, 160–62,
    198–99n
  "Gavriiliada," 39, 41, 42
  Non-fiction, 38–39
  "Queen of Spades," 49–51, 65, 93,
    159, 197n, 201n
  Ruslan and Lyudmila, 39–41, 42
  "Snowstorm," 46–47, 48, 59, 65, 119,
    158, 196n

Radishchev, A. N., *Journey from Petersburg to Moscow*, 21
Reeve, Clara, *The Old English Baron*, 24
Remizov, Aleksei, 66
Richardson, Samuel, *Clarissa Harlowe*,
  56, 198n; *Sir Charles Grandison*, 56
Rousseau, J. J., *Julie, ou la nouvelle
  Héloïse*, 56
Rozhdestvensky, N. V., *Prophetic
  Dreams*, 193n

Samarin, M. P., 54
Scholasticus (or Climacus), Saint John,

Index 215

Ladder of Divine Ascent, 17
Schopenhauer, A., "On Spirit Seeing and Everything Connected Therewith," 133, 134; *The World as Will and Idea*, 133
Schubert, G. H. von, *The Symbolism of Dreams*, 7, 8, 10, 37, 54, 86
Shakespeare, William, *Midsummer Night's Dream*, 5; *Richard III*, 5
Shklovsky, V., 49
Simpson, D., *Discourse on Dreams and Night Visions*, 6
Slonimsky, A. L., 54
Somov, O. M., 24, 25
Song of Igor's Campaign, 19, 193–94n
Sterne, Lawrence, *Tristram Shandy*, 151
Stilman, L. N., 54
Swedenborg, Emanuel, 6, 197n

Tale of Woe and Misfortune, 20
Tangl, E., 54
Todd, W. M., 54, 59
Tolstoy, L. N., 116, 117–46, 148–49, 152
    "Albert," 120
    Anna Karenina, 117, 121, 133, 134–45, 146, 149, 189–90, 203n
    Childhood, 118–19
    Confession, 145
    "Dream" (1857–58), 120–21, 202–3n
    "Dream" (1909), 145
    "Dream of a Young Czar," 145
    Father Sergei, 145
    "History of Yesterday," 119
    "Landowner's Morning," 120
    Master and Man, 145
    "Sevastopol Stories," 152
    "Snowstorm," 119–20
    War and Peace, 117, 121–34, 143, 144, 145, 146, 149, 181–89, 203n
    "What I Saw in a Dream," 145
Turgenev, I. S., 15, 193n

Virgil, *The Aeneid*, 3

Wilson, E., 55
Wordsworth, William, 8

Zhukovsky, V. A., 25–28; "Lyudmila," 25, 27, 28; "Svetlana," 25–28, 29, 32, 34, 36, 48, 55, 59, 69, 148, 153–57, 196n
Zweig, Stefan, 147